"With any hot issue facing Catholics—and certainly when pondering papal authority and its exercise and abuse—it's highly advisable to check with Peter Kwasniewski before rushing to your own conclusion. I find that he always adds additional protein, at a minimum, and often gives you a menu for the entire discussion. This work, in companion volumes, provides the latter."

—**ROGER MCCAFFREY**, Editor, *The Traditionalist*

"Avoiding extremes of 'papolatry' and antipapalism, Dr. Kwasniewski's analysis brings sorely needed balance to contemporary discussions about the role of the papacy in the Church. The first volume helps Catholics rediscover an integrated vision of the office of the pope, not as an autocratic arbiter over the faith but as the servant and defender of Tradition; the second builds up the author's case by concrete reference to the past decade."

—**PHILLIP CAMPBELL**, author of the *Story of Civilization* series

"In hysterical times such as our own, nothing is more important in Church and State than that sane voices be raised and heard. In a period when we are all expected to have immediate opinions on every topic under the sun—no matter how ignorant we may be in this or that area—the result is often a similarly hysterical internal turmoil. Nowhere is this truer than in the Catholic Church under the current pontificate. In the first volume of this work, Dr. Kwasniewski guides us with a sure and sane hand through two millennia of papal history and theology in order to bring us to an accurate understanding of the papacy, showing it to be neither a mere human institution nor another oracle at Delphi. In the second volume he applies these hard-won principles to the various bizarre episodes of the current pontificate. Above all, he shows us how Catholics ought to react to the current crisis in the Church: keeping their eyes on the prize of their eternal salvation. We owe him an enormous debt."

—**CHARLES COULOMBE**, author of *Vicars of Christ: A History of the Popes*

"Dr. Kwasniewski offers an essential resource for coping with the great mystery of our times: how can recent popes, and especially Francis, do so much harm to the Mystical Body of Christ? The answer is not a simple one because we are dealing with a mystery. Avoiding both sophistry and oversimplification, Kwasniewski navigates the safe ground of history and Catholic tradition to build a framework in which we can attempt to live with the mystery until Our Lord decides to heal this crisis."
—**BRIAN M. MCCALL**, Editor-in-Chief, *Catholic Family News*

"In this timely two-volume collection of essays and articles, Peter Kwasniewski gets to grips with the overwhelming scandal facing us today: a Pope who day by day is betraying his divine office and leading the faithful into heresy. It is important to keep the enormity of this before the Church, and to show how it has been made possible by an exaggerated adulation of the person of the reigning Pontiff."
—**HENRY SIRE**, author of *The Dictator Pope*

"Dr. Kwasniewski helps the reader living through the current unprecedented Church crisis to leave behind a widespread and unhealthy hyperpapalism and move on to a Catholic perception of the papacy and its place in the Church. He quotes saintly authorities showing that already back in the thirteenth and fourteenth centuries there was a clear knowledge of the pope being just the 'vicar,' the representative of Christ: he does not supplant Jesus Christ, and he therefore must not change the faith but preserve, clarify, and amplify it—like a good photographer who works on his pictures: he does not change the motifs on it, but increases the contrast and brightens the colors. It is perfectly Catholic to adhere to the teaching of the Church, even when bishops and the pope try to alter it. For, as St. Vincent of Lérins insisted, 'All possible care must be taken that we hold that faith which has been believed everywhere, always, by all.'"
—**MONIKA RHEINSCHMITT**, President, *Pro Missa Tridentina*

THE ROAD FROM HYPERPAPALISM
TO CATHOLICISM

RELATED BOOKS
BY PETER KWASNIEWSKI

Resurgent in the Midst of Crisis
Noble Beauty, Transcendent Holiness
Tradition and Sanity
Reclaiming Our Roman Catholic Birthright
The Holy Bread of Eternal Life
Ministers of Christ
True Obedience in the Church

RELATED BOOKS EDITED
BY PETER KWASNIEWSKI

Are Canonizations Infallible?
From Benedict's Peace to Francis's War
Newman on Worship, Reverence, and Ritual
And Rightly So: Selected Letters and Articles of Neil McCaffrey

The Road from Hyperpapalism to Catholicism

Rethinking the Papacy in a Time of Ecclesial Disintegration

VOLUME 2
Chronological Responses
to an Unfolding Pontificate

PETER A. KWASNIEWSKI

AROUCA
PRESS

ISBN: 978-1-990685-12-5 (paperback)
ISBN: 978-1-990685-13-2 (hardcover)

Arouca Press
PO Box 55003
Bridgeport PO
Waterloo, ON N2J3G0
Canada
www.aroucapress.com
Send inquiries to info@aroucapress.com

Dedicated to cardinals, bishops, priests, deacons,
religious, and laity around the Catholic world
who have suffered due to the results of
the papal conclave of March 2013
and have prayed earnestly
for divine deliverance
and healing

Thou art Peter; and upon this rock I will build my church, and the gates of hell shall not prevail against it... Go behind me, Satan, thou art a scandal unto me: because thou savourest not the things that are of God, but the things that are of men.

Matthew 16:18, 23

And we charge you, brethren, in the name of our Lord Jesus Christ, that you withdraw yourselves from every brother walking disorderly and not according to the tradition which they have received of us.

2 Thessalonians 3:6

I remembered, O Lord, Thy judgments of old: and I was comforted.

Psalm 118:52

TABLE OF CONTENTS

PREFACE
to the Second Volume

MARCH 19, 2022, THE GREAT FEAST OF St. Joseph, was also the ninth anniversary of the accession of Jorge Mario Bergoglio to the throne of St. Peter, and the start of his tenth year in office. In the thirteen and a half years of his reign, St. Gregory the Great (590–604) accomplished a well-nigh superhuman amount of good, which echoed down the centuries. Pope Francis in almost a decade has caused an appalling amount of damage from which it may take centuries to recover. We do not know how much longer this pontificate will last, or the many ways in which Almighty God will draw forth greater good from its evils. One good effect of Francis's pontificate is, however, already apparent: it has forced a fundamental reassessment of the nature, purpose, and limits of the papal office, and for this breakthrough we may and must give thanks to God, the Lord of history.

The first volume of this two-volume set was devoted to the pursuit of this reassessment. The second volume now turns more specifically to Pope Francis himself. *Chronological Responses to an Unfolding Pontificate* gathers my articles and essays on Pope Francis according to the date of their original publication. In this way it serves as a kind of theological diary documenting what it was like to be living through the chaos in real time.

No one who has been attentive to the course of history since the Second Vatican Council would be naïve enough to think that all was well in the papacy until Cardinal Bergoglio was elected. Yet it would be foolish to deny that with Francis we entered into a new phase of what Louis Bouyer once called "the decomposition of Catholicism," a new phase in the extension and application of Modernism.[1] Although prior to 2013 I had already come to see dubious or destructive aspects of the pre-Bergoglian pontificates, I remained a prisoner of neo-ultramontanism and had to be violently shaken awake from that particular "dogmatic slumber."[2] The first five chapters below demonstrate, to my salutary humiliation, that I was not

---

1 See Julia Meloni, *The St. Gallen Mafia: Exposing the Secret Reformist Group within the Church* (Gastonia, NC: TAN Books, 2021); see chapter 62 below.
2 See especially volume 1, chapter 1.

among those more perceptive souls who intuited that Francis was going to be bad news from the moment he appeared on the loggia. My first writings on him are a strained attempt to find Catholic common ground. Soon enough, this pretense had to be abandoned.

We must remember, ponder, and learn from this 266th pontificate.[3] In an age of internet evanescence, the memories of modern Western people become ever shorter. A flagitious deed of one week is swept away by next week's new story. I was deeply disturbed to note, over the years, how quickly the Catholic world seemed to forget about this or that erroneous statement or abusive act of Francis; the constant glut of information buried and hid the past. Forgetfulness or studied silence is not (as some rather too piously express it) a way of reverently covering over one's father's nakedness, as did the sons of Noah; it is a perversion of filial piety that perpetuates a mythology of papal untouchability and even impeccability that plays only too well into the hands of the enemies of Christ and His Church.

No one will be surprised to find herein discussions of *Amoris Laetitia*, the death penalty, Abu Dhabi, Pachamama, and various synods, especially the ones on marriage and family, on youth, and on the Amazon. Articles from 2013 to 2016 are relatively few in number, with none at all in 2017; while the period 2018–2020 shows the most intense engagement. By the start of 2021 I had grown weary and sick at soul over the apparently never-ending errors and scandals of Francis and his court, and felt the need to turn my attention to other intellectual labors and spiritual exigencies. All the same, I believe that the writings from 2013 to 2020 penetrate to the fundamental issues of Bergoglio's theology and praxis and that, accordingly, the work will be and will remain helpful for interpreting his pontificate. I would draw attention especially to the three substantial lectures contained in this volume: one on the change to the *Catechism* on the morality of capital punishment (chapter 40; cf. chapters 13, 14, 16, 23, 41, and 56), the second on the Amazon Synod (chapter 48; cf. chapters 47 and 51), and the third on Modernism from Pius X to Francis (chapter 62). Chapters 59–61 engage more recent issues: the motu proprio *Traditionis Custodes*, the dismissal of Bishop Daniel Fernández Torres, and the Apostolic Constitution *Praedicate Evangelium*. The

---

3   The exact number of popes is and will probably always be a debated question on account of certain confusions in the historical record, but conventionally Francis is considered the 266th pope.

concluding chapter argues that we cannot understand Francis's "program" without seeing it as a recrudescence of the Modernist program condemned by Pius X and Pius XII in the last century.

As most readers will know, many documents have been published over the years, protesting the errors and abuses of Pope Francis and signed by many distinguished individuals. These documents as well as commentary on them, including two pieces of my own, may be found in the book *Defending the Faith against Present Heresies* (Arouca Press, 2021).[4] In a few cases, I have left out articles that would have been relevant to this collection had they not already been developed into chapters of other books. For example, *Ministers of Christ: Recovering the Roles of Clergy and Laity in an Age of Confusion* (Crisis Publications, 2021) treats of Pope Francis's opening of certain "instituted ministries" to women, and *From Benedict's Peace to Francis's War: Catholics Respond to the Motu Proprio* Traditionis Custodes *on the Latin Mass* (Angelico Press, 2021) responds to the infamous motu proprio overturning *Summorum Pontificum*.[5]

As for Rome, what can one say? The Vatican is on a harrowing course of self-destruction. It is enveloped in every kind of disgrace. The pope is cruel and hypocritical, speaking out of both sides of his mouth, taking away with one hand what he bestows with the other, insulting the faithful for evils of which he himself is guilty. Little more than vague humanism, garbled doctrine, and sentimental slogans flow from the mouth of him who should act as the "Vicar of Christ," and yet who dismissed the title.[6]

---

4 Ed. John R.T. Lamont and Claudio Pierantoni; by far the single best resource when it comes to meticulous documentation and evaluation of (most of) the major errors of Francis's pontificate. The two pieces of mine that are included are "Why I Signed the Open Letter Accusing Pope Francis of Heresy" (347–50) and "When Creeping Normalcy Bias Protects a Chaotic Pope" (379–83). The book is available directly from the publisher: http://aroucapress.com/defending-the-faith.

5 Ed. Peter Kwasniewski. This volume contains seventy responses, with six of my own; "The Pope's Boundedness to Tradition as a Legislative Limit" (222–47) is especially pertinent to the theme of the present book. Also relevant is the chapter "The Papacy: In Service of Sacred Tradition" in my *Tradition and Sanity: Conversations & Dialogues of a Postconciliar Exile* (Brooklyn, NY: Angelico Press, 2018), 85–98.

6 See "Pope Francis drops 'Vicar of Christ' title in Vatican yearbook," *Life-SiteNews*, April 2, 2020. My thoughts on Benedict's abdication and Francis's legitimacy may be found in the Preface to, and in several chapters of, volume 1.

Catholics faithful to tradition, as miniscule as they are in earthly terms, are the threat that keeps the power-hungry awake at night, because the latter know their time is limited. Even with all the power on its side, the revolution has never been able to call itself a total success, and as the decades pass, its grip weakens. Nevertheless, a crumbling empire's final efforts at reestablishing hegemony may still cause extensive damage. During this period, we must be ready to imitate those men and women religious who, during the French Revolution or in Communist lands, moved from place to place, dressed perhaps as laity but always continuing their way of life as best they could—adopting any strategy that was necessary for keeping the Faith and pleasing Our Lord.[7] That is how the Catholic Church carries on in the worst periods of history, as the Faith survived in Japan for centuries without the aid of priests. Our times and seasons are in His hands, and He knows what He is about. Vain is the help of man; *adiutorium nostrum in nomine Domini*.

With the exception of the lecture on Modernism (ch. 62), the text of which is published here for the first time, the essays, lectures, and articles in this book were first published at *New Liturgical Movement* (chs. 1, 4, 9, and 30), *Views from the Choir Loft* (chs. 2, 3, and 5), *Rorate Caeli* (chs. 6–8, 40, 45), *LifeSiteNews* (chs. 10–29, 31–39, 41–44, 46–47, 49, 53–56), *OnePeterFive* (chs. 48 and 58), *The Remnant* (chs. 50–52, 57, 59), and *Catholic Family News* (chs. 60–61). Apart from small stylistic corrections and footnotes, they are kept as they originally appeared, although some footnotes have been added; it should go without saying that my views on certain topics (such as Vatican II) have continued to develop since the time these pieces were first published, especially the ones written prior to 2018. To avoid the ungainly sprawl of hyperlinks in the notes, online articles have been referred to simply by author, title, website, and date; when no author is specified, I am the author. Web addresses have been provided for more obscure online locations. Psalms are referenced by their Septuagint/Vulgate numbering.

March 19, 2022
Feast of St. Joseph
Peter A. Kwasniewski

---

7   See Stuart Chessman, *Faith of Our Fathers: A Brief History of Catholic Traditionalism in the United States, from* Triumph *to* Traditionis Custodes (Brooklyn, NY: Angelico Press, 2022).

Pope Francis on the Divine Liturgy

New Liturgical Movement
TUESDAY, JULY 30, 2013

WITH ALL THE TALK OF POPE FRANCIS, this item, courtesy of Robert Moynihan (Letter #78 of this year) should greatly interest the readers of NLM. Toward the end of a recent interview, a Russian journalist asks the pope to comment on the 1025th anniversary, currently being celebrated in Russia, Ukraine, and Belarus, of the baptism of the Rus', the ancient Russian people, centered at the time (988 A. D.) in Kiev. In response, the pope makes a very positive judgement on the liturgy of the Orthodox:

> "They have conserved that pristine liturgy, no?" Pope Francis says. "So beautiful. We [i.e., the Latin Christians] have lost a bit the sense of adoration, they conserve it, they praise God, they adore God, they sing, time does not count. The center is God and that is a richness that I would like to emphasize on this occasion as you ask me this question." (Original Italian: "Hanno conservato quella pristina liturgia, no?, tanto bella. Noi abbiamo perso un po' il senso dell'adorazione, loro lo conservano, loro lodano Dio, loro adorano Dio, cantano, il tempo non conta. Il centro è Dio e quella è una ricchezza che vorrei dire in questa occasione in cui Lei mi fa questa domanda.")

At a moment when many are continuing to wonder about Francis's attitude toward the old liturgy of the Church, it is important to note these words of the pope, which as far as I know have not been singled out by any journalist commenting on this long interview.

Update: In its publication in English of the pope's press conference after World Youth Day, ZENIT gives us the complete response to the Russian journalist's question.

In the Orthodox Churches they have kept that pristine liturgy, so beautiful. We have lost a bit the sense of adoration. They keep, they praise God, they adore God, they sing, time doesn't count. God is the center, and this is a richness that I would like to say on this occasion in which you ask me this question. Once, speaking of the Western Church, of Western Europe, especially the Church that has grown most, they said this phrase to me: "*Lux ex oriente, ex occidente luxus.*" Consumerism, wellbeing, have done us so much harm. Instead you keep this beauty of God at the center, the reference. When one reads Dostoyevsky—I believe that for us all he must be an author to read and reread, because he has wisdom—one perceives what the Russian spirit is, the Eastern spirit. It's something that will do us so much good. We are in need of this renewal, of this fresh air of the East, of this light of the East. John Paul II wrote it in his Letter. But so many times the *luxus* of the West makes us lose the horizon. I don't know, it came to me to say this. Thank you.

2

Pope Francis's Counsel: Do Not Waste What God Has Given Us

Views from the Choir Loft
AUGUST 8, 2013

MANY HAVE COMMENTED ON HOW POPE Francis's preaching seems to be dominated by social justice and the poor. When taking up a theme from the Gospel, he never fails to show how it implies responsibility towards our neighbor. To judge from how some are speaking, it is as if we suddenly have a pope who is "pure horizontalism" in contrast to a predecessor who was "pure verticality"—the one talking about the hungry and the homeless, the other talking about mystery, adoration, and dogma.

As with most popular assessments, this one is superficial and not a little inaccurate. Pope Francis has already preached many times about the life of prayer, the dangers of activism, the primacy of Christ and His Kingdom, the centrality of the sacraments, and other characteristically "Ratzingerian" themes; and those who know Pope Benedict XVI's preaching well know that he was no less insistent and persistent on social themes than Francis has been, even if the media chose to ignore him or aimed their cameras on his red shoes.

Over and above this fair treatment of both popes' emphases, I would like to suggest that it can also be extremely profitable to develop an ability to hear papal teaching in multiple "keys" or "modes." Pope Francis, no less than Pope Benedict, has a way of formulating universal principles of thought and action, and these will be seen to apply to any number of related topics, as long as they share the same pertinent feature.

Take as an example the General Audience on Wednesday, June 5, 2013, when Pope Francis, marking World Environment Day, delivered an address on how important it is to eliminate needless wasting of food and other products. His address was in many ways vintage Ratzinger on the pressing need for a new environmentalism that is true to man's unique nature and vocation to cultivate and care for the garden of creation. What I noticed, however, was a further level of meaning if we listen to his words in a "liturgical key." Pope Francis declared:

> We are often driven by pride of domination, of posses-sions, manipulation, of exploitation; we do not "care" for it [creation], we do not respect it, we do not consider it as a free gift that we must care for. We are losing the attitude of wonder, contemplation, listening to creation; thus we are no longer able to read what Benedict XVI calls "the rhythm of the love story of God and man." Why does this happen? Why do we think and live in a horizontal manner? We have moved away from God, we no longer read His signs.

Now think of what happened in the liturgical reform in the mid-to late sixties. The reformers were men who appeared to think, in an anthropocentric fashion, that they were free to dominate, manipulate, and exploit the liturgy for particular modern aims. They acted at times as if they did not respect the immense gift of tradition we are given to care for. Instead of wonderment at the riches handed down, a contemplative disposition of receptivity and listening to tradition (which are preconditions for discerning the love story between God and man in the Mass and the Divine Office), they chose to think, and therefore to live, in a horizontal manner, which was equivalent to moving away from God through a willful failure to read His signs—the sacred signs of ritual, text, and music that are His exquisite lyric poetry down through the ages.

The crisis, in short, occurred when the Cartesian man who viewed Nature as raw material for economic exploitation via technology became the Consilium man who viewed Tradition as raw material for scholarly exploitation via executive fiat. And as in the former case, what has suffered is man's right relationship with Creation, so in the latter case, what has grievously suffered is the believer's right relationship with Divine Worship.

Pope Francis also said in the same audience:

> We should all remember, however, that the food we throw away is as if stolen from the table of the poor, the hungry!

A few days ago, on the Feast of Corpus Christi, we read the story of the miracle of the loaves: Jesus feeds the crowd with five loaves and two fishes. And the conclusion of the piece is important: "They all ate and were satisfied. And when the leftover fragments were picked up, they filled twelve wicker baskets" (Lk. 9:17). Jesus asks his disciples not to throw anything away: no waste!

In like manner, the solid nourishment that once fed the Christian people was often carelessly thrown away, as missals, vestments, bells, chant books, and other precious goods were pitched into the rubbish—and all this spiritual food was stolen from the table of the poor in spirit, the children of God who never demanded a Marxist revolution that promised a new springtime but delivered a long, hard winter of disorientation, irreverence, and abuse, in which many have died and many others have nearly starved, although they may not realize their plight, as they have nothing else to compare it against.

Jesus, in contrast, desires His disciples to eat their fill from the Church's abundance and be satisfied; the gifts He has given to the Church, His immaculate bride, are possessed of a miraculous power to feed the entire world until the end of time. The Lord commands us to throw nothing away, to waste nothing of what He has given us, to consider nothing trivial, redundant, or meaningless. There is no such thing as "useless repetition," any more than extra fragments of bread are a useless repetition of food. If we were wise, we would not set a lean, sparse table and call it modern; we would put forth a rich banquet of many centuries and call it divine.

3

General and Particular Examen

Views from the Choir Loft

DECEMBER 12, 2013

ONE OF MY FAVORITE SPIRITUAL BOOKS is Dom Jean-Baptiste Chautard's *The Soul of the Apostolate*. In company with countless writers, Chautard strongly recommends the "particular and general examinations of conscience," but seems to assume that the reader simply knows what this is all about. One doubts that many laypeople, especially after the Second Vatican Council, would have a clue about how to carry out this double examination. And one hesitates to google about it, for fear of finding random and superficial material.

When I first came across this passage, I consulted a venerable priest whose opinion has never failed me, and he explained it as follows.

The distinction between general and particular examinations of conscience is made by Saint Ignatius in the first week of his *Spiritual Exercises.* Put simply, the general examination surveys *all* the morally significant actions of the day, so far as we can recall them, while in the particular examination we focus our attention on one particular fault against which we are struggling and the corresponding virtue we are trying to cultivate (because the positive cultivation of a virtue is the most effective way of fighting against the vice that is opposed to it). Saint Ignatius tells us that we should make the particular examination three times a day— morning, after lunch, and after dinner; the general examination, in contrast, is best done just before we go to bed.

This is a simple and lucid template for self-awareness and continual conversion of life. We are all in danger of forgetting or even being totally ignorant of the areas of our lives in which we stand in need of conversion; we are all, in the best of circumstances, notoriously lacking in self-knowledge; we can all use more humility and even humiliation to get the point across that we are far from perfect and yet capable of improvement, with God's help. The particular and general examinations provide a

6

kind of spiritual scaffolding around the day that can help us pay attention to our defects and make progress in correcting them. There does not need to be anything fussy or time-consuming about it: a few concentrated moments of reflection may suffice. But what an opportunity we are missing when we do not pay any attention to how the day has gone and what we might have done differently or better!

Is it fanciful to see, in Pope Francis's numerous recent course corrections,[1] the outward signs of a Jesuit who, in the best tradition of the order's founder, is serenely accustomed to making these examinations and has discovered in himself certain faults or at least areas of improvement? We will never have a sinless or a perfect pope, but we can have a holy one who sets us a good example of continual conversion.

---

1 See Sandro Magister, "Even the Pope Critiques Himself. And Corrects Three Errors," *Settimo Cielo*, November 22, 2013.

4

Why is Vatican II So Vexing?

New Liturgical Movement
JANUARY 13, 2014

OVER THE PAST TWENTY YEARS, I HAVE often encountered or noticed a curious phenomenon. One might refer to it as "Vatican II weariness." Briefly described, it is the attitude of being tired out by the very topic of the Council; not really caring to discuss it because the Second Vatican Council just seems so incredibly long-winded in its documents, so controversial, so trapped in its time period—and, well, can't we just get on with life and stop worrying so much about it?

We had a Year of Faith that was supposed to be dedicated, at least in large part, to a rediscovery and re-reading of the documents of the last Council. Granted, Benedict XVI dropped a bombshell during this Year and pretty much tore everyone's minds off of his original intention. Still, even if he had never abdicated the chair of Peter, wouldn't many people be dragging their feet when it comes to re-reading those sixteen documents? Wasn't the great upheaval of the election of Pope Francis and his megaton interviews a worthy excuse for quietly filing away Benedict's original script for this special Year? At least many people acted that way. A period of time in which we are ticking off many half-century conciliar milestones appears to be unfolding in an atmosphere of surprising indifference.

I have often wondered what is the root cause of this Vatican II malaise. Some traditionalists would say the cause is the muddled and meandering pastoral loquacity of the Council itself; but that, of course, is a begging of the question, since people would have to *read* and *study* the Council first in order to reach a fair judgment that it's muddled and problematic—and that's what we *don't* see happening on a large scale. Your typical liberal will appeal breezily to Vatican II whether he's read a single sentence of it or not.

My theory is that it is precisely those who have abused Vatican II by continually ignoring or even counterfeiting its teaching who have produced a situation in which the same Council is becoming increasingly distant, wearisome, vexed, and irrelevant. For example,

8

had there been a clear and humble acceptance of the teaching of *Sacrosanctum Concilium*, and, therefore, had the Church been free from widespread liturgical abuses and the hermeneutic of rupture that is still the *modus operandi* of most parish communities, there can be no question that the traditionalist movement would have spent far less of its time critiquing Vatican II as such. Put simply: it was not inherently necessary that the Council become a lightning-rod of discontent. It was *made to be that* by the purveyors of its "spirit."

If Vatican II dies the death of an irrecoverable failure, it will be solely the fault of the progressives who thought they could ride the horse of Vatican II all the way home to a "new Church," and who met with considerable success in persuading the world to believe the same lie. As there is one Body of Christ planned from all eternity, sojourning on earth in the unity of faith and charity, and destined to live forever, there cannot ever *be* a "new Church." Those who were content to remain in the one and only Church there is can hardly be blamed for turning a deaf ear to so much tiresome twaddle about the Council. Over time, the historical Council insensibly merged with the virtual or media Council, and as a result, the real teaching, the authentic documents, have become marginalized.

Imagine with me a counterfactual situation in which, because the Council *had* been judiciously received and faithfully implemented, traditionalists of 2014 would be shoring up their spiritual counsels and pastoral plans with frequent citations of the Council, even if they might be uncomfortable with some of the ambiguous language or the novel directions taken in certain documents. But we are now radically polarized, and Vatican II has become a source of dismay because of the liberals and the modernists who insisted on selfishly abusing it for their own agendas back in the 60s and 70s and up to the present. It will be their ignominy in the annals of the Church to be the ones who defeated the hopes of John XXIII by dropping the atomic bomb on the new springtime and leading us into a nuclear winter.

It is no wonder that Pope Francis spoke so highly of Archbishop Marchetto and his correct hermeneutic of the Council. If there is ever to be a future fruitful reception and application of the Second Vatican Council, it will be purchased by that hermeneutic and by no other.

9

5

Pope Francis on Sound Doctrine, Memory, and Adoration

Views from the Choir Loft
JULY 10, 2014

T HROUGH SELECTIVE REPORTING AND A heavy interpretive slant, it has been possible for the popular and religious media to co-opt Pope Francis almost entirely. One of the most common canards now broadcast is that Pope Francis cares but little for the sacred liturgy, so eager is he to reach out to the poor and marginalized; and so, things like the Eucharistic doctrine of Trent, Eucharistic adoration, even the very concept of tradition, mean relatively little to him.

Even if Pope Francis is not a theologian of the liturgy as was his beloved predecessor, however, it is stretching the truth quite a bit to suggest that he does not appreciate—and include in his preaching and writing—many of the fundamental points Pope Benedict XVI strove to emphasize in his teaching. I would like to present a few of these quotations here.

Letter to Walter Cardinal Brandmüller, November 19, 2013:

> As the 450th anniversary of the day on which the fortunate Council of Trent was closed approaches, it behooves the Church to recall with more prompt and attentive eagerness the most fruitful doctrine which came out of that Council convened in the Tyrolese region. Certainly not without cause, the Church has for a long time already accorded so much care to the Decrees and Canons of that Council that are to be recalled and observed, since, when the most grave affairs and questions appeared at that time, the Council Fathers summoned all diligence that the Catholic Faith appear more clearly and be better understood. No doubt, with the Holy Ghost inspiring and suggesting, it especially concerned the Fathers not only to guard the sacred deposit of Christian doctrine, but also to more clearly enlighten mankind, so that the saving work

of the Lord may be poured out onto the whole world and the Gospel be spread through the entire world.

Graciously hearing the very same Holy Spirit, the Holy Church of our age, even now, continues to restore and meditate upon the most abundant doctrine of Trent. As a matter of fact, the "hermeneutic of renewal" (*inter-pretatio renovationis*) which Our Predecessor Benedict XVI explained in 2005 before the Roman Curia, refers not only to the Tridentine Council but also to the [Second] Vatican Council. The mode of interpretation, certainly, places one honorable characteristic of the Church in a brighter light that is given by the same lord Benedict XVI: "She is a subject which increases in time and develops, yet always remaining the same, the one subject of the journeying People of God" (Christmas Address to the Roman Curia, December 22, 2005).

And, as if to answer the question "Why should we intently study and internalize the doctrine of the Council of Trent?," here is what the Holy Father reminded us in his homily for Pentecost Sunday, June 8, 2014:

> The Holy Spirit reminds us, He reminds us of all that Jesus said. He is the living memory of the Church. And while he reminds us, He makes us understand the Lord's words. This recollection in the Spirit and thanks to the Spirit is not reduced to a mnemonic reality, it is an essential aspect of the presence of Christ in us and in His Church.... A Christian with no memory is not a true Christian: he is a Christian in the middle of the road, a man or a woman prisoner of the moment, who does not know how to treasure his history, how to read it and live it as history of salvation.... May the Holy Spirit enliven Christian memory in all of us! And on that day, with the Apostles, there was the Lady of Memory, the one who initially pondered all those things in her heart. There was Mary, our Mother. May she help us in this road of memory.

The Catholic Church, precisely because she is a social body whose glue is tradition, worships publicly in the temple, with the songs and rites handed down—and not for the sake of herself, but always focused on the Lord who is her All. Hence the primacy of adoration, as Pope Francis indicates in his homily for the Feast of St. Cecilia, November 22, 2013:

> The temple is the place where the community goes to pray, to praise the Lord, to give thanks, but above all to adore: the Lord is adored in the temple. And this is the most important point. This is also true for liturgical ceremonies: in this liturgical ceremony, what is most important? The songs, the rites, they are all beautiful... However, adoration is what is most important: the whole community together look at the altar where the sacrifice is celebrated and adore.
>
> Are our temples places of adoration? Do they foster adoration? Do our liturgical celebrations foster adoration?... The temple was a sacred place. we should enter there, in the sacredness that leads us to prayer.
>
> We too need to be continually purified with prayer, penance, and with the Sacraments of Reconciliation and the Eucharist.
>
> In these two temples—the physical temple which is a place of adoration, and the spiritual temple within me where the Holy Spirit dwells—our disposition should be one of true piety that adores and listens, that prays and asks pardon, that praises the Lord.

So, the next time you hear someone assert that Pope Francis is breaking away from everything that came before him, you might want to pull out texts like these as a way of signaling that, at the very least, we are dealing here with a man of many facets, who at times gives vivid expression to core principles of Catholic traditionalists.

6

Saying and Unsaying:
The Synod's Orwellian Atmosphere[†]

Rorate Caeli

DECEMBER 16, 2014

IT SURPRISES ME HOW OFTEN CATHOLICS grasp at straws when it comes to the situation in Rome and in much of the Church's episcopacy these days. It's as if they are working as hard as they can to deny the evidence of their senses and to find absurdly far-fetched explanations that will prevent them from having to draw the obvious conclusions. Let's consider three facts.

1. TO LEAVE SOMETHING UNSAID IS OFTEN TO UNSAY IT.

Many commentators on the interim *relatio* and the final *relatio* noted that these documents were rather inadequate (in varying degrees) when it came to articulating the beauty and blessings of marriage as instituted by God and elevated by Christ and defending its truth and goodness. The documents included this or that true statement, but they did not give the lion's share of attention to the sacrament of marriage itself and its nobility, permanent validity, and abundant graces for the world, nor did they condemn the sins and structures of sin aligned against Christian marriage.

The problem is this: when we purposefully leave something unsaid, and in a context where it *ought* to be said, we are effectively *unsaying* it. To neglect to say something when every circumstance demands that it be said is not merely absent-mindedness, a want of affirmation, but a destructive omission that undermines the truth, a black hole that sucks the light into itself.

This is one of the many lessons we have learned from "the Synod experience"—that experience which Pope Francis declared

---

† The Synod in question here is the Extraordinary General Assembly of the Synod of Bishops in October 2014 on the theme "Pastoral Challenges of the Family in the Context of Evangelization."

to be a good one, but which was good only in the sense that God the Almighty can bring forth good out of evil. One impressive good that has come forth is the worldwide exposure of the serious lack of orthodoxy and virtue in many members of the hierarchy, as well as a renewed admiration for those heroes of the Faith who are willing to suffer calumny and exile. This is a good thing because it chips away at that dreadful, uncatholic and altogether untraditional ultramontanism and subservience to whatever the shepherds dish out to the longsuffering faithful. It is a wake-up call to abandon sheepish passivity and to stand valiantly for the faith of our fathers, as the laity did during the Arian crisis of the fourth century.

2. TO FRAME AN IMPOSSIBLE QUESTION CAN BE A FORM OF MENTAL ABUSE.

Other commentators thought that it was "good" that the pope encouraged the asking of tough questions and open debate on their answers.

The problem is this: many of the questions discussed by the Synod were questions to which the Catholic Faith, not to mention natural law, *already* has determinate, unequivocal, and immutable answers. Raising *these* questions is nothing less than a form of mental abuse, a manipulation of feelings and an effort to sow confusion, doubt, and denial. To ask, as if seriously wondering, whether there can be such a thing as homosexual marriage is already to have surrendered to the enemy of human nature; to ask whether active bigamists can receive Holy Communion is already to do violence to the consciences of Catholics and to blaspheme the Blessed Sacrament. There are certain questions it is not possible to raise as if they were still open questions or as if they were healthy intellectual exercises. This kind of question, if it is not an empty show or *flatus vocis*, implies an epistemological stance, an existential commitment.

3. TO FOLLOW NEOLOGISMS OR TO AVOID TRADITIONAL LANGUAGE IS A KIND OF EXPLOITATION AND DECEPTION.

There are words that signify realities as they are, and there are words that deliberately obscure them. "Living in sin" clearly states that an unmarried man and woman who sleep together are guilty of offending God and harming one another; "cohabitation" is a neutral description that passes no judgment and seems to imply that no judgment should be made. "Concubine" or "paramour" tells us frankly what we are dealing with; "marriage partner" does not. "Adulterous union" calls a spade a spade; with its legal sound, "civil remarriage" decorously papers over the serial polygamy. That Vatican documents should have been besmirched with such "value-neutral" language is a powerful sign of the triumph of factions over fidelity, power over truth, Orwellian thought-control over the liberty of the sons of God.

Should we be surprised? The same thing has happened in the liturgical sphere: instead of the "celebrant," we speak of the "presider"; instead of the "Holy Sacrifice of the Mass," we call it "Eucharist"; instead of "Introit" there is "the opening song." The novel terms are not false in themselves, but they stem from an ideology that wishes to *avoid* the traditional language. There are many such examples, all tending in the same direction. Now, more than ever, we must heed the warning of Josef Pieper, who in his little book *Abuse of Language, Abuse of Power* reminds us that whoever controls language controls reality—a lesson also understood by George Orwell, even if his intuition did not lead him to adore the Logos who alone gives meaning to human speech and reason.

The common denominator between the liturgical reform and the Synod is *accommodationism*: the view that it is the Church's business to adapt herself—her worship, her doctrine, her discipline—to "modern man." That's exactly what Church leaders today are endeavoring to do, with results that all can see.

The social crisis we are seeing in regard to marriage and sexuality is bound up with the spiritual crisis of no longer recognizing who is the bride and who is the Bridegroom, what is sacred and deserving of total reverence, and what is the purity demanded of the one who would dare approach the altar. Generations of Catholics have experienced a liturgy freed from traditions and marked by casual intimacies, just like their sexual morality. Which came first: relaxation and experimentation with the liturgy, or the slackening and abandonment of moral restraints? In any case, we are alive to see the last stage of the revolution: even as the worship of God was redefined according to the purported exigencies of modern man, so today, the same exigencies are driving the redefinition of man as such—an unsurprising outcome that underlines the connection between liturgy and anthropology.

In a world going increasingly mad, Catholics must bring a healing sanity by saying what needs to be said (especially when authorities are unsaying it), exposing and refuting false questions and false conundrums, and using traditional language to call realities by their names.

A Study in Contraſts:
Francis, Benedict, Auguſtine

Rorate Caeli

DECEMBER 22, 2014

I N THE SPEECH DELIVERED AT THE END OF
the Synod, Pope Francis said something puzzling. It was
another one of those invocations of "the God of surprises,"
this time in the midst of a stark opposition between "the letter"
and "the spirit":

> One, a temptation to hostile inflexibility, that is, want-
> ing to close oneself within the written word (the letter)
> and not allowing oneself to be surprised by God, by the
> God of surprises (the spirit); within the law, within the
> certitude of what we know and not of what we still need
> to learn and to achieve. From the time of Christ, it is
> the temptation of the zealous, of the scrupulous, of the
> solicitous and of the so-called—today—"traditionalists"
> and also of the intellectuals.

When I read this, I scratched my head, recalling the quite different
way in which the pope's predecessor, Benedict XVI, had spoken
of the spirit and the letter of the Second Vatican Council, in the
address he delivered only nine years ago today, December 22, 2005:

> The hermeneutic of discontinuity risks ending in a split
> between the pre-conciliar Church and the post-conciliar
> Church. It asserts that the texts [i.e., the letter] of the
> Council as such do not yet express the true spirit of the
> Council. It claims that they are the result of compromises
> in which, to reach unanimity, it was found necessary to
> keep and reconfirm many old things that are now point-
> less. However, the true spirit of the Council is not to be
> found in these compromises but instead in the impulses
> toward the new that are contained in the texts.
>
> These innovations alone were supposed to represent
> the true spirit of the Council, and starting from and

in conformity with them, it would be possible to move ahead. Precisely because the texts would only imperfectly reflect the true spirit of the Council and its newness, it would be necessary to go courageously beyond the texts and make room for the newness in which the Council's deepest intention would be expressed, even if it were still vague. In a word: It would be necessary [on that view] not to follow the *texts* of the Council but its *spirit*. In this way, obviously, a vast margin was left open for the question on how this spirit should subsequently be defined and room was consequently made for every whim.

One notices how clearly Benedict XVI warns against the arbitrary exaltation of a "spirit" and "newness" that are in tension with, if not simply contrary to, the "text" and the "old things"—two categories of things that, when rightly understood, can never be contraries to one another. He warns against the temptation of subjectivism and the inevitable power play that results from it. Who gets to determine *which* "spirit" is the true expression of the Holy Spirit and of the Council? Benedict XVI went on to say that those who speak this way fundamentally misunderstand what a council is all about. It's not a matter of might makes right, as if the truth were subject to a vote and the constitution of the Church to a democratic assembly: "The nature of a Council as such is therefore basically misunderstood. In this way, it is considered as a sort of constituent that eliminates an old constitution and creates a new one."

Certainly for Pope Benedict, there could be no question whatsoever of eliminating the God-given "constitution" of the Church or creating a new one for it; and similarly, as he said and wrote many times, there could be no question of eliminating the traditional liturgy of the Church or creating a new one whole cloth, *de novo*, as if the Church had the ability to repudiate her heritage on the grounds of a surprising new spirit that compelled her to leave behind the old ways.

One of Pope Benedict's favorite authors is St. Augustine, and pondering these matters led me to open up again that great treatise of the Doctor of Grace, *On the Spirit and the Letter*, to see if this work could give me a clue about Pope Francis's turn of phrase. I found what I was expecting, namely, that Augustine, like Benedict

XVI, never pits "letter" and "spirit" *against* one another, but sees the latter as the means by which the former can be actualized and fully lived. The Spirit vivifies the letter and makes it life-giving rather than death-dealing. For Augustine, we are saved not by the spirit alone, nor by the letter, but by following the letter *in the power of* the spirit. Here are some characteristic texts:

> "The letter kills, but the spirit gives life" (2 Cor. 3:6) must be understood in the sense which we have already indicated—that the letter of the law, which teaches us not to commit sin, kills, if the life-giving spirit be absent, forasmuch as it causes sin to be known rather than avoided, and therefore to be increased rather than diminished, because to an evil concupiscence there is now added the transgression of the law.
>
> We are assisted by divine aid towards the achievement of righteousness—not merely because God has given us a law full of good and holy precepts, but because our very will, without which we cannot do any good thing, is assisted and elevated by the importation of the Spirit of grace, without which help mere teaching is the letter that kills (2 Cor. 3:6) forasmuch as it rather holds them guilty of transgression than justifies the ungodly.
>
> Whence it is written in another part of Scripture, "He that increases knowledge, increases sorrow" (Eccles. 1:18)—not that the law is itself evil, but because the commandment has its good in the demonstration of the letter, not in the assistance of the spirit; and if this commandment is kept from the fear of punishment and not from the love of righteousness, it is servilely kept, not freely, and therefore it is not kept at all. For no fruit is good which does not grow from the root of love. If, however, that faith be present which "works by love" (Gal. 5:6), then one begins to "delight in the law of God after the inward man" (Rom. 7:22) and this delight is the gift of the spirit, not of the letter.
>
> For there is no doubt that, without His assisting grace, the law is the letter which kills; but when the life-giving spirit is present, the law causes that to be loved as written within, which it once caused to be feared as written without.

It is therefore apparent what difference there is between the old covenant and the new—that in the former the law is written on tables, while in the latter on hearts; so that what in the one alarms from without, in the other delights from within; and in the former man becomes a transgressor through the letter that kills, in the other a lover through the life-giving spirit.

This is that righteousness of God, which He not only teaches us by the precept of His law, but also bestows upon us by the gift of His Spirit.

For Augustine as for the entire Christian tradition, the law, the letter, the written word, Tradition and traditions, all of these are surpassingly good, useful, and salutary—as long as they are received by one who, raised up by grace, can *truly live* their demands *out of love.* Conversely, the Christian life is inconceivable without these gifts of God that give shape and structure to it. Christianity is not just about love; it is about law animated by love and love directed by law. Thus, to oppose the letter to the spirit as if a zealous maintenance of what is lawful or a certitude about divine law could ever be opposed to following Christ with a generous spirit and a love for one's neighbors is to commit not just a fallacy, but a blasphemy against the goodness of God who gave us *both* the letter *and* the spirit, law *and* charity. Moreover, to suggest that God has in store for us the "surprise" of compromising or undoing His own letter and making adherence to His revealed word a form of hostile inflexibility is to surrender Christian doctrine to the philosophical system of Hegel, where we can expect a steady flow of contradictions as the Absolute Spirit works itself out in history through a process of thesis, antithesis, and synthesis.

Exotic fantasies, the sound of which, on a bishop's tongue, is, to be sure, an unexpected (and undesired) surprise. But the real "surprise" that we need, today and every day of our lives, is the grace to perceive and embrace the unfathomable wisdom contained in the letter—that is, the definite truths of faith and morals that have been revealed for our salvation and handed down faithfully by the Church of all ages. Using their intellects to the full, Catholics zealously follow the definitive letter, the Word of God, thanks to the gratuitous gift of the Spirit. Hegel, as far as we are concerned, may be shown the door.

8

Why Blogs Must Expose the Goings-on in Rome

Rorate Caeli

FEBRUARY 6, 2015

I N AN INTERVIEW PUBLISHED NOVEMBER 5, 2014, Bishop Athanasius Schneider said, apropos the infamous interim report or *Relatio post disceptationem* of the Extraordinary Synod:

> During the Synod there had been moments of obvious manipulation on the part of some clerics who held key positions in the editorial and governing structure of the Synod. The interim report (*Relatio post disceptationem*) was clearly a prefabricated text with no reference to the actual statements of the Synod fathers. In the sections on homosexuality, sexuality and "the divorced and remarried" with their admittance to the sacraments, the text represents a radical neo-pagan ideology. This is the first time in Church history that such a heterodox text was actually published as a document of an official meeting of Catholic bishops under the guidance of a pope, even though the text only had a preliminary character. Thanks be to God and to the prayers of the faithful all over the world that a consistent number of Synod fathers resolutely rejected such an agenda; this agenda reflects the corrupt and pagan mainstream morality of our time, which is being imposed globally by means of political pressure and through the almost all-powerful official mass media, which are loyal to the principles of the world gender-ideology party. Such a synod document, even if only preliminary, is a real shame and an indication of the extent to which the spirit of the anti-Christian world has already penetrated such important levels of the life of the Church. This document will remain, for the future generations and

for the historians, a black mark which has stained the honour of the Apostolic See.[1]

With this judgment, as we know, Cardinal Burke and other prelates concurred.

We have had many reasons to believe that the "funny business" of the Synod extended all the way to the top, but there is no longer any guesswork now that the Synod's General Secretary, Cardinal Baldisseri, admitted candidly, and with no qualifications, that Pope Francis had both seen and approved the *Relatio ante disceptationem* before its publication. It is no wonder, then, that Roberto de Mattei just published an article about Pope John XXII and how his contemporaries reacted to him.[2] We would do well to learn from history.

Sometimes people wonder why *Rorate Caeli* must publish such exposés. Do we specialize in bad news? Are we trying to make people look bad? No, not at all. We report plenty of good news, such as new apostolates of the Priestly Fraternity of St. Peter and new locations for the traditional Latin Mass, bishops who generously feed their flocks with sound doctrine and worthy worship, and heartening manifestations of popular piety throughout the Catholic world. But it is a solemn duty of Christians, yes, of *every* confirmed Christian, to bear witness to the truth in season and out of season, and to cry out like St. Catherine of Siena when good is called evil and evil, good.

Pope John Paul II had seen the trends of our times and anticipated what was coming. He wrote with unmistakable clarity and courage in *Veritatis Splendor* (n. 88 and n. 93):

> It is urgent then that Christians should rediscover *the newness of the faith and its power to judge* a prevalent and all-intrusive culture. As the Apostle Paul admonishes us: "Once you were darkness, but now you are light in the Lord; walk as children of the light (for the fruit of the light is found in all that is good and right and true), and try to learn what is pleasing to the Lord. Take no part

---

1   This and other quotations from the interview may be found at "Bishop Athanasius Schneider: Against Pharisees," *OnePeterFive*, October 14, 2015.
2   *Love for the Papacy and Filial Resistance to the Pope in the History of the Church* (Brooklyn, NY: Angelico Press, 2019), 40–44.

in the unfruitful works of darkness, but instead expose them ... Look carefully then how you walk, not as unwise men but as wise, making the most of the time, because the days are evil" (Eph. 5:8-11, 15-16; cf. 1 Thess. 5:4-8).

This witness [of martyrs to the exceptionless moral law] makes an extraordinarily valuable contribution to warding off, in civil society and within the ecclesial communities themselves, a headlong plunge into the most dangerous crisis which can afflict man: the *confusion between good and evil*, which makes it impossible to build up and to preserve the moral order of individuals and communities. By their eloquent and attractive example of a life completely transfigured by the splendour of moral truth, the martyrs and, in general, all the Church's Saints, light up every period of history by reawakening its moral sense. By witnessing fully to the good, they are a living reproof to those who transgress the law (cf. Wis. 2:12), and they make the words of the Prophet echo ever afresh: "Woe to those who call evil good and good evil, who put darkness for light and light for darkness, who put bitter for sweet and sweet for bitter!" (Is. 5:20).

Anyone who reads (or re-reads) this great encyclical will see how deeply the Church today is mired in a state of civil war over the fundamentals of morality and of the Gospel itself. We are not looking at a mere disagreement over words or "pastoral strategies"; it is precisely the battle between the Catholics who still believe exactly what Jesus Christ taught as the saving truth, and the modernists who, with a magician's sleight-of-hand, explain it away, in deference to "modern man" and his needs (and wants). By the Providence of God, it seems we are being forced at last, slowly and against our will, into the two sides depicted in the Apocalypse of John: the faithful who will cling to Christ even at the cost of their lives, and the worldly who will pay lip-service to Christ while they serve Babylon.

As was his beautiful custom in every major document, Pope John Paul II ends *Veritatis Splendor* (n. 120) with tender yet forceful words inspired by the Blessed Virgin Mary, Mother of Mercy:

Mary shares our human condition, but in complete openness to the grace of God. Not having known sin, she is able to have compassion on every kind of weakness. She understands sinful man and loves him with a mother's love. *Precisely for this reason* she is on the side of truth and shares the Church's burden in recalling always and to everyone the demands of morality. Nor does she permit sinful man to be deceived by those who claim to love him by justifying his sin, for she knows that the sacrifice of Christ her Son would thus be emptied of its power. No absolution offered by beguiling doctrines, even in the areas of philosophy and theology, can make man truly happy: only the Cross and the glory of the Risen Christ can grant peace to his conscience and salvation to his life.

Now, more than ever, is the time to proclaim from the rooftops what the enemies of the Church would wish to hide or silence as they pursue their agenda of destruction. But the strategy that worked so well for them in the past is not going to work now, or let us say, its days are numbered. Faithful Catholics across the world are observing, praying, doing penance—and, yes, *exposing* the works of darkness, whatever their source may be. In this difficult work, in all the suffering that has been inflicted on us by the wolves that prey upon the sheep, the Blessed Virgin Mary is our hope, our confidence, our joy, our protection, our model of absolute constancy and fidelity to Jesus Christ. May she obtain for us the grace to weather any and every storm, for love of Him.

9

St. Thomas Aquinas and Pope Francis on 1 Corinthians 11:27–29

New Liturgical Movement
APRIL 14, 2016

I N HIS GREAT ENCYCLICAL ON SACRED SCRIP-
ture, *Providentissimus Deus*, Pope Leo XIII writes:

> With the age of the scholastics came fresh and welcome
> progress in the study of the Bible.... The valuable work
> of the scholastics in Holy Scripture is seen in their theo-
> logical treatises and in their Scripture commentaries; and
> in this respect the greatest name among them all is St.
> Thomas Aquinas. (n. 7)

It is therefore with complete confidence that we can and should
take up the Angelic Doctor's commentaries on the Apostle to the
Gentiles. These commentaries, from Aquinas's maturest period,
are some of the best reflections of his primary work as a *Magister
Sacrae Paginae* at the university.

Earlier this week at *New Liturgical Movement*, I discussed the
astonishing exclusion of 1 Corinthians 11:27–29 from the postconciliar liturgy (Mass and Office), in spite of the fact that it had
been present in many places in the preconciliar Mass and Office.[1]
Our astonishment will be all the more complete when we read St.
Thomas's probing comments on these verses.

ST. THOMAS AQUINAS'S COMMENTARY
ON 1 CORINTHIANS 11:27–29[2]

*Therefore, whosoever shall eat this bread, or drink the chalice of the Lord
unworthily, shall be guilty of the body and of the blood of the Lord.* [nn.

---

1 The article alluded to, "The Omission that Haunts the Church—1 Corinthians 11:27–29," was subsequently expanded into chapter 13 of my book
The Holy Bread of Eternal Life: Restoring Eucharistic Reverence in an Age of Impiety
(Manchester, NH: Sophia Institute Press, 2020).
2 Phrases in bold are my emphasis.

687–94] *But let a man prove himself: and so let him eat of that bread and drink of the chalice.* [nn. 695–96] *For he who eats and drinks unworthily eats and drinks judgment to himself, not discerning the body of the Lord.* [n. 697]

687. After showing the dignity of this sacrament, the Apostle now rouses the faithful to receive it reverently. First, he outlines the peril threatening those who receive unworthily; second, he applies a saving remedy, at *but let a man prove himself.*

688. First, therefore, he says, *therefore,* from the fact that this which is received sacramentally is the body of Christ and what is drunk is the blood of Christ, *whosoever shall eat this bread, or drink the chalice of the Lord unworthily, shall be guilty of the body and of the blood of the Lord.* In these words must be considered, first, how someone eats or drinks unworthily. According to a Gloss this happens in three ways. First, as to the celebration of this sacrament, namely, because someone celebrates the sacrament in a manner different from that handed down by Christ; for example, if he offers in this sacrament a bread other than wheaten or some liquid other than wine from the grape of the vine. Hence it is said that Nadab and Abihu, sons of Aaron, offered before the Lord "unholy fire, such as he had not commanded them. And fire came forth from the presence of the Lord and devoured them" (Lev. 10:1).

689. Second, from the fact that someone approaches the Eucharist with a mind not devout. This lack of devotion is sometimes venial, as when someone with his mind distracted by worldly affairs approaches this sacrament habitually retaining due reverence toward it; and such lack of devotion, although it impedes the fruit of this sacrament, which is spiritual refreshment, does not make one guilty of the body and blood of the Lord, as the Apostle says here. However, a certain lack of devotion is a mortal sin, i.e., when it involves contempt of this sacrament, as it is said: "but you profane it when you say that the Lord's table is polluted and its food may be despised" (Mal. 1:12). It is of such lack of devotion that the Gloss speaks.

690. In a third way someone is said to be unworthy, because he approaches the Eucharist with the intention of sinning mortally. For it is said: "he shall not approach the altar, because he has a blemish" (Lev. 21:23). **Someone is understood to have a blemish as long as he persists in the intention of sinning, which, however, is taken away through penitence.** By contrition, indeed, which takes

away the will to sin with the intention of confession and making satisfaction, as to the remission of guilt and eternal punishment; by confession and satisfaction as to the total remission of punishment and reconciliation with the members of the Church. Therefore, in cases of necessity, as when someone does not have an abundance of confessors, contrition is enough for receiving this sacrament. But as a general rule, confession with some satisfaction should precede. Hence in the book *On Church Dogmas* it says: "One who desires to go to communion should make satisfaction with tears and prayers, and trusting in the Lord approach the Eucharist clean, free from care, and secure. But **I say this of the person not burdened with capital and mortal sins.** For the one whom mortal sins committed after baptism press down, I advise to make satisfaction with public penance, and so be joined to communion by the judgment of the priest, if he does not wish to receive the condemnation of the Church."

691. But it seems that sinners do not approach this sacrament unworthily. For in this sacrament Christ is received, and he is the spiritual physician, who says of himself: "those who are well have no need of a physician, but those who are sick" (Mt. 9:12). The answer is that this sacrament is spiritual food, as baptism is spiritual birth. Now one is born in order to live, but he is not nourished unless he is already alive. Therefore, **this sacrament does not befit sinners who are not yet alive by grace;** although baptism befits them. Furthermore, as Augustine says in his *Commentary on John,* "the Eucharist is the sacrament of love and ecclesial unity." **Since, therefore, the sinner lacks charity and is deservedly separated from the unity of the Church, if he approaches this sacrament, he commits a falsehood, since he is signifying that he has charity, but does not.** Yet because a sinner sometimes has faith in this sacrament, it is lawful for him to *look* upon this sacrament, which is something absolutely denied to unbelievers, as Dionysius says in *Ecclesiastical Hierarchy.*

692. Second, it is necessary to consider how one who receives this sacrament unworthily is guilty of the body and blood of the Lord. This is explained in three ways in a Gloss. In one way materially: **for one incurs guilt from a sin committed against the body and blood of Christ, as contained in this sacrament, which he receives unworthily and from this his guilt is increased.** For his guilt is increased to the extent that a greater person is

offended against: "how much worse punishment do you think will be deserved by the man who has spurned the Son of God and profaned the blood of the covenant?" (Heb. 10:29).

693. Second, it is explained by a similitude, so that the sense would be: he *shall be guilty of the body and of the blood of the Lord*, i.e., he will be punished as if he had killed Christ: "they crucify the Son of God on their own account and hold him up to contempt" (Heb. 6:6). But according to this the gravest sin seems to be committed by those who receive the body of Christ unworthily. The answer is that a sin is grave in two ways: in one way from the sin's species, which is taken from its object; according to this a sin against the Godhead, such as unbelief, blasphemy, and so on, is graver than one committed against the humanity of Christ. Hence, the Lord himself says: "whoever says a word against the son of man will be forgiven; but whoever speaks against the Holy Spirit will not be forgiven" (Mt. 12:32). And again a sin committed against the humanity in its own species is graver than under the sacramental species.

In another way, the gravity of sin is considered on the part of the sinner. But one sins more, when he sins from hatred or envy or any other maliciousness, as those sinned who crucified Christ, than one who sins from weakness, as they sometimes sin who receive this sacrament unworthily. It does not follow, therefore, that the sin of receiving this sacrament unworthily should be compared to the sin of killing Christ, as though the sins were equal, but on account of a specific likeness: because each concerns the same Christ.

694. He *shall be guilty of the body and of the blood of the Lord* is explained in a third way, i.e., the body and blood of the Lord will make him guilty. **For something good evilly received hurts one,** just as evil well used profits one, as the sting of Satan profited Paul. By these words is excluded the error of those who say that as soon as this sacrament is touched by the lips of a sinner, the body of Christ ceases to be under it. Against this is the word of the Apostle: *whosoever shall eat this bread, or drink the chalice of the Lord unworthily.* For according to the above opinion, no one unworthy would [be able to] eat or drink. But this opinion is contrary to the truth of this sacrament, according to which the body and blood of Christ remain in this sacrament, as long as the appearances remain, no matter where they exist.

695. Then when he says, *but let a man prove himself,* he applies a remedy against this peril. First, he suggests the remedy; second, he assigns a reason, at *for he who eats;* third, he clarifies the reason with a sign, at *therefore, there are many.*

696. First, therefore, he says: **because one who receives this sacrament unworthily incurs so much guilt, it is necessary that a man first examine himself, i.e., carefully inspect his conscience, lest there exist in it the intention to sin mortally or any past sin for which he has not repented sufficiently.** *And so,* secure after a careful examination, *let him eat of that bread and drink of the chalice,* because for those who receive worthily, it is not poison but medicine: "let each one test his own work" (Gal. 6:4); "examine yourselves to see whether you are holding to your faith" (2 Cor. 13:5).

697. Then when he says, *for he who eats,* he assigns the reason for the above remedy, saying: a previous examination is required, *for he who eats and drinks unworthily eats and drinks judgment,* i.e., condemnation, *to himself:* "those who have done evil will rise to the resurrection of judgment" (Jn. 5:29). Not discerning the body of the Lord, i.e., from the fact that he does not distinguish the body of the Lord from other things, receiving him indiscriminately as other foods: **"anyone who approaches the holy things while he has an uncleanness, that person shall be cut off from my presence"** (Lev. 22:3).

IN THE FOREGOING TEXT, WE SEE ST. THOMAS AQUI-nas lucidly expounding 1 Corinthians 11:27–29 in accord with the great majority of Catholic theologians and magisterial documents down through the ages. In striking contrast, we find Pope Francis in *Amoris Laetitia* stating outright (as modern scriptural exegetes are wont to do) that vv. 27–29 are more correctly interpreted in a *social* sense, in accord with the context of 1 Cor. 11:17–34; indeed he goes so far as to dismiss the traditional reading as being out of context and generic:

> 185. Along these same lines, we do well to take seriously **a biblical text usually interpreted outside of its context or in a generic sense, with the risk of overlooking its immediate and direct meaning, which is markedly**

social. I am speaking of 1 Cor. 11:17-34, where Saint
Paul faces a shameful situation in the community. The
wealthier members tended to discriminate against the
poorer ones, and this carried over even to the *agape* meal
that accompanied the celebration of the Eucharist. While
the rich enjoyed their food, the poor looked on and went
hungry: "One is hungry and another is drunk. Do you
not have houses to eat and drink in? Or do you despise
the Church of God and humiliate those who have nothing?" (vv. 21-22).

186. The Eucharist demands that we be members of the
one body of the Church. Those who approach the Body
and Blood of Christ may not wound that same Body by
creating scandalous distinctions and divisions among its
members. This is what it means to "discern" the body of
the Lord, to acknowledge it with faith and charity both in
the sacramental signs and in the community; those who
fail to do so eat and drink judgement against themselves
(cf. v. 29). The celebration of the Eucharist thus becomes
a constant summons for everyone "to examine himself or
herself" (v. 28), to open the doors of the family to greater
fellowship with the underprivileged, and in this way to
receive the sacrament of that eucharistic love which makes
us one body. We must not forget that "the 'mysticism'
of the sacrament has a social character" (Pope Benedict
XVI). **When those who receive it turn a blind eye to
the poor and suffering, or consent to various forms
of division, contempt and inequality, the Eucharist is
received unworthily.** On the other hand, families who
are properly disposed and receive the Eucharist regularly,
reinforce their desire for fraternity, their social consciousness and their commitment to those in need.

Now, it requires no special expertise to see that a social reading
of 1 Cor. 11:27-29 and a moral-dogmatic reading of it are not
incompatible; indeed, it is part of the genius of St. Paul that he
often interweaves the communal, the spiritual, and the sacramental. The problem consists rather in the downplaying or sidelining
of the dominant traditional reading in a document tackling the
thorny question—debated intensely now for some time—of who

should and should not be admitted publicly to the banquet of the Holy Body and Blood of Christ. The classic interpretation of this passage, epitomized in the Church's Common Doctor, is particularly relevant and profoundly needed in our times. A refusal to pay heed to it, or, worse, a dismissive attitude towards it, is symptomatic of precisely that hermeneutic of rupture and discontinuity so keenly diagnosed by Pope Benedict XVI.

And this brings us back to the heart of the problem: the desire to sweep under the rug the demanding message of 1 Cor. 11:27–29, on the necessity of individual examination of conscience and a sincere turning away from mortal sin. Concerning this and other "hard teachings" of Scripture—passages included in the old lectionary but deemed "too difficult" for modern man and therefore excluded from the new one—Peter Kreeft has some incisive words:

> We want it all. We want God *and*... But we can't have God and... because there is no such thing. The only God there is, is "God only," not "God and." God is a jealous God. He himself says that, many times, in his word. He will not share our heart's love with other gods, with idols. He is our husband, and his love will not tolerate infidelity. A hard saying, especially to our age, which is spiritually as well as physically promiscuous. But if we find the saying hard, that is all the more reason to look at it again and look at ourselves in its light, for the fact that we find it hard means that we have not accepted it yet, and need to. It's precisely those parts of God's revealed word that we don't like or understand that we need to pay the most attention to.[3]

---

3   *Making Choices: Practical Wisdom for Everyday Moral Decisions* (Ann Arbor, MI: Servant Books, 1990), 151.

10

Why the *Amoris Laetitia* Controversy Is So Important and Will Not Go Away

LifeSiteNews
JANUARY 9, 2018

S OME PEOPLE I KNOW HAVE MENTIONED that they are weary of the debate over *Amoris Laetitia*. At a recent USCCB meeting, an American bishop said that the richness of this apostolic exhortation has been eclipsed by the excessive preoccupation of the conservative blogosphere with the problems of chapter 8, and that the "narrative" about the document has to be seized back and replenished. I'm sure there are many who wish the whole conversation would just go away.

But I'm afraid that's not going to happen. It's not possible. What's more, it's not desirable. If a banquet is full of delicious and nourishing foods but the wine has a drop of cyanide in it, the meal is still deadly, and the one who prepared it is still responsible for the outcome. Chapter 8, which has provoked a veritable firestorm of confusion and contradiction in moral theology and the discipline of the sacraments, has done vastly more harm than any amount of good the rest of the document may ever accomplish.

The devil is a clever strategist. He knows that the best way to establish error is not to argue for it, but to keep repeating it *ad nauseam,* so that people already disposed to the error will come to accept it without argument as part of the ambiance, and those who oppose it will surrender from sheer exhaustion. This is why we must *never* tire of pointing out the intrinsic error of, and the host of evil consequences that follow from, the proposal to admit to the sacraments of Penance and the Holy Eucharist a "divorced and remarried Catholic," i.e., a Catholic living *more uxorio* (sharing the bed) with someone who is not his or her actual spouse in the eyes of God and the Church. For this is not just one small error. It is an error that, by logical implication, touches and corrupts every aspect of Catholic faith and morals. To take just one example, it would invalidate the divine inspiration and inerrancy of Sacred Scripture.

Proponents of sacraments for already-married persons continuing to live in a sexually active relationship with someone other than their original spouse(s) have never hidden their agenda. This was true during the two Synods (of which the telltale event that sticks in my mind was the theft of the copies of *Remaining in the Truth of Christ* from the mailboxes of the synodal participants). It has remained true in the entire period following *Amoris Laetitia*.

For 2,000 years, the Church has seen certain actions in the realm of human sexuality, e.g., fornication, masturbation, pornography, incest, sodomy, and pedophilia, as intrinsically evil, regardless of intention. Such actions, deliberately chosen, are always and everywhere wrong to do, displeasing to God, and incompatible with grace and inheriting eternal life.

Adultery is no less serious a sin than the others just mentioned. If there are now pastoral situations that allow us to admit adulterers to "penance" and communion without any intention on their part to end sexual relations with someone not their spouse, why would we deny the same sacraments to those who fornicate, masturbate, produce or view pornography, or practice incest, sodomy, or pedophilia? They may feel regrets or even "anguish" about it, but if they have no firm intention of amending their life by God's grace, they do not have *repentance*.

What, after all, is "repentance"? For a murderer or a thief, repentance is being sorry for having killed or stolen, making restitution for the crime, and resolving earnestly not to kill or steal again. For a liar, it is to be sorry for lying and to resolve not to tell lies in the future. For a blasphemer, it is to bewail his blasphemy and firmly intend never to do it again. For a fornicator, repentance is to be sincerely sorry for having had sexual intercourse outside of marriage, and to firmly intend never to do so again.

It is no different with adultery. A person who is "civilly remarried" while his or her sacramental (i.e., only real) spouse is still alive and who has sexual intercourse with the civil partner is committing adultery—there is no way around this fact. Therefore, repentance for such a person is to be sorry for having sinned against fidelity to an indissoluble bond by having slept with someone who is not one's lawful spouse in the eyes of God, and firmly and sincerely to intend never to do it again. This, and nothing else, is the repentance required to make a valid Confession and, *a fortiori,* to be admitted to the Eucharistic nuptial banquet.

This, of course, is exactly what Pope John Paul II taught in *Familiaris Consortio,* grounding it in Sacred Scripture:

> The Church reaffirms her practice, which is based upon Sacred Scripture, of not admitting to Eucharistic Communion divorced persons who have remarried. They are unable to be admitted thereto from the fact that their state and condition of life objectively contradict that union of love between Christ and the Church which is signified and effected by the Eucharist. Besides this, there is another special pastoral reason: if these people were admitted to the Eucharist, the faithful would be led into error and confusion regarding the Church's teaching about the indissolubility of marriage.
>
> Reconciliation in the sacrament of Penance which would open the way to the Eucharist can only be granted to those who, repenting of having broken the sign of the Covenant and of fidelity to Christ, are sincerely ready to undertake a way of life that is no longer in contradiction to the indissolubility of marriage. This means, in practice, that when, for serious reasons, such as for example the children's upbringing, a man and a woman cannot satisfy the obligation to separate, they "take on themselves the duty to live in complete continence, that is, by abstinence from the acts proper to married couples."

This is not legalism or rigorism or any other -ism. It is simply the truth. It is not possible to contradict this Catholic teaching, given consummate expression by John Paul II, without placing oneself outside of the Catholic Faith and at odds with the divine law. It is the very opposite of mercy to create confusion among the faithful about the Gospel's "demands of radicalness and perfection" (*Familiaris Consortio* 33). The Church is a merciful Mother who exercises her mercy by proclaiming the fullness of the truth that saves us from our sins and calling people to conversion, for which God is always ready to provide the grace.

Recently I heard St. Alphonsus Liguori invoked as one who would support Pope Francis's "gradualist" approach. Whatever limited gradualism the patron saint of moral theologians accepted, he would be appalled to find his name used in support of Communion for a man or woman who, *while not intending to forego future adulterous sexual acts,* would still be admitted to Communion. At this point, we are clearly working against the entire doctrine of the sacraments as it has been handed down by the Fathers, Doctors, Councils, and Popes.

Nevertheless, any priest or bishop who still follows the hitherto unbroken doctrine and practice of the Church is now labeled a legalist, a rigorist, a Pharisee, a hater, etc. Moreover, entire episcopates are now divided against each other with regard to who may receive the sacraments. Such a turning against our tradition and against one another can never be from the Holy Spirit. Nor can it be from the Holy Spirit to contradict the perennial magisterium enunciated in such a clear, declarative, and normative way by John Paul II in *Familiaris Consortio, Ecclesia de Eucharistia, Reconciliatio et Paenitentia, Veritatis Splendor,* and other documents. If John Paul II is wrong in what he taught so many times and in so authoritative a manner, then there is no pope who may ever be trusted again when it comes to morality.

"Mercy" is invoked today to cover a multitude of sins, but the Church has never pitted mercy against law or justice. This is the ancient error of antinomianism (nothing new under the sun). Mercy in the New Covenant is extended to the repentant sinner, not to the sinner who clings to his sin. Mercy will be given seventy times seven times to the sinner who repents and falls again out of human weakness, but only as long as he genuinely intended and intends to stop sinning. There has never been any disagreement about this—until now.

The progressives like to invoke the "ancient Church" and pretend that the liturgical reform after Vatican II was a return to ancient practices (which it mostly was not). Curiously enough, the progressives never want to imitate the penitential discipline of the early Church, whereby fornicators or adulterers could be banished *for years* not only from the sacraments but from the church building itself, to be readmitted only if they had done serious penance and had utterly overcome and forsworn their sinful behavior. The reason is simple: ancient Christians really *believed* what they professed, and they zealously kept the Eucharist *away* from anyone who was not worthy of it—worthy in the sense of being among the baptized and living a life in harmony with the Ten Commandments, free from mortal sins. Have we forgotten that Christianity teaches self-denial, asceticism, as the narrow road to perfection, the premise of *all* spiritual development? The Eucharist is not a point of departure but a place of arrival.[1] The point of departure, for the Fathers of the Church, was the rudiments of moral virtue, fasting and abstinence, prayer, the reading of Scripture, and other disciplines, which prepare the soul to partake of the heavenly feast.

Certainly the Church is a "field hospital," and we must bend over backwards to take care of each wounded person who comes our way. At the same time, a doctor does not apply the same remedy to each disease, knowing that a medicine that cures in one case may kill in another. This is how the Church Fathers speak of the Holy Eucharist: it is food for the wayfarer who is living according to God's revealed law; it is deadly for anyone else.[2] It is only when we have a well-founded confidence that we are wearing the wedding garment of charity and sanctifying grace (cf. Mt. 22:11) that we may dare to approach "the divine, holy, pure, immortal, heavenly, life-creating, and awesome Mysteries of Christ" (Byzantine Divine Liturgy). Otherwise, as every liturgical rite says before Communion, we eat and drink "judgment and condemnation."

---

1   See John Paul II, *Ecclesia de Eucharistia*, nn. 35–36.
2   See Kwasniewski, *Holy Bread*, 181–95.

Why It's Impossible for the Catholic Church to Ever Accept Remarriage

LifeSiteNews

APRIL 17, 2018

RICHARD REX, PROFESSOR OF REFORMA-
tion history at the University of Cambridge, writes the
following sobering words in the course of a review of
Ross Douthat's new book *To Change the Church: Pope Francis and the
Future of Catholicism*:

> What we might bear in mind, if we are disturbed by the
> policies of the leaders of the Church in such a situation,
> is that the duties of conscience apply just as much to
> our relationship with the Church as to our relationship
> with the state. If our leaders fail, then we should criticize,
> appropriately and helpfully. If they need to be reminded of
> the truths that have been entrusted to them, then it is our
> duty to remind them. There may well be, there certainly
> will be—as there certainly have been only too recently—
> abuses within the Church and failures by its leaders. Faith
> in the one, holy, catholic, and apostolic Church requires
> us to soldier on, minding our consciences, upholding the
> truth out of love, and avoiding evil and false doctrine.[1]

It is refreshing to find someone speaking the simple truth: given
fallen human nature and the many temptations of the world,
the flesh, and the devil, the clergy—from the Sovereign Pontiff
all the way down to the least parochial vicar—can and will fail,
sometimes dramatically so.

It is undoubtedly Rex's training as an historian that makes
this claim not only uncontroversial but transparently obvious.
I have often thought that the greatest gap in the education of
Catholics today is history. If we do not study, for example, the

---

1   In the April 2018 issue of *First Things*; text also available online.

Arian controversy or the Reformation and Counter-Reformation period, we will not be aware of the extent to which the Church on earth can become confused, corrupted, disoriented, and acutely in need of reform—the *right* kind of reform, which, as Martin Mosebach reminds us, means *returning to form,* recovering the form God intends for His Church. This form includes perfect adherence to the doctrine contained in Sacred Scripture and in Sacred Tradition, as it has been taught through the ages by shepherds exercising the charism of truth.

Rex continues his analysis with a *reductio ad absurdum,* a "what if" argument that leads to an impossible conclusion:

> If, however, the Catholic Church were indeed to abandon or reverse the almost total opposition to divorce that it has maintained across two millennia, then its claim to be the privileged vehicle of divine revelation on moral issues would be, quite simply, shattered. The position of the Church on the indissolubility of marriage is among the most consistent of its traditions. Its scriptural basis is, frankly, stronger than that for the doctrine of the Trinity, for the observance of Sunday as the day of rest, or for the real presence in the Eucharist. To all intents and purposes, it is a mark of the Church. Nor should this claim be theologically surprising. Marriage, as Paul taught, symbolizes the union of Christ and his Church (Eph. 5:31-32). For Christians, the indissolubility of marriage is integral to its symbolic—that is, its sacramental—place in the economy of salvation. If it is terminable, then it can no longer symbolize that perfect union between the head and the body of Christ.

While I'm not sure I understand why Rex says "*almost* total opposition to divorce"—the Church has *never* accepted or tolerated divorce but has always branded it a sin when chosen (rather than when merely suffered)—he is absolutely correct to say that few other teachings are clearer or more consistent from the very beginning until the past few tempestuous years. Christ's uncompromising teaching on remarriage-as-adultery is *so* clear, in fact, that adherence to it is a veritable mark of the true Church, while deviation from it is, all by itself, an indication of heresy, a deviation from the Way, the Truth, and the Life.

Rex insightfully points out that the very sacramentality of marriage, that is, its elevation by God to a grace-bearing sign of the indissoluble union of Christ and the Church, is undermined the moment one calls into question its God-given indestructible permanence. This is true even if one pays lip-service to that permanence but connives at sexual liaisons outside of the original bond and rewards them with admission to the sacraments.

In his final paragraph, Rex delivers the *coup de grâce*:

> If, after all, marriage is not a divine union of male and female in one flesh, dissolved only by the inevitable dissolution of that flesh in death, then the Catholic Church has, in the name of Christ, needlessly tormented the consciences of untold numbers of the faithful for twenty centuries. If this teaching were to be modified in the name of mercy, then the Church would already have been outdone in mercy not only by most other religions but even by the institutions and impulses of the modern secular state. Such a conclusion would definitively explode any pretension to moral authority on the part of the Church. A church which could be so wrong, for so long, on a matter so fundamental to human welfare and happiness could hardly lay claim to decency, let alone infallibility.

The irony is poignant: the neo-ultramontanism that endows every papal word and judgment with infallibility is sawing off the very branch on which it rests. If couples in irregular (i.e., anti-sacramental and adulterous) marriages are, after a period of consultation and "public penance" (whatever *that* means, when there is no intention to live in chastity), allowed to receive sacraments *without foregoing their adultery,* then not only is papal infallibility itself fatally compromised, but the very foundations of the Catholic Faith are destroyed.

It is to Rex's credit that he sees and diagnoses without flinching what so many others blithely ignore or sweep under the carpet. If the Buenos Aires guidelines that permit the above scenario were true, the Catholic Church has been a moral monster worse than anything Protestants have ever imagined, for she will have been demanding for two thousand years a standard of holiness that is not only impossible but unnecessary and even contrary to human flourishing.

Fortunately, this nightmarish conclusion is easily avoided. To the extent that the Buenos Aires guidelines permit what the Church has *always* forbidden on account of divine law, they are false, and any true Catholic will reject them without hesitation.

12

Why Sacred Liturgy's Modernization Has Resulted in Abandonment of Ten Commandments, Gospels

LifeSiteNews
JULY 6, 2018

TOMORROW MARKS THE ELEVENTH ANNI-
versary of the promulgation of Pope Benedict XVI's motu
proprio *Summorum Pontificum,* which has yielded countless
fruits but is still ignored by all too many, who will have to answer
to God for their lack of responsiveness to this wise initiative and
their lack of compassion for the people of God who are thirsty
for liturgy that is palpably sacred.

In light of the unfolding (or perhaps one should say unravel-
ing) of Pope Francis's pontificate, we should revisit words once
spoken by Joseph Cardinal Ratzinger, predating and anticipating
Summorum—words that now have an alarming portentousness:

> I am of the opinion, to be sure, that the old rite should
> be granted much more generously to all those who desire
> it. It's impossible to see what could be dangerous or
> unacceptable about that. A community is calling its very
> being into question when it suddenly declares that what
> until now was its holiest and highest possession is strictly
> forbidden, and when it makes the longing for it seem
> downright indecent. Can it be trusted any more about
> anything else? Won't it proscribe tomorrow what it pre-
> scribes today?[1]

He has asked a question to which, so far, no honest answer
has been given by the Church's leaders. The reason is not hard to
see. Ratzinger dared to say that the Church's very being had been
called into question when Paul VI declared the old Mass forbidden—which in fact he repeatedly *did,* in response to attempts to

---

1 *Salt of the Earth: The Church at the End of the Millennium,* trans. Adrian Walker
(San Francisco: Ignatius Press, 1997), 176–77.

maintain a liturgy the Church had celebrated for 500 years, and in its essentials, for 1,000 years, and in the core of it, for 1,500 years. The longing for this treasure of faith was mocked, stepped on, suppressed, treated as a form of disobedience, arrogance, or neurosis. And the haunting question rises up: "Can the Church be trusted any more about anything else? Won't it proscribe tomorrow what it prescribes today?"

If Paul VI in 1969 can abolish the oldest liturgical rite of Christendom and replace it with a new-fangled rite fashioned by committee according to modern ideas, with the two rites having *very little* in common when one looks at their details, why can't Francis today modify the Ten Commandments or the Gospels? They, too, are awfully old, rejected by vast numbers of people as irrelevant to modern times, extremely provocative, and rather narrow in their fixation on obeying God *or else*. Don't we need to update and modernize the whole of Christianity? If we can do this with what is our holiest and highest possession, namely the Holy Sacrifice of the Mass, we can do it across the board, top to bottom. What is permitted, what is forbidden, what is to be construed as good, what is to be rejected as evil, is simply up to the will of the reigning pontiff.

"Wait a minute," you say. "Aren't you exaggerating things?" No. Have we not seen, in the most dramatic way possible, how that which was yesterday universally taught and understood to be intrinsically evil, namely, attempted remarriage after divorce, is now deemed a step in the right direction, the best some people can do, worthy of reconciliation and holy communion—as if, for all the world, Our Lord Jesus Christ, the apostles, the Church Fathers, and innumerable saints had never condemned divorce and remarriage? Moreover, have we not seen how that which was yesterday universally taught and understood to be permissible under certain circumstances—the death penalty—is now being deemed intrinsically evil?

One could paraphrase Ratzinger this way: "A community is calling its very being into question when it suddenly declares that its holiest and highest sacrament, so far from requiring moral rectitude in the observance of the commandments as always previously taught, may now be received by anyone who, in his or her own mind, feels sorry and sincere, and when it makes the longing for Penance and the Eucharist seem always decent and fulfillable, regardless of what their recipients intend to do next." Yes, that is exactly what is going on, and we are either going to fight against it with all our might, or sign off on the self-destruction of the only institution left in the world that stands for the intrinsic good of marriage and family and the intrinsic evil of all that opposes them.

As Cardinal Bellarmine states:

> In order to resist and defend oneself no authority is required .... Therefore, as it is lawful to resist the Pope, if he assaulted a man's person, so it is lawful to resist him, if he assaulted souls, or troubled the state, and much more if he strove to destroy the Church. It is lawful, I say, to resist him, by not doing what he commands, and hindering the execution of his will.[2]

In 1969 the community centered around Paul VI began its wearisome journey down the road of calling its very being into question, as it chopped away century after century of development in pursuit of an illusory updating that was impossibly supposed to be, at the same time, a return to roots. Where would it all lead? From 2013 onwards, the community centered around Francis has completed this journey by renouncing continuity and non-contradiction. As Ratzinger implied, it cannot be trusted. Those who are looking for a rock of strength rather than a postmodern void had better look elsewhere—namely, to Sacred Scripture and Sacred Tradition as received and taught by the Catholic Church in her authentic Magisterium, which equally binds the lofty and the lowly.

---

2   *De Rom. Pont.* ii.29, quoted by John Henry Newman in his *Letter to the Duke of Norfolk.*

13

Pope's Change to *Catechism* Contradicts Natural Law and the Deposit of Faith

LifeSiteNews
AUGUST 2, 2018

I N THE BOLDEST AND MOST RECKLESS MOVE to date in a pontificate that was already out of control and sowing confusion on a massive scale, the Vatican has announced Pope Francis's substitution, in the *Catechism of the Catholic Church,* of a new doctrine on capital punishment.

Sacred Scripture, Sacred Tradition, and the Magisterium of the Church for 2,000 years have upheld the legitimacy of the death penalty for grave crimes against the common good of Church or State. There had never been any doubt in the minds of anyone on this subject. It was not a point of contention in the Schism between East and West, or in the Reformation and Counter-Reformation, or in the period of the Enlightenment—in short, it was one of those rare subjects on which agreement could be found not only within the Church, but with nearly everyone.

The reason is simple: according to the natural law and Scripture alike, the rulers of a State, acting as representatives of divine justice and as custodians of the common good, may exercise an authority over life and death that they do not possess as private persons. In other words, it is God, always God, who has the right of life and death, and if the State shares in His divine authority, it has, at least *in principle,* the authority to end the life of a criminal. That the State does share in divine authority is the constant dogmatic teaching of the Church, found most explicitly (and repeatedly) in the Encyclical Letters of Pope Leo XIII.

Lest there be any doubts on this matter, Edward Feser and Joseph Bessette published a comprehensive overview of the subject: *By Man Shall His Blood Be Shed: A Catholic Defense of Capital Punishment* (San Francisco: Ignatius Press, 2017). In this hard-hitting book, Feser and Bessette present the natural law arguments in favor of capital punishment, furnish a veritable catalog of citations from Scripture, Fathers and Doctors of the Church, and popes that uphold its legitimacy, and mount a critique of the logical fallacies and doctrinal contradictions—be they those of American bishops, or even of the Bishop of Rome—who attempt to wiggle out of this unanimous witness of faith and reason.

The *Catechism of the Catholic Church,* like Feser and Bessette's book, frequently quotes authoritative witnesses to Catholic doctrine from a period of 2,000 years (and more, if we add Old Testament references). It is hardly surprising, on the other hand, that the new *Catechism* text imposed by Francis cites but one source: a speech that Francis himself gave to participants in a meeting of the Pontifical Council for the Promotion of the New Evangelization on October 11, 2017. Francis, creating doctrine *ex nihilo,* has only himself to cite.

Some may say that Francis is not being revolutionary here, since Pope John Paul II was also opposed to capital punishment. But there is a crucial difference. John Paul II never questioned the admissibility of the death penalty as such; indeed, he could not have done so, because there is no way to reject this penalty without repudiating the foundations of Catholic Social Teaching. Instead, John Paul II recommended favoring the approach of detention, clemency, and rehabilitation. About such prudential issues, Christians and Catholics can indeed disagree with one another, presenting various arguments pro and con.

The matter at hand could not be more grave. If Pope Francis is right, only one conclusion follows: "the Church was wrong in a major issue literally of life and death":

> If such a certain doctrine of the Church (of the possibility of the death penalty at least in some situations), affirmed by Christ Himself in Scripture—when, confronted by Pilate who affirmed his right to inflict capital punishment, told him, "You would have no authority over Me if it were not given to you from above," affirming that it is a power granted to the State in its authority, even if, as all governmental powers, it can be exercised illegitimately and unjustly—can be changed, then anything can be changed. A "development" of doctrine may bring about anything: from the end of the "intrinsic[ally] disordered" nature of

homosexuality to the priestly ordination of women, from the possibility of contraception in "some" cases to the acceptance of the Lutheran understanding of the Real Presence in the Eucharist as a possible interpretation of what the Church has always believed—and so on.[1]

With this move, Pope Francis has shown himself to be openly heretical on a point of major importance, teaching a pure and simple novelty—"the boldness of a personal opinion becoming a completely new and unprecedented 'teaching' of the Church," as *Rorate Caeli* stated. "The current Pope has far exceeded his authority: his authority is to guard and protect the doctrine that was received from Christ and the Apostles, not to alter it according to his personal views."

Francis may be banking on an assumption—false at least for the United States—that most Catholics are already (more or less) opposed to the death penalty, and therefore, that it is an obvious place to commence the *official* program of "renovating" the Church's morality, while not ruffling too many feathers. He sees that if this change to the *Catechism* is accepted, it will be relatively easy to proceed to the other issues mentioned above: a change in the *Catechism* on homosexuality, a change on contraception, a change on conditions for admission to Holy Communion, a change on women's ordination, and so forth.

Whether Francis is a *formal* heretic—that is, both fully aware that what he is teaching on capital punishment is contrary to Catholic doctrine and pertinacious in maintaining his position in spite of rebuke—is a matter to be adjudicated by the College of Cardinals. No doubt exists, however, that orthodox bishops of the Catholic Church must oppose this doctrinal error and refuse to use the altered edition of the *Catechism* or any catechetical materials based on it.

May St. Alphonsus Liguori, patron saint of moral theologians, whose feast is celebrated on August 1st and August 2nd, intercede for the pope and for the entire Catholic Church, that the Lord in His mercy may quickly end this period of doctrinal chaos.

---

1   "What was black is now white: Pope 'changes Catechism' to declare death penalty 'inadmissible in all cases,'" *Rorate Caeli*, August 2, 2018.

14

Pope's Change to *Catechism* Is Not Just a Prudential Judgment, but a Rejection of Dogma

LifeSiteNews

AUGUST 3, 2018

IN THE AVALANCHE OF REACTIONS TO POPE Francis's audacious move to modify the *Catechism* so that it says the opposite of what the Church and every published catechism had ever taught before, there is one line of argument that has surfaced a great deal: "Pope Francis is not making a doctrinal statement about the illegitimacy always and everywhere of the death penalty but merely a prudential judgment about the inopportuneness of its use at this time in history."

In a recent article, Dr. Alan Fimister correctly points out that even if this reading were plausible, the pope has overstepped his jurisdiction by offering an opinion about a contingent matter of political judgment, which is the proper realm of the laity and not of the ecclesiastical hierarchy, as per the teaching of the Magisterium (e.g., Leo XIII in *Immortale Dei*).[1]

As much as I might wish that this interpretation of the papal "correction" of the *Catechism of the Catholic Church* were true, I cannot concur with it, because it fails to do justice to the actual presentation of the new teaching in the revised text of 2267. Let us take each paragraph:

> Recourse to the death penalty on the part of legitimate authority, following a fair trial, was long considered an appropriate response to the gravity of certain crimes and an acceptable, albeit extreme, means of safeguarding the common good.

---

1   See "Pope's change to Catechism on death penalty is distressingly ambiguous," *LifeSiteNews*, August 2, 2018.

The implication here is that it *used* to be thought—indeed, by everyone in the Catholic tradition—that capital punishment could be employed by a legitimate authority. But such a thing can be thought no more. And why?

> Today, however, there is an increasing awareness that the dignity of the person is not lost even after the commission of very serious crimes. In addition, a new understanding has emerged of the significance of penal sanctions imposed by the state. Lastly, more effective systems of detention have been developed, which ensure the due protection of citizens but, at the same time, do not definitively deprive the guilty of the possibility of redemption.

Today, in modern times—so the argument goes—we have made a new discovery, foreign to the earlier philosophical and theological tradition, that human persons have a dignity that cannot be lost, no matter what crime they may commit. This is certainly a surprising claim to make, as, on the one hand, the truth of the *metaphysical* dignity that consists in being made to the image and likeness of God is present from the first page of the Bible and has been universally upheld by all Catholic philosophers and theologians of all centuries, and, on the other hand, the *moral* dignity that consists in living in accordance with that image and likeness can obviously be lost by serious crime. One can never forfeit the right to be treated as a person, but one can forfeit the right to be included as a member of civil society. It is the same with supernatural dignity: a baptized person is forever a Christian, distinguished from the non-baptized by the sacramental character indelibly marked on the essence of his soul; but a Christian enjoys the further dignity of being an adopted son of God so long as he is in a state of sanctifying grace, and thus the one who commits mortal sin forfeits this dignity and, if he dies in that state, will suffer the loss of heaven and the pains of hell.

This second paragraph, although it mentions the contingent issue of reliable systems of detention, is advancing the view that we are now aware of an intrinsic and inalienable dignity of the human person that *must* be respected to the point of never utilizing the death penalty. In other words, the Catholic tradition prior to Francis failed to recognize this dignity and contradicted it in

48

practice by using (or defending the use of) capital punishment. This claim is, to use the classic language of theological censures, at very least temerarious, and more likely proximate to heresy.

Then comes the conclusion Francis has been driving towards:

> Consequently, the Church teaches, in the light of the Gospel, that "the death penalty is inadmissible because it is an attack on the inviolability and dignity of the person," and she works with determination for its abolition worldwide.

All doubt of the nature of this novel teaching is removed by this final paragraph. The reason "the Church" now declares the death penalty "inadmissible"—let us give this word its full force: *unable* to be admitted, incapable of entry (and this is said without qualification of time or place)—is that "it is an *attack* on the inviolability and dignity of the person." It is, in and of itself, contrary to human dignity and the human good. The death penalty is wrong, not because we have better detention systems, and not because modern governments are already too cavalier in their treatment of human life (which is unfortunately true). It is wrong because "the light of the Gospel" shows us that it goes against something always and everywhere true, namely, the inviolable dignity of the person.

If this is not a philosophical and theological assertion, I do not know what is. If this is not intended to be a magisterial statement about what is *intrinsically* right and wrong, I do not know what is. In short, the replacement text for 2267 leaves no room for maintaining that the pope is recommending a mere shift in policy or a temporary adjustment. He is indeed promoting a shift in policy— nothing short of "worldwide abolition." But he is doing so because he believes that the thing in itself is and cannot but be wrong.

This is precisely where he himself is wrong and can be known to be wrong, for two reasons.

First, there is no need to beat around the bush: this new teaching is simply contrary to what the Church has always officially taught. One example among a thousand, taken from the *Roman Catechism of the Council of Trent,* will suffice to illustrate the traditional doctrine:

> The power of life and death is permitted to certain civil magistrates because theirs is the responsibility under law to punish the guilty and protect the innocent. Far from

being guilty of breaking this commandment [Thou shalt not kill], such an execution of justice is precisely an act of obedience to it. For the purpose of the law is to protect and foster human life. This purpose is fulfilled when the legitimate authority of the State is exercised by taking the guilty lives of those who have taken innocent lives. In the Psalms we find a vindication of this right: "Morning by morning I will destroy all the wicked in the land, cutting off all evildoers from the city of the Lord" (Ps. 101:8).

A dogmatic theologian explains:

> In the case of the dogma of the intrinsic morality of the death penalty, the denial of this dogma is formally heretical, since it contradicts a doctrine which is contained in divine revelation and which has been proposed as such by the ordinary and universal magisterium of the Church.[2]

That is, to state that the death penalty is *inadmissible for theoretical reasons,* as we have seen is the pope's position, is contrary to established dogma, and therefore formally heretical.

Second, the new teaching requires a false understanding of "development of doctrine," the wand that enables a magisterial magician to put a frog in the hat and pull out a rabbit. As the letter from the CDF cheerfully and blusteringly tells us: "All of this shows that the new formulation of number 2267 of the *Catechism* expresses an authentic development of doctrine that is not in contradiction with the prior teachings of the Magisterium." Voila, just like that—a rescript rabbit!

But the letter gives away too much. For it claims that the new statement is a development *of doctrine,* so it is *not* just a "prudential matter," a "juridical matter" as some would have it, but a matter of what is true always and everywhere: it is the *doctrine* of the Catholic Church on the death penalty, not its recommended social policy. This logically requires that "inadmissibility" be a roundabout way of saying illegitimacy, and therefore, immorality. (Would not a Catholic who continued to espouse the death penalty, or who meted it out, or who administered it, now have to be considered to be acting immorally?)

---

2   Cited in Steve Skojec, "Heresy in the Catechism. Wolf in the Vatican. No Shepherds in Sight," *OnePeterFive,* August 2, 2018.

The pope has thus avoided the easy road. He could have said "This is not expedient" and left it at that, as did John Paul II. But he chose the high road: "This is now Catholic doctrine, as more fully understood in our times." As Fr. Zuhlsdorf commented, the notion of the development of doctrine in play is clearly not that of John Henry Newman, for whom development refines and expands, but does not undermine or reject, what was taught earlier. When a later teaching departs from an earlier one, it is a corruption, not a development.[3]

Pope Francis is obviously and sadly wedded to a conception of papal authority that has little to do with the First Vatican Council's articulation of the papacy's inherently conservative nature, by which it receives and transmits, in its integrity, the apostolic faith as it passes through the ages—growing in expression, yes, but not morphing into something different or opposed to itself. Tragically, by functioning as a doctrinal maverick, the pope offers to Protestants, Eastern Orthodox, and the entire world the spectacle of a papacy that confirms rather than denies the familiar anti-Catholic caricature of papal positivism and hyperultramontanism that reasonable and faithful people could do nothing other than reject.

---

3   See "Pope Francis changed the Catechism about the death penalty. What next?," *Fr. Z's Blog*, August 2, 2018.

15

Two Strategies Enemies within Church Will Use to Abandon *Humanae Vitae*

LifeSiteNews
AUGUST 14, 2018

S INCE ITS RELEASE IN APRIL 2016, *AMORIS Laetitia* in its eighth chapter has shown itself to be the Trojan Horse by which progressive, liberal, and modernist clergy have been able to introduce old errors, new abuses, and more sins into the City of God. In this fiftieth anniversary year of *Humanae Vitae,* we will see the same clergy utilize two strategies to set aside the perennial teaching contained in that encyclical.

One strategy will make use of the "canonization" of Pope Paul VI. As with John XXIII and John Paul II, this politically motivated canonization is intended to remove Paul VI to a distant pedestal as an "example" of living the Christian life "in his particular circumstances"—i.e., not in *our* particular circumstances. It is paradoxically a way of excluding him from the current conversation by wrapping his life and work in a haze of hagiographical admiration that, in a sense, "discharges" all of our obligations towards his moral magisterium. Those who are manipulating his memory can create a smokescreen behind which they will be more free to do as they please. The same thing happened, of course, with John XXIII, whose canonization cemented in place a carefully contrived picture of him as the great revolutionary of Vatican II, and with John Paul II, whose canonization meant that *Veritatis Splendor, Familiaris Consortio,* and a host of other documents could be sealed up in the reverent tomb of his earthly remains.

The reasoning goes like this: *Humanae Vitae* was understandable in its context, that is, the confusion of the late 1960s, when the subject of birth control was still in its infancy (if you'll pardon the expression), and we should applaud and admire a pope who had the courage to take a stand in defense, as he viewed it, of the goods of marriage. But in the twenty-first century, there is no longer any doubt that "times have changed." The Church has a deeper and broader understanding of the goods of marriage, especially the union of spouses, such that the scholastic and natural-law categories relied on by theologians in the last century are now seen to be simplistic and outmoded. Moreover, the Church in her "motherly compassion" for weak human beings, and in her grave concern for the ecological health of the planet under the pressures of overpopulation, understands that there are competing goods that Paul VI may have overlooked—for he is a saint not due to how well he governed or how true his doctrine is, but because of the goodness of his heart.

So this is one strategy, and the whiff of sulfur is more than noticeable.

The other strategy will be a continuation of the divorced-and-remarried refrain, namely, that the Church's traditional teaching is too difficult for some people in some circumstances to follow. They simply cannot do it; it is "morally impossible" and therefore not required of them.

But Pope Paul VI—well advised on this particular topic, if not always on others—anticipated that very line of argument and cut it off decisively:

> The teaching of the Church regarding the proper regulation of birth is a promulgation of the law of God Himself. And yet there is no doubt that to many it will appear not merely difficult but even impossible to observe. Now it is true that like all good things which are outstanding for their nobility and for the benefits which they confer on men, so this law demands from individual men and women, from families and from human society, a resolute purpose and great endurance. Indeed it cannot be observed unless God comes to their help with the grace by which the goodwill of men is sustained and strengthened. (*HV* 20)

This, in a nutshell, is just what Pope John Paul II would later argue at length in *Veritatis Splendor* and other documents: while fallen man on his own is incapable of following God's law, Christian man with the help of grace is certainly able to follow it, even if there will be faltering and failure, with the need for repentance and continual conversion. Put simply, a Christian is obliged to live *as* a Christian—and God will never deprive any of the baptized of the grace it takes to do that, if they sincerely ask Him for it. If they do not so live, then the Church's motherly compassion consists not in a wink-wink, nudge-nudge toleration, but in reminding them, gently and firmly, of the truth by which we are saved, and of the need for God's help to live according to it.

A different application of the archetypal error of *Amoris Laetitia* consists in maintaining that, even if contraceptive sex is wrong, it is a *lesser* moral evil than other evils such as infidelity, divorce, and abortion, and therefore can be condoned if only to prevent those greater evils. Pope Paul VI once again anticipates this devious dodge and refutes it utterly:

> Neither is it valid to argue, as a justification for sexual intercourse which is deliberately contraceptive, that a lesser evil is to be preferred to a greater one, or that such intercourse would merge with procreative acts of past and future to form a single entity, and so be qualified by exactly the same moral goodness as these. Though it is true that sometimes it is lawful to tolerate a lesser moral evil in order to avoid a greater evil or in order to promote a greater good, it is never lawful, even for the gravest reasons, to do evil that good may come of it—in other words, to intend directly something which of its very nature contradicts the moral order, and which must therefore be judged unworthy of man, even though the intention is to protect or promote the welfare of an individual, of a family, or of society in general. Consequently, it is a serious error to think that a whole married life of otherwise normal relations can justify sexual intercourse which is deliberately contraceptive and so intrinsically wrong. (*HV* 14)

We must be prepared for the Machiavellian and, to speak truthfully, Luciferian strategies of the enemies of human nature, natural law, and holy matrimony. Pope Paul VI will be our ally, if, instead of elevating him to a lofty niche of irrelevance, we allow him to remain near us as the complicated and problematic figure he was, through whom nonetheless St. Peter spoke when he passed on the unbroken teaching of the Church about the intrinsic evil of contraception.

16

When a Pope Politicizes Doctrine He Betrays Teaching of Christ and Church

LifeSiteNews
AUGUST 17, 2018

O N AUGUST 3, *THE CATHOLIC THING* PUB-
lished an excellent piece by David Warren on "Deathgate," as Fr. John Hunwicke names the latest scandal
emanating from the halls of the Vatican: Pope Francis's attempt
to change the teaching of divine revelation and the ordinary universal magisterium of the Church on the moral legitimacy and
therefore admissibility *in principle* of capital punishment, whatever
the prudential limitations on its use might be in this or that
contingent set of circumstances. Warren writes:

> The damage that is done, and will be done, by this lat-
> est breach of "papal etiquette," is broader and will be
> broader than first appears. Beyond the creation of a
> precedent for altering Church teaching by papal fiat, it
> confirms the politicization of our doctrine. Henceforth,
> and for the foreseeable future, the Holy See (even after
> Bergoglio's demise) is re-oriented to social and political
> issues.... [T]he rewrite of paragraph 2267 of the *Catechism*
> brings into scandal all the previous social doctrine of the
> Church.... Now we accept the alteration of the teaching
> itself, because it is not in accord with "the times."

What makes the teaching of Jesus Christ rise above all centuries
and all cultures, Warren continues, is that we find in His words a
timeless wisdom equally applicable to the ever-varying situations
of temporal life. Christ did not come to earth to abolish the death
penalty; he calmly stated Pilate's sin in putting an *innocent* man
to death with the genuine power he had been given "from above,"
even as Christ willed that He should suffer His Passion between
two malefactors who knew they had been put to death for good

reason. Although St. Paul converted after recognizing his guilt in persecuting the Mystical Body of Christ, he never failed to teach reverence for civil authority, which does not hold the sword in vain, but uses it to punish evildoers. Fathers and Doctors, Popes and Councils form an unbroken consensus of two millennia in favor of the inherent legitimacy of capital punishment, even when individuals among them were strongly opposed to its use in practice.

Warren then says:

> The wisdom of restricting ourselves to Christian inspi-
> ration—to what can be apprehended in Scripture and
> Tradition from our beginnings—was previously understood.
> Perhaps the greatest (and most monstrous) achievement
> of modernity was to unhinge this.

Modernity has put asunder what God has joined together: the sources of divine revelation and the actual exercise of Christian teaching in the form of catechesis, mystagogy, homiletics, theology, and liturgy. All forms of teaching should never depart from "what can be apprehended in Scripture and Tradition from our beginnings," and the single greatest error, the characteristic error of modern times, is to allow ourselves to drift further and further from these *givens,* until we reach a point where, with towering hubris or daft naivete, we start teaching something different, at cross-purposes, and finally, contradictory.

In this way a preacher, be he an ordinary priest, a bishop, or even the pope, becomes like a man sawing off the branch on which he is sitting. For a pope to politicize our doctrine, yoking it to modern Western secular liberalism, while deliberately surrounding it with clouds of confusion—"Is it a doctrinal change? Is it only a prudential judgment? Is it a new category? Catholic rabbis, get ready to write your endless commentaries!"—is to betray the luminously supernatural character of Christ's teachings and the Catholic tradition that emerged organically from them.

David Warren is right: the pope's re-writing of the *Catechism* has established a baleful precedent. But so too have *Amoris Laetitia,* and *Evangelii Gaudium,* and *Vultum Dei Quaerere,* and many other acts of this pontificate. The pope continues to destabilize the doctrinal and sacramental integrity of the Roman Catholic Church. It is high time that the faithful stopped making excuses for him simply because he happens to be pope. It is precisely *because* he is pope that his heterodoxy is inexcusable. Now, more than ever, Christ's faithful must know the Catholic religion well, relying on approved traditional sources which concur with one another over the span of many centuries. The faithful must speak clearly and without compromise. Above all, they must pray for the pope and the entire hierarchy, that they may bring the unadulterated message of divine revelation to the modern world.

17

Medical Journal: If Pope Francis Can Change Doctrine on Death Penalty, Why Not Abortion?

LifeSiteNews

AUGUST 20, 2018

I N THE MEDIA COVERAGE OF "DEATHGATE"—
that is, the pope's emendation of the *Catechism* so that it states
that capital punishment is always and everywhere inadmissible, as being contrary to human dignity and the Gospel—many
authors have pointed out that if Francis comes to be seen as
having authority to change a part of Church teaching that has
been stable for millennia, people will naturally expect other parts
to fall within the scope of his power. This impression will especially affect moral matters, where modern democratic convictions
and social conventions are far removed from Christian teaching.

The Lancet—one of the most prestigious medical journals in the
world and second only to the *New England Journal of Medicine* in
global readership—published an editorial in its most recent issue
that demonstrates how much confusion the pope is causing by
his routine interference with longstanding Catholic teaching. The
editorial discusses the recent Argentinean senate vote:

> Just a week before the abortion vote, the Vatican reformed
> its position on the death penalty, declaring it inadmissible in all cases. Thus, Pope Francis seems comfortable
> changing doctrine based on modernised social norms with
> regard to the rights of prisoners. But he offers no such
> accommodation to women's reproduction.[1]

The author, Richard Horton, who seems highly piqued about the
affair, interprets the "reform" of the position on the death penalty
to be a significant shift: a change in *doctrine* "based on modernised
social norms with regard to the rights of prisoners." The author

1 *The Lancet*, vol. 392, issue 10147, August 18, 2018, p. 532; www.thelancet.com/journals/lancet/article/PIIS0140-6736(18)31801-4/fulltext.

then draws the conclusion that the pope is acting inconsistently by refusing to take into account modern social norms in regard to "women's reproduction."

Of course, the argument is fallacious no matter what we make of the change to the *Catechism,* for the question of the *use* of capital punishment (not the inherent right to use it) has always been murkier and more controverted than the right to life of the unborn. Believing Catholics have disputed when and where criminals convicted of serious crime should be put to death, but they have never disputed the exceptionless prohibition on killing unborn babies. Thus, the editor of *The Lancet* is clearly out of his depth when he leaps from a reform in the one area to an "accommodation" in the other.

Nevertheless, what this editorial shows is how easily and, one might say, understandably, a huge number of theologically illiterate people will misinterpret what the pope has done and invoke it as justification for many other changes that the liberal establishment has long desired of the Church. The manner in which Pope Francis changed the *Catechism* leads the simple astray, foments confusion within the flock, and transmits a false picture of the Catholic Church and her magisterium. The pope is compounding the crisis of the West by throwing fuel on an already raging forest-fire of liberalism, in a dereliction of his duty to lead the nations to Christ and consolidate them in the truth of the Faith.

Horton's editorial makes for a magnificent example of the sheer illogicality, not to say cold cruelty, that reigns in the secular world, where a woman's "rights and bodily autonomy" are held to warrant an absolute power over the life and death of an unborn baby human—even though the *child's* body is certainly not *her* body! The Catholic Church is reproached for the prevalence of unsafe abortions, when in reality it is the responsibility of governments to prevent *all* abortions and the responsibility of a network of social organizations to come to the aid of mothers in need.

Richard Horton will, in any case, have to reconcile himself to living with his indignation, since the Catholic Church will never budge an inch on the question of so-called "reproductive rights." But that he is so frustrated and confused, and that he nurtures false hopes, is squarely the fault of a Jesuit from Argentina whose motto—quoting his own words—seems to be: "Make a mess."

18

If Pope Francis Covered Up McCarrick Abuse, Then He's Neither "Holy" Nor a "Father"

LifeSiteNews

AUGUST 27, 2018

SHOULD WE BE SURPRISED AT ARCHBISHOP Carlo Maria Viganò's detailed testimony about Pope Francis covering up ex-Cardinal McCarrick's abuse?[1] We have seen this level of mendacity and depravity coming for years. From the first moment of his papacy, Pope Francis showed disdain for papal traditions, a sign of disrespect for the duties and limits of his office. His minimalist and lackluster celebrations of Mass suggested that for him, the liturgy was not "the source and summit of the Christian life."

His torturous and often doctrinally suspect homilies exposed an uncatholic mind. His sloppy interviews with newspapers and on airplanes sowed confusion about basic Christian teachings. "Who am I to judge?" appeared in every newspaper and eventually on thousands of pieces of online merchandise as a message of liberation from God's commandments. The sweet name of "mercy" was co-opted for an agenda of secularization. The word "Pharisee" became the favorite taunt for anyone who still believed in the Bible or any identifiable version of Christianity.

The papally rigged synods on the family and their spawn, *Amoris Laetitia*—authoritatively clarified by the Buenos Aires guidelines— bestowed papal honors on the normalization of adulterous liaisons. Changes to the annulment process fast-tracked the granting of "Catholic divorce." Internal reorganizations and initiatives at the

---

1   See "Pope Francis covered up McCarrick abuse, former US nuncio testifies," *LifeSiteNews*, August 25, 2018. The text is also reproduced in *A Voice in the Wilderness: Archbishop Carlo Maria Viganò on the Church, America, and the World*, ed. Brian M. McCall (Brooklyn, NY: Angelico Press, 2021), 35–55.

Vatican weakened the anti-abortion message and muddied the waters of *Humanae Vitae* even in its anniversary year. Notorious anti-Catholics were invited to the Vatican, given a platform, and applauded.

The moment anyone got too near to the wretched truth about Vatican financial corruption, the supposedly "reform-minded" pope ensured that the threat was removed—be it the C-9 cardinal who was conveniently framed or the professional external auditors who were summarily fired.

The pope's condemnation of homosexuality was never better than ambivalent; the traditional teaching seemed to be heading for the same dustbin as capital punishment. (If you don't like what Church tradition has to say, why not just change the *Catechism*, while speaking the magic words "Abracadabra, development of doctrine"?) The handling of the global sexual abuse crisis, as seen in the situation in Chile, demonstrated a flaccid commitment to justice at best, and a trend towards complicity at worst.

And now this news, which has rightly created shockwaves around the globe, a collective astonishment at the depths of alleged wickedness in high places.

It is not only that we lack justice in Casa Santa Marta; we have dwelling there what appears to be a calculated, premeditated resolve to support, honor, and promote injustice. It is not only that we have a "trend towards complicity"; the upper echelons of the Vatican are the factory where the evils are being manufactured, with an efficiency Henry Ford would marvel at. The ineluctable progress of events is unmasking Pope Francis more and more as a facilitator of that lavender mafia in whose limp-wristed bureaucratic grip the Church on earth is suffering strangulation. Bergoglio's Vatican is a kind of sinkhole in which the worldly accommodationism of the Second Vatican Council and the worst ideas and behaviors of the postconciliar rebellion have gathered in concentrated form.

An article I published at *OnePeterFive* on August 15 contained the following statement: "To hear well-meaning people say Bergoglio must impanel some investigative body to set things right [in the USA] is Alice in Wonderland lunacy. It's like putting Himmler in charge of Nuremberg."[2] For some, this was too strong a statement. How dare I say such a thing about "the Holy Father"?

---

2   See volume 1, chapter 17: "No Matter How Bad You Think the Corruption Is, It's Worse."

Today, in light of Viganò's revelations and so many other pieces of evidence, I stand by that statement, and a thousand others like it. For he shows no probable signs of being holy, nor is he acting like a father. A holy father would not treat Catholics the way Francis has treated them. A holy father would not mislead his children into sin about the mysteries of sexuality, marriage, and the Blessed Sacrament. A holy father would not oppress those of his children who found spiritual strength in the recovery of family traditions, while sponsoring and promoting children who rebel against the family, or even strangers who care nothing for it. A holy father would not tolerate *for a moment* the eldest children in his family when they are caught grossly abusing the littlest; he would strip them of all dignities and put them out.

Who knows what is going on within the convolutions of his own mind? God alone knows. What *we* know is that God has permitted this period of tribulation for the testing and strengthening of the faith of His servants, to see if we will be loyal to His revelation, His commandments, His gift of tradition, His righteousness, come what may.

Divine Providence has tested Christian fidelity many times in the Church's long history, be it with the gruesome tortures and bitter exiles of Roman or pagan persecution, rampant clerical immorality and corruption, doctrinal chaos and compromise, or simply the terrible hardships of war, famine, plague, and disasters that our fallen world will never be without. "Blessed is the man who remains steadfast under trial, for when he has stood the test he will receive the crown of life, which God has promised to those who love him" (Jas. 1:12).

19

Why Viganò's Testimony Will Go Down as the Clarifying Moment of Francis's Papacy

LifeSiteNews
SEPTEMBER 4, 2018

T HE MONTH OF AUGUST OPENED WITH A bang—and closed with a nuclear detonation. On August 2nd the world learned of Pope Francis's disdain for the witness of Scripture and the ordinary and universal magisterium of the Church on the death penalty as he took it upon himself to "develop" into oblivion over 3,000 years of Jewish and Christian teaching. On August 25 the world learned of Pope Francis's disdain for justice, victims of abuse, and the eradication of the homosexual elite. In the space of a single month, Catholics beheld the prodigy of a pope who neither guarded orthodoxy of doctrine nor protected the faithful from the predation of wolves.

We *knew* it was bad before, but something has changed. Comparisons are not easy, but I suppose it would be like thinking your country is ruled by Mussolini and discovering it is actually ruled by Stalin. Before Viganò, people could persuade themselves to believe with faint and remote hope that Bergoglio might "come around" and do something about the sexual abuse crisis exemplified in McCarrick, that he might "wake up" to the gravity of the situation and respond as befits the Vicar of Christ. Now, it appears that he himself is the enabler, the patron of criminals, the head of a religious Mafia that has occupied the vineyard of the Church.

There are, it is true, some people who reacted with "I knew it all along! From the very day he stepped out on the balcony of St. Peter's . . ."—and it could be that they were gifted with a preternatural intuition. I was uncomfortable from the very first Angelus address in which he praised the theology of Walter Kasper. There are also those, who, like olympic ostriches practicing the sport of extreme head-burying, continue to defend the pope at all costs (including the cost of their intellectual honesty).

But for the vast majority, it has been a moment of awakening: the scales have fallen from our eyes, the scales that prevented us from seeing clearly the magnitude of the problem and therefore assessing the magnitude of the solution required. As some like to say, it is a "clarifying moment."

As such, it is also a moment of decision: decisions about who we are and what we believe as Catholics, how we will relate to wolves in sheep's clothing, where we will turn for truth and salvation, and why we will remain faithful in spite of the infidelity of those who were *graced by God* with the office of teaching, governing, and sanctifying.

We can see more clearly than ever that we do not and must not lean on men, no matter how lofty their titles, but on Our Lord Jesus Christ, the head and rock of the Church. We see that our religion, in its holy worship, its perennial doctrines, and its life-giving code of morals, is not a man-made edifice subject to constant manipulation but a God-given revelation to which we must submit ourselves and remain unbendingly true.

It may be that the best effect of August 2018 is that it prompts sincere Catholics—those who still wish, above all, and in spite of all, to follow Christ the King in His one, holy, catholic, and apostolic Church—to ask painful questions not just about the past *five* years, but about the past *fifty* years. What has made this pontificate and its attendant chaos possible? Is it a stray chastisement permitted for the purification of our sins? Or is it the fruition of an entire program, the distillation of decades of ambiguous doctrine, catechetical waffling, worldly accommodationism, strategic secularization? Are we not beholding the fully consistent manifestation of "the spirit of Vatican II" that not only willfully outstripped the texts of the Council but had already permeated the conciliar assembly in the well-documented machinations of the progressive European bishops who dominated the proceedings and whose spiritual descendants are today running the show?

Today's "clarifying moment" is a divine judgment on the evils that were set in motion decades ago, evils from which we can no longer hide if we wish to be rid of them for good, or at least cleanse our lives of their poisonous influence. All of the evils—evils of liturgical deformation, evils of immoral behavior, evils of heterodox teaching—share one thing in common: *each and every one of them is based on a rejection of Catholic tradition.*

In times of distress, the only safe path to follow is the tried-and-true path of tradition, that which was handed down and accepted by all Catholics until the postconciliar rupture, and which has never ceased to be followed and transmitted by that portion of the faithful who, over the past half-century, held fast to their inheritance. Concretely, this means traditional liturgy and sacraments, traditional catechisms, traditional examinations of conscience, traditional devotions and spirituality. One can *never* go wrong with such things in and of themselves, whereas one may frequently go wrong with their modern substitutes.

We do not want ersatz Catholicism but real Catholicism. August 2018 has dramatically proclaimed that the former is totally bankrupt. It is up to us to draw the right conclusions and to act accordingly.

20

When Will Catholics Wake Up and See the "Mess" Pope Francis Has Made?

LifeSiteNews

SEPTEMBER 13, 2018

T HEY SAY THAT POPE PIUS X'S FAVORITE bedside reading was *The Soul of the Apostolate* by Dom Jean-Baptiste Chautard. I am beginning to wonder if Pope Francis's favorite bedside reading is Niccolò Machiavelli's *The Prince*. Authors like Ross Douthat, Phil Lawler, and Henry Sire have provided copious documentation of the pope's Machiavellian *modus operandi*. It may help to recall, in the midst of Viganògate, a few egregious examples from the past that demonstrate how it works.

We remember when the pope deliberately washed the feet of women, against the universal liturgical law that limited the washing of feet to men. Then he changed the law to allow for the inclusion of any baptized member of the faithful—and proceeded to violate his new law by washing a Muslim's feet. Even if one argues that the pope, as the highest legislator, is not bound by these laws in the same way as his subjects are, he should (as popes in the past have done) set the first and best example of observing Church discipline, since others will, in fact, take their cue or their justification from him. Thus, his public actions contrary to discipline are meant to transmit a spirit of contempt for law, with the message that subjective motives of "charity" or "mercy" can and should lead to the practical neutralization of Church discipline.

We have seen the same contempt, message of neutralization, and stirring up of confusion in regard to the German bishops' disputes over whether communion should be given to Protestant spouses of Catholics. The pope first feinted to the left, favoring the liberal bishops, then feinted to the right, seeming to support backpedaling from the CDF, and finally let it be understood that the bishops could do whatever they pleased, even if the result will be a *cuius regio eius religio* checkerboard of dioceses with contradictory policies.

Then, in his manner of modifying the *Catechism of the Catholic Church* as well as in the new content that was ordered to be inserted, Pope Francis pushed through another victory for progressivism by effecting a change in doctrine, or initiating a motion towards that end, without having used a form of language that is unequivocally heretical. We saw that he did precisely the same thing in *Amoris Laetitia* (taken together with the Buenos Aires guidelines), in his revisions to the annulment process, and in many other cases, using techniques such as equivocation, studied ambiguity, internal contradiction, false quotation, and stalling tactics between phases to accomplish his purposes.

Again and again he displays this duplicity, playing off one side against the other, keeping people guessing—and keeping employed an army of anxious conservative Catholics who rabbinically reshape each act or statement. But a situation in which it is thought necessary to bend over backwards again and again to defend the pope against undeniable appearances of doctrinal rupture and moral corruption is already a crisis of unprecedented scope. It means, at very least, that this pope has permanently lost the trust of many, and has therefore introduced a strong note of instability into the very office of the papacy, since future popes will be governing from a weak foundation. All of this coming from a pope who told youths at a Mass in 2015 to "make a mess." [1]

There are still some Catholics who are digging in their heels. They refuse to believe that any pope can be as bad as this pope would have to be, if the most natural "reading" of things turns out to be true—so it must not be true! "Perhaps all of these doctrinal contradictions and moral meanderings and policy flip-flops are being misreported or misunderstood. Let's circle around and defend the pope at all costs from these naysayers, scandalmongers, and calumniators!" By doing this, they are effectively consigning their heads to a permanent vacation in the sand. This is one kind of coping mechanism: it effectively denies that there is a problem. It is like a child who puts his hands over his ears and says some

---

1   See Philip Pullella, Daniela Desantis, "Pope closes South America trip urging youths to 'make a mess,'" *Reuters*, July 12, 2015.

loud nonsense in order to avoid having to hear what an adult is saying to him.

There is another group I have known, a smaller and more rarefied one, made up of intellectuals who have convinced themselves that whatever the pope is saying must either be true (since he is, after all, the vicar of Christ, and we want to be on *his* team, right?) or have the wherewithal to be deftly rendered true by clever scholastic distinctions about the level of authority of a given statement, the location of a prepositional phrase, a faulty translation into French, etc. This is, I believe, a psychological coping mechanism for not dealing with the now notorious fact that we have a pope who is somewhat like a truck with failed brakes careening out of control down a steep mountain and heading for a mighty crash.

By this point, people who evade the truth about Francis are oddly like the Pharisees who, instead of surrendering to the divine reality of Our Lord, argued ceaselessly about their human traditions in the interpretation of the Law and whether or not He was violating this or that aspect of it. In other words, rather than face up to the big reality, they sought refuge in their Jewish scholasticism. In our present case, the big reality is not something good and holy like Our Lord in the midst of His disciples, but something sinister and repugnant, like Judas stealing from the common purse, betraying with a kiss, and hanging himself.

But, as many have pointed out, this situation is no cause for despair. It is, on the contrary, a dramatic and long-overdue end to an unsustainable exaltation of the papal office, where the pope is cast as a combination Delphic oracle, globetrotting superstar, dynamo of doctrinal development, and standard meter bar of orthodoxy. This is not only contrary to Catholicism, it is corrosive of it, because it replaces the primacy of inheriting the deposit of faith from divine revelation through apostolic transmission with the primacy of papal voluntarism. Such a distortion of the dogma of *Pastor Aeternus* could only end in flames.

21

Pope Francis Is No Longer Hiding His Strategy for Manipulating Outcome of Youth Synod

LifeSiteNews

SEPTEMBER 18, 2018

I N ADDITION TO THE DELEGATES ELECTED by the world's episcopal conferences, the upcoming Synod on Youth has been given 39 special delegates appointed directly by Pope Francis.

This list includes several of his close allies in the hierarchy: Cardinal Marx of Munich, President of the German bishops' conference; Cardinal Cupich, who has said that the Church has more important business than dealing with the abuse crisis, such as environmentalism and immigration; Cardinal Tobin, who denies having known anything about McCarrick, in spite of evidence of hundreds of clergy who knew "all about it"; Father Antonio Spadaro, editor of *La Civiltà Cattolica,* famous for tweeting that in theology (modern theology?), 2+2=5; and Archbishop Vincenzo Paglia, president of the deconstructed Pontifical Academy for Life and grand chancellor of the gutted John Paul II Institute in Rome.

All of these figures have been in the spotlight for their hetero-doxy, and all have angrily denounced Catholics who oppose the pope's progressive agenda.

In some ways, this delegate development is not surprising. In another way, however, it is appalling. Many of these men have given evidence of being shameless liars (to use Viganò's terminology) by denying knowledge of now ex-Cardinal McCarrick's predations or by denying that the abuse crisis is primarily a consequence of active homosexuality in the clergy. Like the recent Vatican photo of the private papal meeting on abuse which shows everyone relaxed and smiling, or the now extensive string of papal homi-lies in which the pope compares himself to the silent Christ in His Passion and writes off his critics as accusers like Satan, this development is one more nail in the coffin of any reasonable expectation Catholics might have to see the pope or any of his senior officials take seriously either the abuse scandal or the devastating report of Viganò.[1]

As regards the upcoming Synod itself, there's not even an attempt anymore at hiding (as had been the case with the two synods on marriage and family) the papal strategy for manipulating its outcome. Now it is in broad daylight. On September 17, Pope Francis released a new document, an Apostolic Constitution *Episcopalis Communio* governing the structure of the Synod of Bishops, which turns the Synod into a permanent body, somewhat like a parliamentary form of government, and, more worrisomely, amplifies the "magisterial" force of the final document produced by a Synod. In other words, the process by which synodal progressivism will be able to modernize Catholic dogma and morals has been accelerated. One wonders if Pope Francis is worried about how many years he's got left, and wants to make sure that he changes as much as he can, as quickly as possible.

We already know, from events held in advance of the Youth Synod, that it will represent a one-sided view of youth and what they need and what the Church should give them. Even George Weigel, who has been an outstanding proponent of papal authority over the years, has criticized the upcoming Synod on Youth, saying that there's likely to be nothing to it but conventional sociology and that the Church seems to be apologizing for her challenging moral teachings.

What is most obvious is that the new traditional voice among practicing Catholic youth will be utterly ignored and stifled, treated as if it does not exist. This is because Francis and his allies would strongly prefer that it not exist.

Will nothing come of the McCarrick affair? Will it be business as usual? Will the Youth Synod, the Amazon Synod, and a whole host of future Synods irrevocably alter the face of Catholicism? That is what the pope and his Vatican would like the most; but that is not what they are going to get. As Fr. Zuhlsdorf wrote:

---

1 Some opponents of Viganò's testimony argue that the Vatican's McCarrick report (November 10, 2022), released over two years after the whistle was blown, clears Pope Francis of wrongdoing and even implicates Viganò. This has been contested by many critics of the report, including the archbishop, who points to its systemic flaws (see *Voice in the Wilderness*, 69–87).

"A great deal of the clean-up of The Present Crisis will be (must be) driven by lay people, who have, above all, numbers, and who have, ultimately, the money."[2] And, most importantly, who seem, at this time, to have a monopoly on the orthodox Faith.

Think of it this way. I would wager that at least 75% of believing and practicing Catholic laity today—by "believing and practicing," I mean Catholics who know the basics of their faith and accept the Church's teaching on such countercultural issues as divorce, homosexuality, contraception, and abortion—are by now opposed to the progressivist and modernist program of Pope Francis. Perhaps the number is even higher. In contrast, probably not more than 50% of the lower clergy are skeptical of it or opposed to it. Maybe 25% of the world's bishops and 15% of the cardinals are hesitant about it or opposed to it.

What this suggests to me is that, at this time in history, the higher one's position in the institutional hierarchy, the more likely one is to be corrupted and compromised, while simple lay believers are far more likely to be outspokenly committed to traditional faith, morals, and liturgy. This is where future Catholic laity, priests, and religious will come from—not from the Synod machinery of the new German-Italian Axis.

Instead of praying for the success of another rigged Synod, perhaps we need to pray for a real chastisement from God to wake up the Church in its heady echelons. We might consider using the so-called cursing Psalms that were excised from the new Liturgy of the Hours.[3]

In the end, God will have the last laugh (see Ps. 2:4). And those who are faithful to him will join in, because everyone can now see how manipulated it all is, and that the Synod is speaking for no one but its progressive organizers.

---

2   "Lay Rage in Chicago, Mary Eberstadt takes names, and Fr. Z rants," *Fr. Z's Blog*, September 18, 2018.
3   See "The Omission of 'Difficult' Psalms and the Spreading-Thin of the Psalter," *Rorate Caeli*, November 15, 2016.

22

How Vatican's Deal with Communist China Fits into Pope Francis's Larger Agenda

LifeSiteNews

SEPTEMBER 21, 2018

A S THE WORLD'S GREATEST EXPERT IN Chinese population policy, Steven W. Mosher is intimately familiar with the political ins-and-outs of the Communist regime. In particular, with his knowledge of Chinese and his frequent travels to the country, he has devoted years of careful observation and study to the question of how the Communists treat religious groups, and, in particular, Catholics.

I heard Mr. Mosher speak in Virginia this summer on Chinese topics and was impressed by his detailed knowledge and the sobriety of his judgments. Like faithful underground Catholic laity, clergy, and bishops in China, Mosher is utterly opposed to the Vatican-Beijing deal, a "provisional agreement" of which was signed over the weekend.[1] Doing us a great service, Mosher summarized the grave situation in an article at *OnePeterFive*.[2]

The Vatican-Beijing concordat will secure for the Catholic Church an evanescent prestige at the supposed normalization of diplomatic relations and an apparent victory in the regularization of the Church's hierarchy and sacramental provision on the mainland. It will secure for the Communist government a freedom in naming bishops that would have been the envy of centuries of lay rulers in the European Middle Ages who attempted to arrogate for themselves authority over investitures. Anyone who has studied how communist governments work (as Mosher has done) knows that they have no qualms about breaking their word before the ink is dry on the paper. Why should the conscience of a dialectical

---

1   Diane Montagna, "Vatican signs 'provisional agreement' with China on appointment of bishops," *LifeSiteNews*, September 22, 2018.
2   See "Vatican to Allow Beijing to Name Bishops," *OnePeterFive*, September 15, 2018.

materialist atheist bother him? He does not believe in the divine law or in the natural moral law.

Such an "agreement" means that for the first time in the Church's existence, the Communist Party that rules a country will choose the bishops with Vatican approval. This means that the "Chinese Catholic Patriotic Association" will thereby be regularized, even though it supports Communist coercive population regulations and its first and primary loyalty is to the Chinese Communist Party.

Therefore, Beijing will continue to persecute true orthodox Catholics with impunity, but now, thanks to the Vatican's kowtowing to secular power, these Catholics will be made to look disloyal and recalcitrant—come to think of it, just like conservative and traditional Catholics have been made to look in the "free" Western world, when they refuse to fall into lockstep conformity with the juggernaut of secularism cosponsored by the United Nations, the European Union, and the Vatican. In this perspective, the Beijing deal is one side of a coin whose flip side is the pervasive modernization of morals, ranging from the repudiation of intrinsically evil sexual acts to the redefinition of capital punishment as an intrinsically evil act and the exaltation of environmentalism as the central arena of virtue.

Thus we have yet another key to interpreting this papacy's larger agenda. The soft approval of Communism implied in this sell-out of the underground Catholic Church, which has been fighting at the cost of great suffering for decades to remain faithful to the fullness of Catholicism (including in some places the retention of the traditional Latin Mass!), harmonizes with many other pro-Marxist and pro-socialist statements and actions of Francis's pontificate; and this, in turn, complements the policy of Freemasonic *laïcité* or secularism (a secular state "is better than a confessional state, because confessional states always end badly," as Francis said),[3] Pistoian liturgical modernization (in his words: "we can affirm with certainty and with magisterial authority that the liturgical reform is irreversible"[4]), and the modernist rejection of dogmatic stability and moral absolutes (seen in a range of statements on "development of doctrine" and on sexual morality).

---

3   See Joseph G. Trabbic, "The end of the Catholic state?," *Catholic World Report*, February 20, 2017.
4   Elise Harris, "For Pope Francis, 'the liturgical reform is irreversible,'" *Catholic News Agency*, August 24, 2017.

This China deal fits in perfectly with the attempted deconstruction of Catholic identity, the postmodern exaltation of fluid norms, and the assault on Catholic fidelity that has marked this pontificate from day one. Indeed, it simply revives and grossly amplifies the tragic *Ostpolitik* of Pope Francis's predecessor Pope Paul VI, who betrayed and humiliated József Cardinal Mindszenty in pursuit of further alliances with the Communists. It is hardly surprising that Pope Francis will attempt to canonize Paul VI next month, in an exercise of self-admiration like those with which he has been regaling us in his recent homilies in which he compares himself to the silent Christ and his accusers to Satan.[5]

As Gerhard Cardinal Müller preached at a priestly ordination in Rome on Saturday, September 15, 2018:

> The Church, founded by God and made up of human beings, is, according to its human side, in a deep, manmade crisis of its credibility.... Not clericalism, whatever that may be, but the turning away from the truth and moral lawlessness are the roots of the evil.... The real danger to today's humanity is the greenhouse gases of sin and the global warming of unbelief and the decay of morality when no one knows and teaches the difference between good and evil.[6]

One last thought: Why will the Communist-sponsored "Chinese Catholic Patriotic Association" (CCPA) be able to be in "full communion" and its clergy "regularized," while the Priestly Fraternity of St. Pius X (SSPX) isn't? To me, the answer is plain as day: because the CCPA is enthusiastic about the secular state, Vatican II, and the Novus Ordo (which it introduced into China!), and adapting morality to situations ("situational ethics"), while the SSPX stands for integralism, perennial doctrine, the traditional Roman Rite, and exceptionless moral norms. In other words, in a total inversion of Catholicism, we are seeing the complete opposite of what should be the case. May the Lord in His mercy rescue us from those who claim to be acting in His name.

---

5 See Dorothy Cummings McLean, "Pope makes yet another cryptic reference to 'Great Accuser' amid Viganò allegations," *LifeSiteNews*, September 18, 2018.
6 My translation from "Korruption der Lehre zieht immer die Korruption der Moral nach sich," *kath.net*, September 17, 2018.

23

Why I Can Never Teach Pope Francis's New Teaching on Death Penalty

LifeSiteNews

OCTOBER 3, 2018

I T'S HARD TO BELIEVE THAT THE CHANGE TO the *Catechism,* which caused such a tempest at the time, happened only two months ago. The inexorable whirl of events under this pontificate has already buried the subject in the news cycle and in people's minds. It's just one more milestone in the long forced march towards the Church of Tomorrow. But we should not make the mistake of letting our interests be dominated by the latest news, such that we cease to ponder "the method to the madness."

Consider the difference between the new *Catechism* text and the speech of October 11, 2017, on which it was based and to which it refers (as the *only* cited source for the revision). In the speech, the pope spoke his mind freely:

> It must be clearly stated that the death penalty is an inhumane measure that, regardless of how it is carried out, abases human dignity. It is *per se* contrary to the Gospel, because it entails the willful suppression of a human life that never ceases to be sacred in the eyes of its Creator and of which—ultimately—only God is the true judge and guarantor.

Here, the pope claimed that the death penalty *in and of itself, in principle,* is contrary to the Gospel, which must mean contrary to divine law or natural law or both, and therefore intrinsically immoral. This is heretical teaching, and we can be sure the pope knows this—but he also knows how few Catholics know enough theology to be able to identify a heresy even if it sprang up and hit them in the face.[1] Moreover, he knows that most of the officials

---

1   See Roberto de Mattei, "Whoever says death penalty is evil in itself 'falls into heresy': Church historian," *LifeSiteNews,* August 3, 2018.

who surround him are either cowards or climbers, so he will get no challenges from that quarter.

The new *Catechism* text, however, features cleverly crafted language: "The Church teaches, in the light of the Gospel, that 'the death penalty is inadmissible because it is an attack on the inviolability and dignity of the person'" (citing the same speech). *Inadmissible.* A vague, fuzzy, roundabout word that has no pedigree in moral theology, which speaks of that which is moral or immoral, right or wrong, or right in some circumstances and wrong in others.

As its author knew it would, "inadmissible" sent Catholics scuttling in all directions to try to figure out what it means. Is it a practical or a theoretical claim? A prudential limitation or a principled exclusion? And the apologist network began cranking out its predictable "explanations" to show that, once again, in spite of all appearances to the contrary, in spite of contradictions everyone can point to, *nothing* has really changed and *everything* is all right! The more earnest kept scratching their heads, demanding endless clarifications and signing endless petitions and producing endless talmudic commentaries to show how to square the circle.

Dr. Joseph Shaw put it well: "In this case, the mouse-hole of ambiguity conservative Catholics need to crawl through to maintain the continuity between the two editions of the *Catechism* is humiliatingly small. When they have crawled through it, moreover, they will be ignored."[2]

Meanwhile, in spite of such efforts (and even, in a way, due to them), the pope's overarching goal—to transmit the signal that Catholic doctrine is perpetually debatable and developable into new and unforeseen evolutionary forms, malleable and adjustable to the Zeitgeist—has already been triumphantly achieved in the minds of the vast majority of Catholics and non-Catholics. Fr. Hugh Somerville Knapman points to the harm of this way of thinking:

> Looking at this more contextually, perhaps an even greater concern is the phenomenon of change itself. Since the middle of the twentieth century the Church has suffered a constant, and often quite bewildering and ultimately

---

2   "The death penalty for the prestige of the Papacy," *LMS Chairman*, August 5, 2018.

unnecessary, series of changes to teaching and liturgy. Large-scale change leads to an expectation of more. And more. Everything is perceived, often wrongly, as open to change. When change is valued for its own sake, nothing is safe. Recently Professor Stephen Bullivant, and other commentators, have noted how the negative reaction to *Humanae Vitae* in 1968 was conditioned by the widespread expectation of change in Church teaching on artificial contraception, an expectation fostered and exacerbated by the dizzying changes unleashed on the Church in the 1960s. Thus, this change to the text of the *Catechism* appears as a regrettable perpetuation of a culture, a hermeneutic, of change. It is not what we need right now.[3]

And yet, it is deliberately what we have been *given*. The Lord's rhetorical questions—"What man is there among you, of whom if his son shall ask bread, will he reach him a stone? Or if he shall ask him a fish, will he reach him a serpent?" (Mt. 7:9-10)—have, alas, been answered in a non-rhetorical manner.

I would like to make this clear: I will never teach to *anyone*—my children, my friends, my students, my readers, my audiences—the stuff that Francis has commanded to be put into the *Catechism*. I will gladly teach that capital punishment is often not the best solution; I'm willing to admit that it may deserve to be curtailed in modern Western democracies. But I cannot, in good conscience, declare that capital punishment is "contrary to the dignity of man" or ruled out by "the light of the Gospel." I could not do this without rejecting revelation and the Catholic faith. It is in the name of obedience to the Lord of life and death, the divine author of the State and the source of its punitive authority (cf. Rom. 13), that I refuse my consent to this false teaching, and I sincerely hope that such refusal will be the norm rather than the exception.

Now is not the time for obsequious ultramontanism, which would be like pouring gasoline on a fire. Now is the time for saying "enough is enough." As for me and my house, we will serve the Lord in the Catholic Faith to which thousands of catechisms have borne unanimous witness for centuries.

---

3   "Death in question," *One Foot in the Cloister*, August 3, 2018.

24

"LGBT" Appears for the First Time in a Vatican Document

LifeSiteNews

OCTOBER 4, 2018

AS REPORTED HERE BY OUR ROME COR-
respondent, the working document for the Youth Synod
underway at the Vatican contains the first use, in an
official Vatican document, of the acronym "LGBT."[1] Why is this
a big deal?

The term "LGBT" was coined by secular activists to describe
what they consider to be a range of acceptable sexual orientations
or lifestyle preferences: lesbian, gay, bisexual, and transgender.
The slang use of "gay" is already something that no one should
buy into, since the shattered lives and angry advocacy of homosexuals is manifestly contrary to the original positive meaning
of the word.

More broadly, to say or write "LGBT" in a way that seems
intended as a description that accurately represents reality is to
embrace the ideology behind it, the construction of a universe
other than the one God created. It is one thing to mention the
acronym in order to critique it, but to mention it neutrally or
positively is already to admit its false premises.

In his letter to the Ephesians (5:3-4), St. Paul enunciates a
principle about Christian discourse, whether in writing or in
speech: "But fornication, and all uncleanness, or covetousness, let
it not so much as be named among you, as becometh saints; nor
should there be obscenity, foolish talk or coarse joking, which are
out of place, but rather thanksgiving." Or, as the Amplified Bible
translates and comments: "But immorality (sexual vice) and all
impurity (of lustful, rich, wasteful living) or greediness must not

---

1   Diane Montagna, "Cardinal: We're not removing 'LGBT youth' from
Vatican Synod working text," *LifeSiteNews*, October 1, 2018.

even be named among you, as is fitting and proper among saints. Let there be no filthiness (obscenity, indecency) nor foolish and sinful (silly and corrupt) talk, nor coarse jesting, which are not fitting or becoming; but instead voice your thankfulness [to God]."

In other words, Christians are not even supposed to *talk* about foul and disgusting things unless they are forced to do so for the sake of refuting error and defending the truth. This is the reason why Christians are also morally required not to watch TV shows or movies that display sexually immoral acts: if such things shouldn't even be *mentioned* among those who are called to be saints, what would St. Paul say about *watching* them and taking them into our imaginations and memories?

Thus, we see that in the Bible, as well as in Church documents, immorality is dealt with either by circumlocution or in discreet and modest ways. If the Church is going to talk about psychological diseases and sins, she is obliged to use accurate terminology already given to her within the Christian tradition, accompanied by correct judgments about their degree of sinfulness and the harm they cause. Therefore, no document that claims to express the mind of the Church or of her pastors may talk about sexual disorders in a neutral, sociological manner, let alone with seeming tolerance, approval, or encouragement.

The neutral, sociological use of "LGBT" by the Synod organizers exemplifies the process, long under way, of "moving the needle" on normalcy. Fifty years ago, homosexuality was barely mentioned except in thick tomes of moral theology. It was one of those things that Christians didn't talk about, as per St. Paul's recommendation. As the decades wore on and the secular culture gradually "destigmatized" homosexual behavior, we saw it mentioned in Church documents, albeit always with clear condemnation. In recent decades, vague and misleading psychobabble about homosexual, bisexual, or transgender "inclinations" has crept into the discourse, muddying the waters still further.

Pope Francis catapulted the process to the next level with his infamous "Who am I to judge?" remark.

And now the Youth Synod, which was organized by and is being driven by a small faction of ultraprogressive ultramontanists, has moved the needle further by its premeditated adoption of the anti-Catholic (actually, anti-human nature) concept of "LGBT."

For Catholics who follow the patent teaching of Scripture that God created human beings as male and female *only*, two sexes ordered to one another *only*, and that any kind of sexual activity outside of marriage between one man and one woman is foreign to virtue, personal happiness, and the good of society, the appearance of the ideologically loaded "LGBT" in a Vatican document is a moment of dishonor before God and the world.

We do not yet know where the discussions at this Synod will go, but we have every indication, in small details as in larger ones, that it has been rigged from the start, just as the Synods on the Family were rigged.[2] The final document—which, thanks to a move by Pope Francis, may now be rapidly rubber-stamped as "magisterial"[3]—is likely to be either bad or weak. Neither outcome is worthy of Christ or of His immaculate Bride.

2   See Edward Pentin, *The Rigging of a Vatican Synod? An Investigation into Alleged Manipulation at the Extraordinary Synod on the Family* (San Francisco: Ignatius Press, 2015).
3   See chapter 21.

25

Cardinal Ouellet's Letter Confirms the Very Problems Viganò Has Identified

LifeSiteNews
OCTOBER 8, 2018

CARDINAL OUELLET'S RESPONSE TO ARCH-bishop Viganò[1] is obviously a document of great serious-ness that attempts to respond to the latter's revelations and allegations. Both the eminent position of its author and its severe content compel those who are investigating the truth of the matter to take it seriously as part of the many documents that the McCarrick case has occasioned.

But if the Prefect of the Congregation for Bishops (and therefore one who has been involved in the appointments in recent years of some of the Church's most controversial liberal prelates) thinks his letter is going to be enough to shut the door on Viganò's account, he is mistaken. There are three things that give one pause about this letter.

First, although Ouellet accuses Viganò of essentially "going over to the dark side," he never invokes a higher authority in support of his own claims. That is, unlike Viganò, he does not say his conscience is compelling him in the sight of God and that he swears before God to the truth of what he is reporting. For Ouellet, it seems the guiding rule is: "Trust me. I'm an important person. I have access to the pope. All that I'm saying is true and all that Viganò is saying is false."

I'm sorry, but with so much evidence of real lying and cover-up on the part of hierarchs of the Church, "just take my word for it" is not going to cut it anymore. If someone, even the highest authority in the Church, were to say to you: "The Synod of Bishops on the Family was run with perfect transparency, fairness, and

---

1   Diane Montagna, "Cardinal Ouellet to Abp. Viganò: your testimony was 'political' and 'extremely reprehensible,'" *LifeSiteNews*, October 7, 2018.

collaboration," would you buy it? Of course not. Truth has its claims on our human reason.

More particularly, since there are already many reasons to distrust Pope Francis's handling of this and other disciplinary and doctrinal affairs, saying that "the Holy Father assures me" and "has given me permission to say this" and "will ensure all documents are thoroughly searched" is about as convincing as Cardinal Wuerl and Cardinal Tobin saying "they didn't know" there were serious problems with their predecessor McCarrick. Does anyone really expect intelligent people to believe this kind of thing? It reflects sadly on the breakdown of trust under this pontificate to note that many Catholics fear and even expect (again, not unreasonably) that incriminating documentary evidence will be or has already been shredded. Conveniently, investigations will discover nothing!

Second, if some have criticized Viganò's letter for being "over-the-top" distrustful and disrespectful of Pope Francis, unfortunately this letter by Ouellet is "over-the-top" sycophantic, even papolatrous. He undermines his credibility by speaking of the Holy Father as of a veritable Messiah who has only labored selflessly, with heavenly purity, for the Kingdom of God: "a true shepherd, a resolute and compassionate father, a prophetic grace for the Church and for the world ... "

Yes, by all means, we want to remain in communion with the Successor of Peter—and nothing in Viganò's letter suggests that he repudiates this Successor or would wish to sever communion with him. But do we have to crawl on our knees to lick the boots of the fisherman? Ouellet undercuts his case by showing that, in his eyes, this pope can do no wrong (at least no *serious* wrong), and on the contrary, is the God-given prophet for our times. Would that this were so, but it cannot simply be assumed as a kind of geometrical axiom.

Along these lines, our eyebrows rise when Ouellet claims that his own "interpretation of *Amoris Laetitia*"—namely, an interpretation that favors access to holy communion for those living objectively in adultery, contrary to divine law—"is grounded in this fidelity to the *living tradition,* which Francis has given us another example of by recently modifying the Catechism of the Catholic Church on the question of the death penalty."

Again, Your Eminence, with all due respect, no one on earth can excuse Catholics from the solemn duty they have before God to follow the *settled and established* tradition of the Church, not to mention Sacred Scripture and the ordinary universal Magisterium, all of which measure, delimit, and control the so-called "living" tradition—whether about divorce and "remarriage," the legitimacy of the death penalty, or any number of issues. The loaded phrase "missionary reform" in Ouellet's final sentence is another signal that he is thinking along the lines of a hermeneutic of rupture and discontinuity. For Catholics concerned about the novelties of this pontificate, such sweeping language will not incline us to meekly drop our objections.

Third, Ouellet's letter is strangely, one might say eerily, bereft of believably genuine acknowledgment of the sheer amount of damage done by McCarrick and others like him in the Church. He writes:

> How is it possible that this man of the Church, whose incoherence has now been revealed, was promoted many times, and was nominated to such a high position as Archbishop of Washington and Cardinal? I am personally very surprised, and I recognize that there were failures in the selection procedures implemented in his case.

"Incoherence" is as weaselly a word as "inadmissible."[2] How about "vicious behavior"? The prefect says he is "very surprised." I dare him to look a victim of abuse in the eye and say: "I am personally very surprised that this could have happened to you. There must have been failures in our procedures." A little frank discourse here would have gone a long way towards giving Ouellet ground to stand on, but he is so intent on slamming Viganò that he forgets the gravity of the matters about which Viganò is indignant in the first place.

Let's put it bluntly: No one reading this letter by Ouellet can believe that he cares about the extent of the moral corruption of homosexuality in the hierarchy, that he recognizes it and its fallout as a crisis, and that he and his Vatican associates intend to exterminate it. Rather, reading between the lines, one senses that the only man who is really in trouble is Viganò himself.

---

2   See chapter 23.

As Edward Pentin pointed out, not once in Ouellet's letter is Viganò referred to as a bishop; and in one chilling moment, the prefect appeals to him to "return to communion" with the pope. This suggests that Viganò has already been stripped of his episcopal dignity and excommunicated, or that this will soon take place. Given that such severe penalties have been rarely administered even to bishops of monstrous moral corruption, the implicit message is that no crime whatsoever can compare with that of challenging the Dictator Pope.

All told, Cardinal Ouellet has accomplished two things with this letter. First, he will have equipped progressive and "conservative" Catholics with the perfect excuse for discrediting and discounting Viganò's testimony; hence, whatever truth is contained in it will have an even harder time gaining a foothold and prompting overdue reforms. Second, and ironically, he will have strengthened the conviction of many that it is precisely a blind adulation of Church leadership that has led us straight into the lion's den of the current abuse crisis.

26

Why Pope Francis's Method of "Discernment" Could Lead Souls Away from God

LifeSiteNews

OCTOBER 10, 2018

WE HEAR A LOT OF TALK FROM THE nucleus of postconciliarism, Pope Francis, and the cloud of Jesuit electrons that orbit him, on the theme of "discernment": the need for a new discernment in today's world; for discernment of the needs of youths, minorities, immigrants, women, or what have you; for discerning the surprising ways of the "God of surprises" in a Church still ossified with too much tradition (as if there were much left!).

One of the most perceptive Catholic commentators, James Kalb, published a brilliant article at *Crisis Magazine* on October 3 called "The Pope as Supreme Being," in which he pointed out the pitfalls of a subjectivist and absolutist reliance on a process of so-called "discernment," unmoored from rock-solid principles on which it must rest. The danger is all the more pressing when the one calling the shots for the worldwide Church sees himself as—and is lauded by his adulatory supporters as—free from constraints, whether it be the teaching of Scripture and Tradition, the witness of his predecessors and of all the Councils (not just the last one), or the doctrine of the great theologians.

The problem with making an airy appeal to St. Ignatius of Loyola and his emphasis on discernment of spirits is that St. Ignatius himself would have been the first to disown moral and doctrinal subjectivism and an absolutism of authority. His *Spiritual Exercises* are firmly grounded in immovable first principles, as any science must be if it is going to reach true conclusions, or any art if it is going to produce useful and beautiful works. The "room" needed for individual application is opened up by the power of the principles themselves, which, as long as they are adhered to, ensure that discerners will never stray beyond the boundaries of the Faith.

Let me offer a concrete image of what I am talking about. The art of navigation involves four elements: a set destination; a proposed path for reaching it, based on a good map; a knowledge of how to find the path "in the wild" by determining where one is in reference to fixed points; and an attentive knowledge of surroundings and changing circumstances. Navigation would be impossible if there were not fixed compass points and fixed features like the stars.

In the Catholic Faith, the destination is given to us already by Our Lord Jesus Christ: eternal life with Him. We reach this goal by a living faith in His Passion, into which we enter by the sacraments of His Church and ongoing conversion of life in prayer and good works. Our map is the Catholic Faith as taught by the Fathers, Doctors, Councils, and Popes, which hundreds of catechisms reliably sum up (it requires no doctorate to learn the *Baltimore Catechism* and live by it). Our four compass points—the north, south, east, and west of our spiritual globe—are Sacred Scripture, Sacred Tradition, the authentic Magisterium, and the lives of the saints. It is *always* with reference to these compass points that we can make our way confidently across whatever stormy seas lie between our current position and our destined port.

Notice how the work of "discernment" concerns only *one* of the four elements of navigation: attentive knowledge of and reaction to surroundings and circumstances. The goal, the way, the map, the objective requirements of navigation—all these are not matters of flexible assessment but matters of authoritative knowledge based on givens. Without those givens, the entire project is over and done. It would be easier for a ship to reach a harbor by setting out in a random direction on the Atlantic than for a Christian to reach heaven by means of a path not already plotted out, as it were, according to the givens of our Faith.

And that brings us back to the problem of the modern (not traditional) Jesuit conception of discernment. For here we are dealing with a vision in which the ultimate goal of the Christian life is itself unclear: is it eternal life in heaven, or worldly goals like environmentalism, immigration, international peace? The way, too, is unclear: is faith in Christ and membership in His Church necessary for salvation, or is it all about, let's say, good will, camaraderie, the search for a "transcendent Other"? The map has been, at best, ignored, at worst, run through the shredder since the Second Vatican Council, and few there are who make any reference to it—or worse, an attempt is made to rewrite the map.

Worst of all, those entrusted with navigating the vessel seem to think they can make their way without consistent and continual reference to the fixed points of the spiritual compass, as they dismiss major teachings of Scripture, jettison ecclesiastical and even apostolic traditions, turn a deaf ear to the great Councils of the Church (such as the Council of Trent, the most doctrinally substantive of all of them), and replace the great cloud of witnesses of unequivocally Catholic saints with the cloudy witness of more recent "saints" who are fast-tracked to canonization in order to legitimize this modern style of navigating, which, in reality, should be seen for what it is: the criminal negligence of drunken captains.

There is no discernment of spirits when the principles of discernment are up for grabs and always shifting. Indeed, one cannot help wondering *which* "spirits" such an anti-methodical method will end up following. The infernal spirits are those who have failed to attain the supernatural end for which they were created; who are banished to the outer darkness without sun, moon, and stars (Christ, Mary, and the saints) to navigate by; and who seek to draw down into their own disorder men who will not submit to the humble yoke of Christ, who is "the same yesterday, today, and forever" (Heb. 13:8).

27

A Parish Priest Explains
How Pope Francis Is
Undermining His Ability
to Teach Moral Truths

LifeSiteNews
OCTOBER 11, 2018

O NE OF THE BENEFITS OF WRITING REG-
ularly on the internet is that I receive a fair number of
notes from readers with whom something I've published
has struck a chord. I hear disproportionately from priests, religious,
and seminarians who are struggling to live a faithful Catholic
life—above all, liturgically—in the midst of a hostile wasteland,
with wolves on one side and hyenas on the other.

A priest recently wrote to me about the challenges created for
him by the pope's rough manhandling of settled Catholic doctrine
in regard to capital punishment (about which I have written a
number of times: that Francis's new text is not in accord with the
truth; that it cannot be defended; and that it should be neither
taught nor adhered to).[1] Here is what he said, apropos the last
of these articles:

> Thank you so much for writing this article. It seems odd
> that this subject has received such little attention. I've
> not found anyone who thinks Pope Francis' actions are
> problematic. Until now, I have always taught that despite
> some sinful popes and bishops, none has ever officially
> proclaimed an error to be truth. The teachings of the Mag-
> isterium cannot be "overturned" like an unconstitutional
> law. Teachings can be expanded or elaborated on to account
> for new developments or discoveries, but not reversed.
>
> To my knowledge, no encyclical with a declarative state-
> ment to establish, explain, and define the [new] teaching
> was issued. It's simply inexplicable that an act is morally

---

1 See chapters 13, 14, and 23.

good/allowable for thousands of years, to become today an intrinsic evil. This event leads me to believe that Francis has no clue about the workings of the Magisterium or the Holy Spirit!

One of my concerns is the damage this kind of thing does to my ability to teach moral truths. It's essential for the faithful to have absolute confidence in the accuracy of the Church's teachings. I fear similar errors will follow from the current Vatican in regard to teachings on marriage, human sexuality, and ordination. If a pope can simply bypass common sense, convention, and tradition to revise the *Catechism,* all moral teachings are questionable.

This good priest is quite correct. The faithful deserve clear and consistent moral guidance that is not peppered with contradictions, ambiguities, doubts, and loopholes, otherwise they will turn away from the Church either to a secularism that has no rules except self-gratification or a sect that has strict (but not always correct) rules. For man cannot live without some principle to live by, and he will live either by true principles such as those Christ has given us through His Church, or by false principles such as self-love, political messianism, or sectarian codes. The extent to which the Vatican appears to be operating by all three—the messianic complex of the great leader, the sectarian creed of liberal Protestantism, and the self-love that places modern differentness over traditional commonality—is therefore most appalling, and presents the single greatest challenge to pastoral care, Church renewal, and evangelization that the Church has yet seen in the post-Tridentine period.

In responding to the priest, I expressed my agreement with his analysis. What the pope is doing *is* terribly destabilizing, not only for Catholic pastors today, but for the future work of all of his successors. The papacy has become far too politicized, as if each conclave is a new parliamentary session electing a new prime minister to steer the country's affairs in a liberal or conservative direction. This is certainly not the vision of the pope as the staunch guardian of doctrinal orthodoxy and the determined upholder of ecclesiastical traditions that Church history reveals to us at the papacy's best moments, nor is it the theological vision of the papacy discussed at and taught by the First Vatican Council.

In my opinion, Pope Francis has not attempted to engage his *full* magisterial authority to teach anything, let alone something erroneous. After all, if we look at the conditions under which earlier popes have signified their intention to teaching infallibly, we will see an exceptional care taken to use the most solemn language coupled with threats of the most dire punishments. (This prompts me to wonder if any modern pope, inasmuch as he buys into the false ideas about justice and mercy first enunciated by John XXIII in the run-up to Vatican II, would ever be able to muster the courage or clarity to issue a solemn pronouncement that could be *known* to be an infallible statement!)

As for teaching error, either the Holy Spirit would prevent the pope from doing so (e.g., by bringing about his death prior to the act of teaching error), or in the moment he uttered the error, he would *ipso facto* cease to be pope. For this latter scenario to play out, the error would have to be manifest to all, e.g., "Jesus Christ did not actually rise physically from the dead on Easter Sunday; he only rose spiritually, inasmuch as the early Christians were inspired to follow his example in their hearts." If a pope ever came out and said such a thing, and it was clear that he was not insane or joking, it would be time for the cardinals to book their plane tickets to Rome. (Actually, if he was insane or joking, it would *also* be time for them to book their tickets.)

Let us hope, for the sake of preserving the little sanity we have left, that Our Lord does not permit us to capsize into still murkier and rougher waters than those in which we are currently sailing.

I return now to the issue raised by my correspondent. There is *no question* that the death penalty is permissible in some circumstances, and that is because the death penalty is taught by God to be, and is accepted by Catholic tradition as, a legitimate exercise of punitive and retributive justice on the part of the state, which has its authority from God, the Lord of life and death. One is allowed to argue that those circumstances no longer obtain, but one *cannot* say the thing in itself is evil. That, indeed, would be heresy, and one notes that Francis did not dare to say this explicitly in the new *Catechism* text. But he *implies* it, which is hardly less damaging, for all the reasons we have seen.[2]

---

2   See chapter 17.

Are you a Catholic tempted to tear out your hair and say: "Wait a minute, if the pope can't be trusted, who can?" There *is* a way out of this perplexing situation. It involves admitting forthrightly, as most Catholics in history would readily have done, that the pope is not above the law, not above tradition, not above the theological witness of the Fathers and Doctors, but in communion with them and, in a sense, subordinate to them. Therefore, one may *always* be confident believing and teaching what has been held "by everyone, always, and everywhere" prior to this time of confusion.

28

Saying Church Is in a
Francis-fueled "Crisis"
Isn't Polarizing, but Reality

LifeSiteNews

OCTOBER 18, 2018

A RASH OF PUNDITS WILL ALWAYS BE ON hand who tell us that talking about a "crisis" in the Church is needlessly emotional and polarizing language. They seem to be addicted to optimism at any price, not realizing that their smiling message sounds increasingly hollow, their analysis fake, and their applause lame.

This becomes more and more apparent with the giant hammer-blows of the Viganò testimonies, with the third one (just released[1]) shattering the feeble defenses of the ultramontanists for whom Pope Francis is the new Prophet who is leading us (at last!) into the Promised Land of the Second Vatican Council. In reality, never have the papacy and the Vatican been more corrupt in the 2,000-year history of the Catholic Church—and I say this as one who has read deeply about other moments of crisis and corruption in Church history. We have seen popes and curias of venality, ambition, and lust, but never those vices *plus* continual doctrinal innovations and oppressive liturgical banality. Even Alexander VI upheld Catholic doctrine and celebrated the solemn pontifical Mass with splendor!

It is true that *elsewhere,* to *some* extent, things are getting better—as, for example, in the religious communities and parishes that use the traditional Mass and sacramental rites—but we cannot honestly speak of a turnaround when every poll that is taken indicates fewer and fewer Catholics who accept the Church's teaching (or who even *know* that teaching) on any issue remotely controversial, from the truth of the Real Presence to the evils

---

1 Diane Montagna, "Archbishop Viganò issues third testimony, refutes accusations of Cardinal Ouellet," *LifeSiteNews,* October 19, 2018; cf. *Voice in the Wilderness,* 62–68.

of contraception, abortion, and homosexual acts. A majority of self-identified "Catholics" are in favor of legal recognition of homosexual "marriage" and many other sexual deviations contrary to biblical teaching and hitherto unbroken magisterial doctrine.

One could go on about the complete catastrophe in catechesis, the decline and fall of most of the Catholic schools, the self-serving bureaucratization of curias and chanceries, the abysmal state of sacred music and the fine arts—but what would be the point? Anyone with eyes to see and ears to hear can tell that, apart from a remnant of more or less traditional Catholics, the Church is in the throes of a desperate disease called modernism, and the prognosis is looking grim.[2]

I received this email from a priest in Europe and, from what I have seen, it may be taken for a typical situation—the very situation Viganò depicts in his latest testimony:

> Dear Sir: English is not my mother language, so I apologize for the grammar mistakes.
>
> I am an assistant priest in a parish. The parish priest is gay and has a partner (not openly, but everybody knows). He has been the priest of that parish for more than 20 years. He is very diplomatic and he never proclaims any heresy. But after this 20 years, he has conveyed to the congregation a spirit of absolute moral relativism (and also of doctrinal relativism, since he never speaks about the doctrine of the Church).
>
> Last Sunday, I told the parishioners what is going on in the Church and I explained the letter of Mgr. Viganò. I also said that I had no trace of doubt that Mgr. Viganò is telling the truth. Many parishioners were not able to accept the message. They were furious with me and threatened to leave the Church if I continued to speak like that about the pope. It was a frontal attack to their "feel good gospel" that has been taught to them.
>
> It made me clear again how evil this homosexual practice is and what its effects are on the faithful, even when it is not explicitly proclaimed or defended. It is a worldly spirit that ruins the sound spirit of faith. I do not know how things will continue. I have said that I will

---

2   See chapter 62.

not change my attitude towards this situation and that I will continue to tell the truth, even when this truth is inconvenient. I am sure that Heaven will help me, but still I am grateful for your prayers.

No, things are not getting better; they are getting worse, much worse under this pontificate than they have ever been in the history of the Church, *as regards what is essential*. Sure, in earlier centuries we may have suffered from axe-wielding barbarians torching villages, immoral Renaissance pontiffs bestowing benefices on illegitimate offspring, plague-laden rats sowing foul disease across Europe, or charismatic heretics shattering the unity of Christendom, but never have we seen a pope gone so far off the rails, the magnitude of financial scandals involving the Vatican, the enormity of an embedded homosexual network across the globe—it is all rather like seven demons rushing in to fill an ecclesiastical house swept clean and left empty after the Council.

If we thought we had escaped or would escape post-Vatican II malaise by the contiguous pontificates of John Paul II and Benedict XVI, as if finally the ship was going strong over the waves, the message of history has been: "Not so fast. You suffer from a lack of realism about how deep the rot had penetrated into the wood, how far the errors had extended, how much the 'petty magisterium' had deviated. *It's time to wake up.*"

As for me, then, I regretfully but more truthfully stick with the language of crisis. And we will never find a solution to our crisis until we recover our Catholic identity through the celebration *everywhere* of the traditional Latin liturgy, with the doctrinal orthodoxy and moral strength it embodies, represents, and encourages. When the Holy Sacrifice of the Mass, the Divine Office, and the sacramental rites of the Church are once again offered in prayerful majesty to God's glory and the benefit of Christians, then—and only then—will come that "new springtime" about which postconciliar popes have spoken with such baffling confidence. Only then will the New Evangelization begin in earnest, with the Mass of the Ages as its pulsing heart.

29

How U.S. Bishops Should Have Responded to Vatican Hijacking Their Meeting on Abuse Crisis

LifeSiteNews

NOVEMBER 16, 2018

I T WAS WITH THE PROVERBIAL WHIMPER that the recent USCCB meeting in Baltimore went out. The hoped-for and indeed expected bang was thwarted by forces without and within.

The Vatican commanded a halt to the United States bishops taking steps about the clerical abuse crisis and its episcopal component. In a particularly obnoxious example of the Peronist "style" of this papacy, the intervention—apparently known only to Cardinal Cupich, papal confidant and *de facto* head of the USCCB—canceled out subsidiarity, interfered with the legitimate jurisdiction of bishops, and cynically stepped on the very synodality that bishops were forced to vote for in last month's rigged Youth Synod.

In this move, we saw an egregious return to the ultramontanist behavior of treating bishops as if they were vicars of the pope, rather than true shepherds who rule their own dioceses in Christ's name and by His authority. The pope certainly has universal jurisdiction, but individual bishops do not rule on his behalf or by his leave. They rule by a right proper to themselves, which can be removed for bad behavior, but is otherwise inviolable, immediate, and non-transferable.

Put simply, bishops *must* rule their dioceses; they cannot pass the buck to someone else. They, and not the pope, are officially and normatively in charge of their particular portion of Christ's Church. To act otherwise would be running away from the sheep and letting the wolves take over. Sadly, it would seem that the wolves have long since moved in and set up shop. It was disappointing, to say the least, that the U. S. bishops were not able to muster the courage to remind the Vatican of a few basic truths of ecclesiology enshrined in canon law, Church tradition, and (just saying) the documents of the Second Vatican Council.

There were forces within, too, that sabotaged the effectiveness of this plenary meeting. The attempt to frame a respectfully earnest request for all the McCarrick documentation was torpedoed by bureaucratic filibuster and the soft mockery of semi-lavender prelates. Thanks to the leftward-leaning tilt of the pushiest high-ranking members of the American episcopacy, the apparent lack of desire in the conservative minority to stand up to them, and the perpetual self-doubting hesitations of the greater number, the U. S. bishops as a whole could not agree on so much as an initial approach to the disciplining of abusive, complicit, unresponsive, or incompetent bishops. It was a very expensive, time-consuming way to say: "We don't know what we're doing; we're not sure where we're going; and what's more, we're content to leave things as they are, as long as we get to act as errand-boys for the pope."

How different a world it would be if a number of U. S. bishops had stood up and said:

> We're tired of this liberal, confusing, autocratic, Machia-vellian, and destructive leadership in the Church, and all its pomps and works.
>
> We're tired of "official theology" that contradicts magisterial doctrine.[1]
>
> We've had enough of the McCarrick cover-up and, in general, the hypocrisy and corruption exposed by Viganò, whose testimonies have not only *not* been refuted, but have ended up being vindicated by all the attempts to respond to them (which is why the sound of crickets still predominates).
>
> We're done with playing bellboys to a super-bishop rather than taking responsibility for our own flocks, individually and corporately.
>
> And most of all, we're thoroughly sick of an endless stream of unsolicited rambling Vatican documents thick with sociologese and thin on the radical demands of the

---

1   On the expression "official theology" and its significance, see Thomas Pink, "Vatican II and Crisis in the Theology of Baptism," published in three parts at *The Josias*, November 2, 5, and 8, 2018.

Gospel. From this point on, we could care less about exhortations, letters, sermons, press conferences, or curial blather. We have more important and more urgent things to do, like teach catechism, feed the hungry, celebrate the sacraments worthily and beautifully, support marriages and families, bring non-Catholics into the one true Church, reach out to people who are lost and wandering in the wasteland of modernity—and above all, *save souls.* That is our job: to save our own souls and the souls of the faithful entrusted to us, feeding them with sound doctrine, pure morals, and a truly *sacred* liturgy.

So, unless you send us a pithy *ex cathedra* definition *de fide et moribus* with a tiara on top and a side of anathemas, we're done wasting our time on the UN-EU chaplaincy that today's Vatican has become. We've got several lifetimes of work to do just cleaning up our own act, the mess in our own backyard.

Now *that* would have been a plenary meeting to remember!

Perhaps, if things keep getting worse, we may see something of this scenario play out, after all. As I like to say: stranger things than this have happened in the 2,000-year history of the Church.

30

Consecrated Buildings and Their Officially Sponsored Profanation

New Liturgical Movement
DECEMBER 10, 2018

THE *RULE* OF ST. BENEDICT HAS AS ONE of its many virtues the ability to capture an entire vision of things in one lapidary phrase. There is not a single wasted word; what Benedict means to say, he says with vigor, brevity, and clarity. A splendid example is chapter 52, "Of the Oratory of the Monastery," where the Patriarch writes:

> Let the oratory be what its name implies, and let nothing else be done or kept there. When the Work of God is finished, let all go out in deep silence, and let reverence for God be observed, so that any brother who may wish to pray privately be not hindered by another's misbehavior. And at other times also, if anyone wish to pray secretly, let him just go in and pray: not in a loud voice, but with tears and fervor of heart. He, therefore, who does not behave so, shall not be permitted to remain in the oratory when the Work of God is ended, lest he should, as we have said, be a hindrance to another.[1]

I have often wished that this text would be carved into wood or stone and mounted at the door of every Catholic church throughout the world, printed in every bulletin, and preached from every pulpit, with such unfailing regularity that the pervasive anteliturgical and postliturgical chitchat by which the reverent silence of the temple of God is globally snatched away Sunday after Sunday might begin to be suppressed and reduced to naught. I don't know if it would work, but I've often wondered why so few pastors ever make the attempt to restore "deep silence" to

---

1   *The Rule of Saint Benedict in English and Latin,* trans. and ed. Abbot Justin McCann, O. S. B. (Fort Collins, CO: Roman Catholic Books, n.d.), 119.

our churches. It may have to do with a sinking feeling that the good habits of preconciliar days are gone forever and will not return among the cellphone barbarians in the pews; it may have to do with a simple loss of belief in the church as a sacred place. Considering that many suburban churches fall somewhere along the spectrum between a Jet Propulsion Laboratory and a beige-carpeted conference center, it may not be surprising that the sense of sacrality is faint, even absent.

Earlier in the *Rule*, in chapter 19, "On the Discipline of Psalmody," St. Benedict bears witness to the dignity of the church and of the *opus Dei* that takes place in it, deducing thence what our inner and outer attitudes should be:

> We believe that God is present everywhere and that *the eyes of the Lord in every place behold the good and the evil* (Prov. 15, 3); but let us especially believe this without any doubting when we are performing the Divine Office. Therefore, let us ever remember the words of the prophet: *Serve ye the Lord in fear* (Ps. 2, 11); and again, *Sing ye wisely* (Ps. 46, 8); and, *In the sight of the angels will I sing to thee* (Ps. 137, 2). Let us then consider how we ought to behave ourselves in the presence of God and his angels, and so sing the psalms that mind and voice may be in harmony.[2]

This text helps us to grasp two lessons: the sacred liturgy is the time when, by God's own design and good pleasure, we are most of all held to be standing in His divine Presence, yielding up our minds and hearts to Him; and the oratory or church in which we are doing this "Work of God" is a place *like no other*, a place consecrated for the sole purpose of worshiping God. In a well-known passage, Augustus Welby Pugin conveys this point with Victorian lavishness:

> [The church] is, indeed, a sacred place; the modulated light, the gleaming tapers, the tombs of the faithful, the various altars, the venerable images of the just,—all conspire to fill the mind with veneration, and to impress it with the sublimity of Christian worship. And when the deep intonations of the bells from the lofty campaniles, which summon the people to the house of prayer, have

---

2   McCann, 66–69.

ceased, and the solemn chant of the choir swells through
the vast edifice—cold, indeed, must be the heart of that
man who does not cry out with the Psalmist, *Domine, dilexi
decorem domus tuae, et locum habitationis gloriae tuae.*[3]

Drawing on the insights of Benedict and Pugin, we might state
this principle: The church building is the most sacred space we
have; as a result, it is *there* that we will learn—or not learn—the
meaning of the distinction between sacred and profane.

If there is not a strong sense, upon entering a church, of passing from one domain to another, of leaving the world (to some
extent) and entering a different realm, of going from an earth-
bound atmosphere in which we are at ease to a celestial temple
that calls forth reverential fear, I am afraid there will usually be
nothing else that offers an equally powerful communication of
the distinction. There are, to be sure, other ways to evoke the
distinction, such as the sound of Gregorian chant even in a Mass
celebrated outdoors or in a humble tent; but the sacred space,
the "oratory," is normally the most obvious, impressive, durable,
stable, all-encompassing sign of the sacred that we have. It either
says to you: "This is God's house, where you will meet Him in
a special way—tread quietly, watch and pray"; or it says "This is
just a building, where you can amble around, talk, text, take selfies,
joke, sleep, or eat a snack."

Eminent liturgical theologian Msgr. Nicola Bux writes in his
book *No Trifling Matter*:

> Jacob understood, once awakened from sleep: "Indeed,
> the Lord is in this place." He became conscious of the
> fact, he was afraid, and said: "How awe-inspiring is this
> place! This is none other than the house of God, this
> is the gate of heaven."[4] The divine presence pushes the
> patriarch to fashion the stone, on which he had slept
> and received the dream, into a stele, the primitive altar,
> and to anoint it on top. We would say: to consecrate it.

---

3   Pugin, *Contrasts*, 5, quoted in Richard Kieckhefer, *Theology in Stone:
Church Architecture from Byzantium to Berkeley* (New York: Oxford University
Press, 2004), 141.
4   This verse, of course, is the Introit for the Mass of the Dedication of
a Church.

God, in fact, had established his abode, his house; for this reason he changed the name and called that place Bethel, in Hebrew, house of God. That stone founded the house of God.

Consecration renders the Lord always present in a place made by human hands, and increases reverent fear and devotion for the abode and house of God. Consecration changes the designated use of the place: it cannot be used for profane purposes.

But unfortunately today things are not always like that! And so God leaves us, is not with us, does not protect and accompany us in the journey of life, does not feed us, does not make us return safe and sound to our home.[5]

Later on, Bux speaks at greater length of the grave significance of the consecration of a church—something that *changes* it objectively and permanently. His words are worth quoting in full:

Though much emphasized as regards the effects and the changes it calls forth in the place that has been chosen for the purpose, the dedication of a building to Christian worship is very quickly forgotten these days: in fact, one is frequently present at the profanation of everything that was offered to the Lord with such a rite....

In the Ordinary Form of 1977, the Mass of dedication underlines the will of the ecclesial community to dedicate the new building to divine worship, in an exclusive and perpetual way. In particular, the presence of the sacrament and the altar do not permit any other use; in fact they are there to recall to us that the church is the sign of the heavenly sanctuary where Jesus Christ has penetrated, in order to appear before the sight of God on our behalf (Heb. 9, 24).

Liturgists would say that for the sake of the truth of the sign, a church cannot be employed for purposes other than worship, on pain of gravely offending the Lord to whom it has been offered. Besides, its dedication is rightly commemorated every year on the anniversary day, especially within the church that was consecrated. It is

5   Nicola Bux, *No Trifling Matter: Taking the Sacraments Seriously Again* (Brooklyn, NY: Angelico Press, 2016), 27.

therefore a grave error that, in practice, the consecration we have just described is emptied of meaning in our day by the actions of priests themselves, with the holding of events incompatible with the sacred place: concerts, performances, ballets, meetings of every type, which at one time were done outside or "in front of the temple," as the Latin word *pro-fanum* recalls; the phenomenon of using churches for concerts of not only sacred but also profane music seems unstoppable. Acts that are not sacred, and normally done elsewhere, bring with them a profanation of the church....

Welcome cannot be given to profane actions of this type, or to any others, in the place where the divine mysteries are celebrated. How is it possible that bishops and priests have forgotten that such a place as that, so often built with sacrifice by the faithful, has been "dedicated"—a word that recalls the act with which something very personal is offered to someone who is loved. To dedicate something means that it is no longer mine, but his. If I were to take it back, that would be a betrayal. It is a grave matter, because we take from God that which is his, what we ourselves had sworn we would give him. The rite itself of dedication shows that it is a kind of oath or vow, that is, a sacred act. What need is there for such solemnity, if afterwards the sacred place is employed for profane uses?

Liturgists exalt the rite of dedication, but in contradiction with that, they go silent and speak not a word in the face of the transformation of churches into multi-purpose halls. This is worse than what was done by totalitarian atheist regimes, which had transformed these places into theaters, gymnasiums, and stores. It is a very serious phenomenon, because it means, first, that the sense of the church as a place offered to God, for the worship owed him, has been lost; we have consecrated something, and then we take it back in order to do purely human things there. In the second place, we favor in this way the eclipse of the divine presence, because in the church we practice activities proper to a theater or an auditorium, such as speaking, eating, applauding, and other attitudes typical of places of entertainment. When a church becomes a theater where people laugh, applaud, and shout, it then becomes difficult to demand, for the same place, the proper attitudes for worship: listening, recollection, silence, adoration, because the conviction that one is standing in a versatile locale has taken root. That conviction leads to obscuring the principal and characteristic function of a church, which is adoration, and to prohibiting kneeling for prayer, either when the liturgy is being celebrated in the church, or outside the liturgy. But in reality, the church remains a place of presence and prayer, and of silence, even when there is no liturgy being celebrated.[6]

Two of the most egregious postconciliar examples of the contempt for sacred space that Bux laments were furnished, *horribile dictu*, by a cardinal and by the pope. The more recent, as reported last week by *InfoVaticana* and *Rorate Caeli*, was the "World AIDS Day" rock concert held in St. Stephen's Cathedral in Vienna, under the auspices of the cardinal archbishop, who sat in the front row and was photographed before and after with the performers.

Quieter but no less scandalous was the papal luncheon held *inside* the basilica of St. Petronius in Bologna on October 1, 2017, as thousands who stood in the nave watched the pope enjoy a meal with his invited guests.[7]

Although the parallels are not exact, one cannot help thinking of the desecrations of the Hebrew temple recorded in the Old Testament, and of Belshazzar's feast, who, I am sure, was also smiling pleasantly until the horrifying hand began to write on the wall. The sober words of Bux strike at the core of this callous secularism: "A church cannot be employed for purposes other than worship, on pain of gravely offending the Lord to whom it has been offered.... Acts that are not sacred, and normally done elsewhere, bring with them a profanation of the church.... It is a grave matter, because we take from God that which is his, what we ourselves had sworn we would give him."

---

6   Bux, 189–93.

7   The luncheon is listed on the Vatican itinerary for the trip: "Solidarity lunch with poor people, refugees and prisoners in the Basilica 'San Petronio,'" www.vatican.va/content/francesco/en/travels/2017/inside/documents/papa-francesco-cesena-bologna_2017.html, accessed March 22, 2021.

Our Lord ate with sinners and publicans, yes—*but not in the Temple.* What he did to those pursuing secular business in the Temple is rather well known, and we could allow the painting by Cecco del Caravaggio to stand in for a thousand words.

Bux reminds us of what the Soviets did at the end of World War II as their armies came through central Europe. They often chose to stable their horses in churches, to show their contempt for the space and what it represented. In this they imitated the Protestants who, at the time of the Protestant Revolt, ransacked churches, took the sacred hosts out of the tabernacles, and threw them to horses and dogs.

It is not at all surprising that the same pope who denies *in practice* the distinction between worthy and unworthy communions should be the one who violates *in practice* the distinction between a consecrated and an unconsecrated place; nor that the one who has elevated Paul VI to the altars should be the one who disdains the meaning of the very rite of dedication that pope promulgated. Such things are fully consistent with the modernist theology of those who, as Ratzinger explains, deny the very distinction between the sacred and the profane, arguing that with the coming of Christ, everything and everyone has *already* been redeemed, is already blessed—is, as it were, automatically *in* Christ. If God is already all in all, then in a certain sense, to borrow a phrase from Dostoevsky, "all things are permitted."[8] A church is no more special than the Church of which it is a sign; if *extra ecclesiam nulla salus* is incorrect, so must be *intra ecclesiam nullum profanum.*[9]

Bux addresses this very point:

> There is no place more apt than a church for bringing people who so desire—and there are many of them!—to an encounter with God. The Church must not be considered as "the liturgical space" and nothing more than

8   And this is actually true of those who are fully redeemed: the blessed in heaven. Since their wills are in perfect conformity with God's and, seeing Him face to face, they can no longer desire evil, it follows that they may do whatever they wish, and it will be good.

9   For a thorough explication of the claims made in this paragraph, see Pink, "Vatican II and Crisis in the Theology of Baptism"—essential reading for understanding the transformation in Catholic theology and liturgy in the twentieth century.

that! Is it possible that there are no available places for concerts, theatrical performances, and other such things? *Then we should not be surprised that the sense of the sacred, the sense of the divine presence, has been lost.* Few today know what sacred and holy mean. The "theology of secularization" considers that everything is sacred and that there is nothing profane, and so it wishes us to believe that the dedication of a church is not a consecration; it can also be used for profane activities.[10]

In his book *Signs of the Holy One*, Fr. Uwe Michael Lang documents how the category of the sacred was undermined in Rahner and Teilhard, among others. After all, "properly understood," which means by way of a patristic *ressourcement* filtered through a Modernist prism, Christ's Incarnation was a cosmic redemption, a recapitulation of the whole universe; so why reduce the effects of redemption to only a few old buildings, or, for that matter, a few old rites? The whole temple of creation has been consecrated, dedicated; grace can be accessed anywhere. Teilhard seems to say that the sacraments are just "expressions," particular upwellings of this cosmic grace that surrounds and permeates us. It is, needless to say, but one step from this view, which sounds vaguely pious, to a total secularization of the Church that evacuates God altogether.

I believe these observations help us put into a larger context the disturbing lightshows that have been projected on the façades of various churches in Rome in recent years, showing wild animals running across them, or the building dissolving and toppling over, as if we live in a new era in which the institutional Church will be overcome by a borderless, uninhibited, open-ended "luv," the contemporary world's substitute for grace. If this sounds very much like a rehash of 1968, with the false prophet Herbert Marcuse bloviating in the wings, rest assured: it is.

Yet it is worse the second time around. The surge of revolutionary emotions in late 60s could be pardoned as an eruption of uncontrolled immaturity exacerbated by peculiar social circumstances. Today's antinomianism, which is not ashamed to usher into the temple of God shirtless artistes with electric

---

10   Bux, *No Trifling Matter*, 193–94, emphasis added.

guitars or platters laden with lasagna, is premeditated, theoretical, programmatic, and totalitarian. I do not necessarily attribute this perfection of profanation to any one human agent; but an intelligence of exceptional power must surely lie behind it.

31

For Today's Catholic Prelates, There Is Nowhere to Hide

LifeSiteNews

JANUARY 2, 2019

FOR A LONG TIME, THE POPE AND THE bishops were seen as "men apart," occupying a lofty sphere that no layman could dare enter, with a special standing that blocked all criticism. This attitude has a reasonable foundation: we are dealing here with the successors of the apostles, with those who represent Christ the Good Shepherd on earth, teaching, ruling, and sanctifying in His name and by His authority.

However, it is an attitude that has its limits, too, when we remember that we are dealing not with Christ Himself, nor with the irreplaceable Apostles who sit on the twelve thrones, but with fallen men who can either live up to their high calling or fail badly in it.

In past ages, sinful prelates often lived "high off the hog" at the expense of the laity, and there was little enough that could be done to expose them, influence them, or shame them. In like manner, holy and courageous prelates might be praised locally, and perhaps their reputation would eventually spread (especially after their death, when a *cultus* would begin for the holiest of them), but again, there was a practical limit on the reach of their good influence.

Today, however, the situation has changed dramatically, thanks to the media. It is no longer possible for a bishop to do good quietly or to do evil quietly. Already this was true in the age of newspapers and magazines, but the internet has exponentially intensified the bright spotlight shining on the public actions and statements of any bishop. He cannot hide. He must make a choice: be *boldly* good; be *boldly* evil; or look indifferent, disengaged, cowardly.

As many downsides as it undoubtedly has, the internet has become, in a sort of clumsy way, a winnowing fork and a threshing floor (cf. Mt. 3:12). True, the laity still do not have, and will never have, any *direct* authority in regard to the hierarchy. But *moral* authority they do have, wielding the weapons of exposure, protest, and withdrawal of support.[1] They may and should continually call on their shepherds to give good example, to remain faithful to the teaching of Christ and His Church (not the latest fashionable modernized doctrine from the Vatican), to deal promptly with evils, to acknowledge and repent of evils, and to promote "all that is true, noble, right, pure, lovely, admirable, excellent, praiseworthy" (cf. Phil. 4:8).

The internet has made it common knowledge that (as a friend put it to me) billions of dollars in damages have been paid out for the crimes of certain sick members of the clergy. Was this the purpose for which *you* earmarked *your* diocesan contributions? What about your forefathers, who toiled for their bread, saved it up, and gave it generously to their local church for the love of God? Did they want it to be used for the building of beautiful churches and the upkeep of worthy clergy, or did they think that lawyers' fees, professional PR agents, payoffs, and huge court settlements for victims were just as good a purpose?

As Fr. John Zuhlsdorf succinctly stated: "It is time to cut off all funds and channel them only to trustworthy traditional causes."[2] Today's informed laity should not give a red cent to anything run by, sponsored by, or recommended by any diocese or the USCCB until bishops start acting like St. Ambrose, St. Athanasius, and St. John Fisher, instead of hacks for the Democratic Party.

At present, sadly, this outcome does not seem too likely. In November, the U.S. bishops made themselves a spectacle by birthing, on center stage before the eyes of the world, a particularly noxious fruit of hyperpapalism: the spineless abandonment of genuine episcopal responsibility. "In the prophets of Jerusalem also I have seen a horrible thing: they commit adultery, and walk in lies; and they strengthen the hands of evildoers, so that none doth return from his wickedness: they are all of them become unto me as Sodom, and the inhabitants thereof as Gomorrah" (Jer. 23:14).

---

1 See "Five ways Catholic laity can powerfully influence Church for good from within," *LifeSiteNews*, November 8, 2018.
2 "Read and weep: Soviet style 'psych' tactics used against priests by bishops," *Fr. Z's Blog*, September 25, 2018.

As the pope and bishops dither and show their utter incapacity (or even unwillingness) to deal with the crisis they themselves have caused, and as the approaching February meeting promises to be "more of the same," the voice of the faithful continues to rise up, like the rolling of thunder as the storm draws nearer. The hammer blows of lawsuits, investigations, document raids, and criminal sentences will fall more and more relentlessly on the shoulders of the perpetrators, collaborators, and connivers.

Meanwhile, true heroes of the Faith, like Bishop Joseph Strickland, will rise up and be distinguished for their counterwitness. May the Lord send us *many more* in our hour of need.

32

Pope's Rebuke of Traditionaliſts Better Applies to Vatican II Zealots Stuck in 1960s

LifeSiteNews

JANUARY 10, 2019

I N THE EARLY YEARS OF THE FRANCIS REGIME, the world was treated to a wide and colorful array of insulting language from the Vicar of Christ directed at Catholics faulted for remaining "intransigently faithful" to tradition, with the implication that these were not like himself: a 1970s progressive, full of admiration for the United Nations and the European Union. In recent times the flood of insults has somewhat subsided. The pontiff has even warned us against the dangers of indulging in this verbal sport.

We might nevertheless wish to revisit an earlier official papal document, the Apostolic Exhortation *Evangelii Gaudium* of November 24, 2013, where the then-new pope furnished a classy definition of those who exemplify what he called "self-absorbed promethean neopelagianism." They (he says)

> ultimately trust only in their own powers and feel superior to others because they observe certain rules or remain intransigently faithful to a particular Catholic style from the past. A supposed soundness of doctrine or discipline leads instead to a narcissistic and authoritarian elitism, whereby instead of evangelizing, one analyses and classifies others, and instead of opening the door to grace, one exhausts his or her energies in inspecting and verifying. (n. 94)

He then says that this mentality, like "gnosticism" (whatever *that* means), "are manifestations of an anthropocentric immanentism" (whatever *that* means), and concludes: "It is impossible to think that a genuine evangelizing thrust could emerge from these adulterated forms of Christianity."

While it is undeniable that such a tendency, or at least the temptation to it, can exist in any Christian at any time—and therefore also in communities that pride themselves on being "traditional" to one degree or another—one would be remiss if one failed to acknowledge a monumental fact: it is precisely a self-absorbed and neo-pelagian spirit that has infiltrated nearly all celebrations of the Novus Ordo. None other than Joseph Ratzinger condemned the sociological conception of liturgy as "a work of this particular community," one that trusts in the power of its active participation and feels superior to over 1,500 years of Latin liturgy because it "observes certain rules," namely what popes have promulgated in the past 50 years, and "remains intransigently faithful to a particular Catholic style from the past," namely, the 1960s and 1970s, in which Catholicism seems to be fatally trapped, like the mastodons of yore trapped in tar pits.

No doubt, a genuine evangelizing thrust could not emerge from such an adulterated form of Christianity. This perhaps explains why, at least in the Western world, the strongest growth is being seen in parishes, oratories, chapels, and religious communities that are expressly committed to "soundness of doctrine and discipline," which—surprise!—turns out to *open* doors to the grace of conversion. In a phrase used by a priest of the Fraternity of St. Peter, we see people "falling in Eucharistic love"![1]

The old Latin Mass is explicitly anti-Pelagian, categorically rejects Moralistic Therapeutic Deism, and clearly reflects the true nature of sacrifice and the negative theology (sin, hell, penance, etc.) that is reduced or obscured in the new liturgical books. Considered in itself, it is altogether a better antidote to the disease sketched out in *Evangelii Gaudium*. In no way could the Mass that sanctified St. Gregory the Great, St. Thomas Aquinas, St. Ignatius of Loyola, and Blessed John Henry Newman ever be written off as "a particular Catholic style from the past."

If a traditionalist gets a bit drunk, so to speak, on the rich drink poured out for him by tradition, and is tempted to think himself at the end of the path when he is only just beginning to slough off the mortal coil of modernity, let's rebuke him, but have mercy; if he "exhausts his energies" picking splinters out of

---

1   See Fr. Armand de Malleray, FSSP, *Ego Eimi—It Is I: Falling in Eucharistic Love* (Manchester, NH: Sophia Institute Press, 2022; originally published in 2018).

others' eyes, let him be kindly and calmly corrected. These are incredibly confusing and difficult times, and most sheep are doing their best without the guidance of shepherds worthy of the name.

The "good" traditionalist may consider himself "superior" precisely and *only* in this respect, that he submits his soul to be formed by a liturgy in which the tendencies Francis condemns are not inherent; that he emphatically does *not* trust in his own powers but in the universal tradition of the Church; that he trusts the power of Christ shown, lived, and poured forth in the traditional liturgy and its attendant devotions.

Our greatest concern should rather be for the masses of Catholics whose ordinary liturgical experience forms in them nothing other than neo-Pelagian, self-absorbed tendencies. Though I can't prove it, I have a hunch that if you surveyed the average attendant of a Latin Mass (the average "traditionalist"?) and a typical Novus Ordo congregant, the "neopelagiometer" would sound the alarm much sooner over the latter than over the former.

Let us return, then, to the quotation from Pope Francis, and let us speak forthrightly: it is a tendentious caricature, a portrait of the worst traditionalist in his worst moment. It targets the traditionalist who is bitter and spoiled, not the one in healthy bloom. In this sense, it is unjust and mean-spirited towards the large number of Catholics who are striving to love the Lord and their neighbor with the aid of traditional practices of the Faith. It would be as absurd to accept this portrait as it would be to say, about Catholics who attend the Novus Ordo, that all of them are tambourine-touting, liturgical dance-promoting, helium-balloon-sporting, lukewarm relativists.

But then, Pope Francis has shown the world that he has a tendency to be a manipulator, an ideologue, a dictator, and a relativist about dogma, so perhaps it is not worthwhile to take too seriously the problematic things he says.

33

The Pope's Remarks about Sex Ed Are Either Naïve or Nefarious

LifeSiteNews

JANUARY 30, 2019

MOST CATHOLICS ARE PROBABLY AWARE by now of Pope Francis's airplane press conference comments about why schools need to provide "sex education" to children.[1] I will admit that this past six years have battle-hardened me into a capacity for hearing and processing bad news, but even so, occasionally this pope of surprises can still make my jaw nearly fall from its socket.

Either Pope Francis knows nothing about what sex education materials look like nowadays, in which case he should have kept silent on the subject, or he *does* know what these materials look like, in which case he is recommending the tools of sin.

It isn't as if the Church's Magisterium has not offered considerable guidance on this question, always laying emphasis on caution, modesty, discretion, and above all, chastity. In response to the concept of "sex education" when it was first gaining ground in the 1920s *for married couples*, Pope Pius XI memorably said in his great encyclical *Casti Connubii*:

> Wholesome instruction and religious training in regard to Christian marriage will be quite different from that exaggerated physiological education by means of which, in these times of ours, some reformers of married life make pretense of helping those joined in wedlock, laying much stress on these physiological matters, in which is learned rather the art of sinning in a subtle way than the virtue of living chastely. (n. 108)

More pointedly, in 1929 Pope Pius XI's encyclical *Divini Illius Magistri,* which has been called the "Magna Carta" on the Christian

---

1   Diane Montagna, "Pope Francis: 'We must provide sex education in schools,'" *LifeSiteNews*, January 28, 2019.

education of youths, expressly takes up the question. Strikingly, it is as if Pius XI is responding precisely to the dangers and errors contained in his successor's position. And that they are truly dangers and errors cannot be denied, in light of the following authoritative exposition:

> 65. Another very grave danger is that naturalism which nowadays invades the field of education in that most delicate matter of purity of morals. Far too common is the error of those who with dangerous assurance and under an ugly term propagate a so-called sex education, falsely imagining they can forearm youths against the dangers of sensuality by means purely natural, such as a foolhardy initiation and precautionary instruction for all indiscriminately, even in public; and, worse still, by exposing them at an early age to the occasions, in order to accustom them, so it is argued, and as it were to harden them against such dangers.

> 66. Such persons grievously err in refusing to recognize the inborn weakness of human nature, and the law of which the Apostle speaks, fighting against the law of the mind; and also in ignoring the experience of facts, from which it is clear that, particularly in young people, evil practices are the effect not so much of ignorance of intellect as of weakness of a will exposed to dangerous occasions, and unsupported by the means of grace.

> 67. In this extremely delicate matter, if, all things considered, some private instruction is found necessary and opportune, from those who hold from God the commission to teach and who have the grace of state, every precaution must be taken. Such precautions are well known in traditional Christian education, and are adequately described by Antoniano when he says: "Such is our misery and inclination to sin, that often in the very things considered to be remedies against sin, we find occasions for and inducements to sin itself. Hence it is of the highest importance that a good father, while discussing with his son a matter so delicate, should be well on his guard and not descend to details, nor refer to the various ways in which this infernal hydra destroys with its poison so

large a portion of the world; otherwise it may happen that instead of extinguishing this fire, he unwittingly stirs or kindles it in the simple and tender heart of the child. Speaking generally, during the period of childhood it suffices to employ those remedies which produce the double effect of opening the door to the virtue of purity and closing the door upon vice."

Perhaps Pope Francis or one of his defenders would reply: "Ah, but that is someone speaking in 1929. Today, everything is different." He might play once again the "novelty card" as he did in his October 11, 2017 speech against capital punishment, in which the word "new" was mentioned sixteen times, as a way of driving home that the Church must teach not only what is old, but also what is new, fresh, never seen before...

Human nature does not change; the demands of virtue do not change; the harm of premature and improper exposure to sexual topics, outside of the confines of the family, remains the same; the permanent damage sins of impurity cause in souls, in friendships, in families, in society as a whole, remains ever the same. Nothing *of substance* has changed between 1929 and 2019. All that has changed is that our world has become ferociously promiscuous, mired in morose delectation, addicted to carnal pleasure, steeped in iniquities that weaken the will and blind the reason. All of these effects were known to the Desert Fathers of ancient Christianity, who predicted all the consequences of self-indulgence. Far from needing to be up-to-date, we would be far wiser to look back and recover their wisdom.

I'm sorry, but as a parent myself, as a friend of many good Catholic parents, and as a lifelong educator of young people, my reply is unshakably firm: "What Pope Pius XI taught in his encyclicals *Casti Connubii* and *Divini Illius Magistri* more than adequately covers the issue of 'sex education.' I am content with old truths that nourish, and have no need of new opinions that poison."

34

Troubling Signs that Satanism Is Infiltrating the Catholic Church

LifeSiteNews

FEBRUARY 6, 2019

PEOPLE ARE UNCOMFORTABLE TALKING about Satanism, but there are so many whispers about its inroads these days that the subject is at last coming out into the open. Since Satan-worshiping tends, of its very nature, to be done in darkness, it is hard to get hold of solid evidence about who may be involved, and how pervasive it may be. In his lengthy interviews with Taylor Marshall on YouTube, abuse victim James Grein hints at possible Satanic elements in connection with McCarrick, the St. Gallen group, and others involved in the wave of scandals that has overtaken the hierarchy, including the papacy.

Should we be surprised about this? In a way, yes, and in a way, no.

The most powerful churchmen will suffer the greatest temptation to ally themselves with the "angel of light" who attempts to rival God and overthrow His order—an order most apparent in the differentiation of the human race into male and female, and the ordering of sexual activity to procreation. Any powerful man in the Church, if he does not bend all his effort to sanctifying his soul and body in accord with supernatural virtue, will be drawn to defile his soul and body with unnatural vice. Those who are not totally committed to Christ will find themselves sliding down into the party of His archenemy.

That a choice must be made between the way of life and the way of death holds true for all Christians, but it holds true *especially* for priests and bishops, the shepherds of the flock. The hired shepherd, of all men, requires the most humility, for he is working around the clock to watch over and preserve sheep—sheep that do not even belong to him! How humiliating; how grating; how unworthy of the shepherd's own life goals. This is why a good shepherd shines with self-sacrifice, while an evil shepherd stinks of egoism. We should worry more about the "smell of the shepherd" than we do about the "smell of the sheep."

The recent news regarding the promotion by Pope Francis of Argentine bishop Gustavo Oscar Zanchetta to a senior position at the Vatican despite, it appears, already-known serious accusations against him is yet another example, among so many, of how this pope surrounds himself with unsavory characters.[1] So far from being committed to moral reform, he empowers those who are morally compromised, while distancing or disgracing those who are morally strong.

In Revelation 22:15, when Jesus lists those who will be excluded from the heavenly Jerusalem, the list includes various sinners, such as sorcerers, whoremongers, murderers, idolaters, and liars. However, *first* on the list is "dogs." Does Jesus have a problem with "man's best friend"? Hardly. The term "dog" is also used in Deuteronomy 23:17 in a list of unclean things that cannot be brought into the temple in the earthly Jerusalem: "Thou shalt not offer the hire of a strumpet, nor the price of a dog, in the house of the Lord thy God, whatsoever it be that thou hast vowed: because both these are an abomination to the Lord thy God." God makes it clear that the Israelites must not bring filthy things to the temple as offerings. The earnings of prostitutes ("strumpets") and male cult prostitutes ("dogs") are strictly prohibited and are to be excluded.

Therefore, the first people in the Book of Revelation's list who are to be definitively excluded from the heavenly Jerusalem are male sodomites. These, then, are the dogs who must be excluded from the kingdom, both on earth and in heaven.

"Thy kingdom come, Thy will be done, *on earth as it is in heaven.*" That which can never be received into the heavenly kingdom is

---

1   See Maike Hickson, "Report: Pope Francis knew about Argentina bishop's sexual misconduct prior to Vatican promotion," *LifeSiteNews*, January 20, 2019. In February 2022, Bishop Zanchetta was found guilty and sentenced to four and a half years in prison. See Pierre Boralevi, "Argentinian bishop previously defended by Pope found guilty of sexually abusing seminarians," *LifeSiteNews*, March 4, 2022; Joan Frawley Desmond, "Argentinian Bishop's Conviction Spotlights Pope Francis' Role in Case," *National Catholic Register*, March 21, 2022. Many other examples of Francis's promotion or protection of unsavory characters and heretics are given in Lamont and Pierantoni, *Defending the Faith*, 140–45.

likewise forbidden on earth; that which God will always punish in eternity must also be punished in time, to the extent possible. For the Church on earth is called to be holy as the Lord is holy, and to overturn all idols in order to follow Him alone. We see nothing else than this in the Acts of the Apostles; in the Desert Fathers; in the early monks and nuns; in the long line of saints, whether contemplatives removed from the world or ministers actively involved in its governance, who defend the harmonious order of God's creation and the still more marvelous beauty of the redemption Christ obtained for us against the dissonance of its demonic enemies.

Pretending that we, in our time, are not witnesses to and participants in a battle of unprecedented magnitude and intensity between angelic armies of good and evil would be delusional. With the help of Satan, the enemies of Christ and His Church have breached the walls and comfortably sit on episcopal thrones and run curial offices while they advance the destruction of confessional Christianity.

It is better to know what is really happening: this is both somber and liberating. It frees us from the wearisome exercise of pretending we're in a new age of the Spirit unleashed by the last Council, and enlists us in the company of the holy angels whose help we urgently need.

Actually, we *are* in a new age of the spirit. The problem is, it's the wrong spirit, and his name is legion, for they are innumerable. If you are not already praying the St. Michael Prayer every day, it's time to start; if you are praying it, persevere. The season of pretended niceness is over. The guns are loaded; it's all-out warfare.

35

Has Pope Francis Rejected the Supreme Sacrifice of Martyrs Who Resisted Islam?

LifeSiteNews

FEBRUARY 21, 2019

T HE *ROMAN MARTYROLOGY* BEGAN AS AN ancient listing of the names of martyrs on their *"dies natalis,"* that is, their birthday into heavenly glory. It was organically added to, century after century, as the martyrs in their triumphant march were joined by confessors, doctors, monks, hermits, friars, virgins, widows, kings, queens, and others down through the ages. This book is a liturgical book because it is recited or chanted as part of the equally ancient office of Prime. (It is customary to read the following day's list of saints, which mentally prepares us for First Vespers of any great feast that may be coming, and in general, puts us in mind ahead of time of the saints we wish to remember.) It, too, transmits the Faith of the Church, and continues to be used by religious, clergy, and laity who adhere to the *usus antiquior* or older form of the Roman Rite.

Tragically, in spite of its antiquity and its integral role in the sevenfold daily praises of God, the office of Prime was abolished at the Second Vatican Council. The liturgical reform produced a new version of the *Martyrology* that bears about as much, or as little, connection with its predecessor as the *Novus Ordo Missae* of 1969 does to its predecessor, the *Missale Romanum* of 1570. Due, moreover, to the abolition of Prime, the new *Martyrology* has never found a secure foothold, and is extremely rarely used today—one sign of which is the rarity of the Latin *editio typica* and the lack, even today, of an English translation. Ironically, the old *Martyrology* in its last edition from 1956 is widely available in multiple new English editions.

When all is said and done, the *Martyrology* is a catalogue of victors, so beyond its loud proclamation of the truth of the communion of saints, its exaltation of Christian states of life, and its testimony to the prevalence of miracles in the life of the Church, we do not find many instances where it bears witness to specific doctrines. However, the traditional *Roman Martyrology* speaks loud and clear on certain matters, and one of them is highly pertinent to the confusion in which we find ourselves today—namely, the severe judgment on Islam found in its pages.

As I was reading the *Martyrology* for today, February 21, my eyes rested on the following entry:

> At Damascus, St. Peter Mavimenus, who said to certain Arabs who came to him in his sickness: "Every man who does not embrace the Catholic Christian faith is damned as Mohammed, your false prophet, was" and was slain by them.

Unlike Pope Francis, who co-signed with a Muslim leader a declaration that asserts, inter alia, that God wills a plurality of religions,[1] St. Peter Mavimenus spoke the truth with simplicity and fortitude. In his words are condensed the only proper Christian attitude towards Islam: an unequivocal repudiation of its errors, which are all the more dangerous to the degree that some truths of natural religion and some fragmentary truths of revelation are mingled in with them. The assertion to which Francis placed his signature is erroneous and heretical, as Dr. John Lamont and Bishop Athanasius Schneider have shown.[2]

This is far from being the sole passage in the old *Martyrology* that proclaims the age-old enmity between Catholics and Muslims. Indeed, *every month of the year* brings its reminders. The Church traditionally commemorates Catholic martyrs to Islam on January 14, January 16, February 19, March 11, March 15, April 17, April 18, May 16, June 5, June 7, June 13, June 26, June 28, July 11, July 16, July 19, July 20, July 22, July 27, August 6, August 20, September 15, September 19, September 27, October 10, October 11, October 22, November 6, November 24, and December 17. Still other entries speak of Catholics who resisted the Saracens or the Arabs but did not lose their heads for it.

1　See Diane Montagna, "Pope Francis under fire for claiming 'diversity of religions' is 'willed by God,'" *LifeSiteNews*, February 5, 2019.

2　See John Lamont, "Francis and the Joint Declaration on Human Fraternity: A Public Repudiation of the Catholic Faith," *Rorate Caeli*, February 10, 2019; Bishop Athanasius Schneider, "The Christian Faith Is the Only Valid and the Only God-Willed Religion," *OnePeterFive*, February 8, 2019.

Here are some examples of the entries to be found in the old *Martyrology*:

> In Morocco, Africa, the passion of the five proto-martyrs of the Order of Friars Minor, namely, Berard, Peter and Otho, priests, and Accursius and Adjutus, lay-brethren; who for preaching the Catholic faith and because of their rejection of the Mohammedan Law, after divers torments and mockeries, were beheaded by the Saracen king. (January 16)

> At Cordova in Spain, St. Eulogius, Priest and Martyr. On account of his fearless and outstanding confession of Christ, he was scourged and beaten with rods, and finally beheaded in the Saracen persecution. He merited to have part with the martyrs of the city for he had written of their fight for the faith and wished to join them. (March 11)

> At Cordova in Spain, St. Perfectus, Priest and Martyr, who was beheaded by the Moors for disputing against sect of Mohammed, and courageously professing his faith in Christ. (April 18)

> At Cordova in Spain, St. Aurea, Virgin, sister of the holy martyrs Adulf and John; for a while she apostatized through the persuasion of a Mohammedan judge, but, quickly repenting of what she had done, she overcame the enemy in a second contest by the shedding of her blood. (July 19)

> At Cordova in Spain, St. Paul, Deacon and Martyr, who rebuked the heathen princes for Mohammedan impiety and cruelty, and preached Christ with great courage: by their command he was slain, and passed to his reward in heaven. (July 20)

> At Cordova in Spain, the holy martyrs Adulf and John, brothers, who were crowned with martyrdom for Christ's sake in the Arab persecution. Their sister, the blessed Virgin Aurea, was inspired by their example to return to the faith, and later suffered martyrdom bravely on July 19. (September 27)

Near Ceuta in Morocco, the passion of the seven holy martyrs of the Order of Friars Minor, namely, Daniel, Samuel, Angelus, Leo, Nicholas, Ugolino and Domnus, all of whom were priests except Domnus. There they suffered insults, bonds and stripes from the Saracens because they preached the Gospel and put to silence the sect of Mahomet; finally, they were beheaded and thus obtained the palm of martyrdom. (October 10)

Perhaps most haunting of all, given the current circumstances, is this entry:

At Monte Cassino, blessed Pope Victor III, who as the successor of Pope St. Gregory VII shed a fresh luster on the Apostolic See, and with God's help gained a famous victory over the Saracens. (September 16)

Like St. Pius V, Bl. Victor III *fought* the Muslims, rather than capitulating to them, as his successor Francis does with his attitudes on European immigration and his willingness to enter into agreements that confuse Catholics who are already pickled to the gills in religious indifferentism.

In Robert Reilly's *The Closing of the Muslim Mind: How Intellectual Suicide Created the Modern Islamist Crisis*, we learn of the great struggle within Islam from the ninth to the eleventh centuries between the Hellenized Muslims who valued the role of reason and the fundamentalists (as we would recognize them today) who held it in suspicion or denigrated it. The latter obviously won the victory, and since then, the phrase *"en sha'Allah"* denotes everything in Islam—"if God wills it." As Pope Benedict XVI argued in his Regensburg Address, God is reduced to nothing but pure will.[3]

There is a curious and disturbing connection here, as we watch the same reductionism happening to the office and role of the pope. Instead of being seen as a voice of the *Logos*, a witness to reason and revelation as they echo through time in the Church, the papacy becomes a sheer exercise of volition: authority reduced to will-power. As in Islam God is reduced from loving wisdom to almighty will, so in the Vatican the pope is reduced from a

3   See the Lecture of the Holy Father Benedict XVI in the Aula Magna of the University of Regensburg, September 12, 2006: "Faith, Reason and the University: Memories and Reflections."

servant of perennial doctrine to a domineering engineer of change. No one, then, should be surprised that this pope was able to sign the document on human fraternity in the UAE: a papacy of will enters into agreement with a religion of voluntarism.

We enter into dangerous waters indeed when our faith, founded upon Sacred Scripture, Sacred Tradition, and the confident use of reason, is made subject to the will of an individual with an agenda, and treated as a commodity that can be negotiated at the table of interreligious dialogue.

Here we have an obvious clash between the traditional faith of the Church, represented by the *lex orandi* of her *Martyrology,* and the novelties propounded by Francis, who endeavors to introduce a new *lex credendi* on adultery, sacramental access, capital punishment, and religious pluralism—and who finds his path clearer because of widespread lack of access to the older liturgical books, which enshrine the constant belief of Catholics.

36

How the Eight Daughters of Lust Influenced Vatican's Sex Abuse Summit

LifeSiteNews

FEBRUARY 26, 2019

L AST WEEK'S FAILED SUMMIT ON SEX ABUSE showed to the world the spectacle of high-ranking prelates denying obvious connections between clerical abuse and homosexuality and filling the air with lofty sentiments as cheap as the paper they were written on. It is by now clear that Pope Francis has no intention whatsoever of disempowering the cronies who encircle him and eat out of his hand. Meanwhile he pours out his ire on any who dare to question his and others' handling of the situation.

"A man is known by the company he keeps." The list is long, and getting longer every day, of the criminal clergy whom Bergoglio has tolerated or promoted, from his time in Argentina down to the present moment: cardinals (McCarrick, Murphy-O'Connor, Coccopalmerio[1]), bishops (Zanchetta,[2] Piñeda, Maccarone, Marx, Maradiaga), and priests (Grassi, Inzoli, Corradi[3]). As if this were not enough, he thwarts efforts at discipline.[4] "McCarrickism" is still alive and well.[5] All the dots have been well connected.[6]

---

1   See Maike Hickson and John-Henry Westen, "Source: Vatican cardinal was at drug-fueled homosexual party, and Pope knows it," *LifeSiteNews*, October 10, 2018.

2   See Marco Tosatti, "'Hot Photos'—The Vatican Knew about Zanchetta but Still Promoted Him," *OnePeterFive*, February 22, 2019.

3   See Manuel Torres, "'The pope ignored them': Alleged abuse of deaf children on 2 continents points to Vatican failings," *NOLA.com*, February 19, 2019.

4   See Maike Hickson, "Vatican Source: Pope dismissed Cdl. Müller for following Church rules on abuse cases," *LifeSiteNews*, August 29, 2018.

5   See Fr. Alexander Lucie-Smith, "McCarrick has gone. But McCarrickism lives on," *Catholic Herald* (UK), February 19, 2019.

6   See Meloni, *St. Gallen Mafia*.

We have resources in our Catholic tradition to understand at least part of what is going on in the Church today.

St. Gregory the Great, pope from 590 to 604, gave us a major work of theology entitled the *Moralia in Job,* a commentary on the Book of Job best appreciated for its profound insight into ethics and the spiritual life. In the thirty-first book of the *Moralia,* St. Gregory speaks of "the eight daughters of lust." These are "blindness of mind, thoughtlessness, inconstancy, rashness, self-love, hatred of God, love of this world, and abhorrence or despair of a future world."

When St. Thomas Aquinas explains the meaning of these "daughters," he says that lust hinders the operation of the intellect in four ways.[7]

First, it interferes with the grasping of a good end (this is "blindness of mind"). Lustful people do not see clearly the true good; they stumble around, chasing after shadows and illusions, taking what is evil as if it were good. Outsiders can see this loss of vision quite clearly, but those who are given to sensuality become unaware of the spiritual good. If they think of it or discuss it at all, it is in an abstract and distant manner, because there is no feeling for it anymore. The most shocking manifestation of this blindness is the support for abortion found among the unchaste, whose disordered attachment to sex has blinded them to the dignity of other persons. For such people, children are a nuisance or interruption.

Lust also hinders counsel or discernment of the proper course of action; this is why it propels its victims into foolish choices that ultimately tear them apart, as we are also seeing in the Church's hierarchy (this is "rashness"). In a way similar to that of a wrathful person who destroys himself by carelessly rushing into the fray, a man in the grip of passion acts stupidly. He ultimately becomes his own worst enemy.

Lust hinders good judgment to such an extent that it obliterates the memory of justice (this is "thoughtlessness"). We often catch sight of this thoughtlessness in the inadequate, tone-deaf, bureaucratic responses made by hierarchs to abuse victims, or even the lack of any response at all—indications that they themselves may be under the influence of sexual vice.

Lust hinders the ability of a man to resist his concupiscence even if his reason or someone else urges him to resist (this is

---

7   *Summa theologiae* II-II, qu. 153, art. 5.

"inconstancy"). The copious data we now have about pedophiles and homosexuals indicates that, left to their own devices, and without earnest efforts at reform and conversion, they will be incapable of not pursuing their lecherous inclinations. As Aristotle says, this does not make them guiltless, because they were responsible for allowing the vice to grow in the first place.

Lust affects the will in four ways as well.

Desire for the *end*, which ought to take the form of charity for God above all, for neighbor, and for oneself, is twisted into disordered "self-love," which places gratification of one's lower self (the passions and senses) above any other object of love—even the good of one's higher self (the mind). There immediately flows from this disordered self-love a "hatred of God," because God forbids the desired pleasure that is contrary to His law. This perfectly explains the contempt for the divine law that we see with alarming frequency on the part of Church hierarchs, who would rather modify or expunge the sixth and ninth commandments than submit to them out of love for God. The frequent abuse of the sacred liturgy, which is almost always connected with a hatred of spiritual and divine things, is also tied in with this effect of lust.[8]

Desire for the right *means* to a good end is corrupted by lust in two ways. Lust plunges a man into "love of this world" because he clings to the means to worldly pleasure, such as filthy lucre, which he ought rather to resist and purge from his life. For the same reason, lust causes "despair of a future world," because the unchaste man is, and at some level *knows* that he is, far from God. "Through being held back by carnal pleasures, he cares not to obtain spiritual pleasures, since they are distasteful to him," writes St. Thomas.

Because of ingrained habits of lust on the part of large numbers of men and women in the Western world today—including, obviously and tragically, members of the clergy—we should hardly be surprised to see all eight daughters busily at work. St. Peter Damian (1007–1072) in his own day saw the same corruption, and fought against it with all his might, regardless of the personal cost or the threats made against him.

We who are aware of what is going on must stop at nothing until the episcopacy and the Vatican are purified of this disease.

---

8   See John Monaco, "The 'Other' Abuse Crisis in the Catholic Church that No One is Talking About," *Medium.com*, February 21, 2019.

37

Six Years In, Francis Has Shown Himself to Be the Most Troubling Pope in History

LifeSiteNews

MARCH 19, 2019

I F A PICTURE IS WORTH A THOUSAND WORDS, then the photomontage below tells quite a tale, on this, the sixth anniversary of Pope Francis's papal inauguration on March 19, 2013.

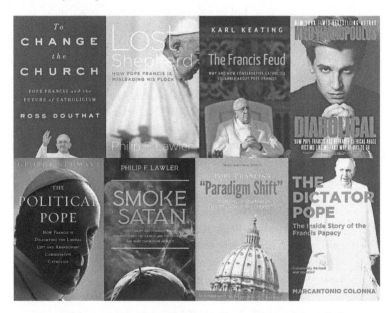

As we know from the seldom dull annals of Church history, many popes have deserved, and received, abundant praise or bitter criticism from their contemporaries or from later ages. On the one hand, the papacy shines, like a jewel-studded crown, with dozens of saints who shouldered their burden of governance with heroic generosity and dedication. The papacy's record in this regard puts to shame the record of any other institution; indeed, no series of rulers of any earthly empire or kingdom can hold a candle up to it for longevity, stability, constancy, and virtue. On the other hand, as history shows, the papacy—though protected from definitively committing the Church to error—is not, after all, protected from moral failings or intellectual debility, from catastrophic political blunders in pursuit of policy or from excessive friendliness to the Church's enemies.[1]

Martin Mosebach vividly describes how we find both sides of the papacy illustrated in the first pope:

> Even those hostile to the papacy would have to admire the shape and construction of this office that, from the beginning, has preserved it—in the person of Peter—from crises. As the successor and representative of Christ, as the Rock on which the Church is to be built, even the most capable office-bearer is bound to fail. For this office of "confirming his brothers in faith" Christ chose the very disciple who, while he had always shown courage and vitality, failed when it came to acknowledging his Master. "Then he began to curse and swear"—the evangelist, describing Peter's apostasy beside the fire in the High Priest's courtyard, leaves us in no doubt as to the seriousness of this betrayal.
>
> By choosing Peter, Christ shows that the office of representative requires no special intellectual gifts and talents, no firmness of character and no proven stability—which means that every man is equally fitted and unfitted for this office. Christ became man and therefore every man is equally equipped to represent him. No pope can betray Christ more than Peter did in that courtyard, no pope can follow Christ more than Peter, who got himself crucified on his account. The choice of Peter establishes the clear distinction, in the Church, between the office and the person. It is this principle that makes it possible to encounter the incarnate, grace-bestowing Christ even in unworthy human beings. The choice of Peter also makes concrete the Catholic anthropology that sees man as weak and sinful, and yet called to pursue the highest perfection.[2]

---

1   See volume 1, chapter 2.

2   *Subversive Catholicism: Papacy, Liturgy, Church*, trans. Sebastian Condon and Graham Harrison (Brooklyn, NY: Angelico Press, 2019), 29–30.

Today, we are required more than ever to lean hard on "the distinction between the office and the person." The papacy deserves our veneration and our adherence; the incumbent pope may or may not be worthy of his office and may, in fact, be a major scandal, a stumbling block to the faithful and to those outside the flock. Christ does not and will not abandon His Church, even when churchmen abandon Him. The Head of the Church is and always remains Jesus Christ. The phrase "Vicar of Christ" brings this out quite clearly: a vicar is one who stands in for someone, who represents *Him,* and has authority solely from and for *Him.* No only does this concept steer clear of hyperpapalism, it undermines it in principle by showing the pope to be a stand-in for the actual eternal Head of the Church. The pope represents this Head on earth—and he can badly fail in his duty.

Mosebach rightly reminds us of a truth that, in healthier times, might seem a truism: man is weak and sinful yet called to pursue the highest perfection. The pope, more than any other, is reasonably expected to pursue this highest perfection, not only to set a good example for the other shepherds and sheep, but more particularly to secure his own salvation and the good of the flock entrusted to him.

Alas, we see weakness and sinfulness abounding at the Vatican and throughout the Church. The evidence of corruption has become so multifaceted and voluminous that it is impossible to deny it. The prophet Jeremiah has words for a situation like this: "My people have been lost sheep. Their shepherds have caused them to go astray" (Jer. 50:6).

The photomontage above puts before us an unprecedented number and variety of book-length critiques published over the past few years, documenting the doctrinal aberrations and failures of Pope Francis, which are cause for the greatest alarm and the most fervent prayer and penance. We pray that where sin abounds, grace will abound all the more.

Meanwhile, we know that the evils under which we suffer must be temporary; the only states that last forever are heaven and hell, which are not of this world. We may also take comfort and courage in the knowledge that God will not be mocked, but has already prepared in His eternal wisdom the doom that will come upon those who lift themselves above their humble status as successors, not replacements, of the apostles: "As for your terribleness, the pride of your heart has deceived you, O dweller in the clefts of the rock, holding the height of the hill. Though you should make your nest as high as the eagle, I will bring you down from there, says the Lord" (Jer. 49:16).

To high-ranking prelates enjoying favor, influence, and power, the prophet cries out: "You also, O madmen, shall be brought to silence; the sword shall pursue you" (Jer. 48:2)—be it the sword of civil authorities or the sword of inevitable death.

> A sword against the oracle priests, that they may become fools! A sword against her mighty men, that they may be destroyed!... For it is a land of images, and they are mad over idols. Therefore wild beasts shall dwell with hyenas in Babylon, and ostriches shall dwell in her. (Jer. 50:36–39 ESV)

The "land of images" might call to mind disturbing light shows on the façades of Roman churches; madness over idols calls to mind the frenetic chasing after the "values" of European liberalism, the abstract "ideals" of modernism, and the "cult" of liturgical change. The "wild beasts," those who live by their carnal passions; the "hyenas," those who make incessant noise about progress; the "ostriches," those who bury their heads in the sand denying that there is a crisis[3]—all these will find themselves cast off to Babylon. It is only a matter of time.

An infallible law of the moral order guarantees, and the world's history copiously illustrates, that evil necessarily consumes itself, and its protagonists end up destroying each other: "The mighty man has stumbled against the mighty; they have fallen both of them together" (Jer. 46:12). The mountain of literature critical of the Bergoglio pontificate and curia offers a somber witness, for our time and for future ages, to the inundation of wickedness in high places, and urges us to persevere in the Christian battle against the world, the flesh, and the devil.

---

3 See chapter 28.

38

Bishops Who Deny or Distort Catholic Doctrine Betray Christ and His Church

LifeSiteNews
APRIL 2, 2019

IETRICH VON HILDEBRAND ONCE WROTE: "It is sad enough when people lose their faith and leave the Church; but it is much worse when those who in reality have lost their faith remain within the Church and... are giving to Christian revelation the interpretation that suits 'modern man.'"

Bishops like Peter Henrici,[1] Walter Kasper,[2] Reinhard Marx,[3] Lorenzo Baldisseri,[4] Óscar Andrés Rodríguez Maradiaga,[5] and Bruno Forte[6] embrace contemporary sociological, psychological, and philosophical theories that, in their view, "necessitate" major changes in Catholic doctrine or practice. They seem unaware (or worse, unconcerned) that there is such a thing as *faith*—radical, saving faith. Believers in Christ are willing to die for the least article of the Apostles' Creed, as the faithful at the time of the Arian crisis were willing to lose everything rather than allow their Lord and God to be insulted by the tainted rationalism of their opponents.

The theological virtue of faith enables one not only to know the truth of what God has revealed but also to *savor* it, and thus to

---

1 See "Catholics who hold fast to truths of faith are now condemned as 'fundamentalists,'" *LifeSiteNews*, November 28, 2018.
2 See Thomas Heinrich Stark, "German Idealism and Cardinal Kasper's Theological Project," *Catholic World Report*, June 9, 2015.
3 See Carl E. Olson, "Cardinal Marx promotes false news about blessings and 'homosexual unions,'" *Catholic World Report*, February 3, 2018.
4 See Chris Jackson, "Secretary General of Synod on the Family: 'The Church is Not Timeless,'" *The Remnant*, May 7, 2014.
5 See Steve Skojec, "Cardinal Maradiaga: The Vatican's Silliest Villain," *OnePeterFive*, May 31, 2017.
6 See "Meet Archbishop Bruno Forte," *Athanasius Contra Mundum*, October 21, 2014.

come to a deeper understanding of the relationship of the mysteries to one another and to their singular origin, the Blessed Trinity. This means, in addition, an ongoing adaptation of the mind to the mysteries as expressed in the traditional dogmatic formulas. Note well: it is not the mysteries that need to be adapted to the human mind (as the Modernists would have it), but rather the human mind that must conform itself to the mysteries, submitting to their demands, humbly bearing their yoke. This is the narrow path trodden by the saints in their pilgrimage to the beatific vision.

What Henrici & Co. exemplify is the triumph of modern rationalism, which will not submit to a predetermined external rule and allow it to measure the mind in a lifelong tutelage. In them we see the attitude of "we know better" that will finally turn upon Jesus Christ as it has already turned upon His Church, and will reject Him as it has already rejected her.

This, I believe, is what we are seeing in the Kasper phenomenon: without it being said explicitly, the real message of the past several Synods in Rome is that Modern Man, having "come of age," no longer needs the severe and restrictive teaching of Jesus Christ, which (to make matters worse) was embellished and encrusted with unreasonable demands by the medieval misogynistic and gamophobic Church. Modern man lives for liberty, independent judgment, and self-expression, and he will have it, regardless of what the Gospel and Catholic doctrine may say. Far from being heroic, adherence to Christ's "narrow way" is destructive of personality, freedom, human rights, and maximal self-expression.

Needless to say, this is a monumental lie, worthy of Satan himself, who seems to have many friends in high places these days. Even Pope Paul VI, whose disastrous liturgical reform is, so to speak, "the gift that keeps on giving" in the postconciliar crisis, was not benighted enough to overlook the entrance of "the smoke of Satan," the spirit of *non serviam,* into the Church.

The *Catechism of the Catholic Church* was intended to be a "sure norm" for knowing and transmitting the Faith. The words "sure norm" are those of Pope John Paul II, in the Apostolic Constitution by which he promulgated the *Catechism.* It should surely disturb us that John Paul II's successor Francis felt free to modify the content of the same *Catechism* to make it say that which *no one* in the Catholic tradition has ever said before—indeed, to say that which is contrary to both Testaments of Sacred Scripture: that the death penalty is *"per se* contrary to the Gospel," "inadmissible," perhaps even "intrinsically evil."[7] Even John Paul II, who was personally opposed to the use of the death penalty, knew full well that he could only say that it was prudentially ill-advised or unnecessary—not that it was something to be categorically excluded or condemned in principle.

How great an irony of our times, then, that the fabled "sure norm" of the *Catechism* has itself been taken hostage by the Modernist proponents of a falsely-conceived "development of doctrine."[8] Wisely did the great Catholic convert Orestes Brownson write in July of 1846:

> The Church is not here to follow the spirit of the age, but to control and direct it, often to struggle against it. They do her the greatest disservice who seek to disown her glorious past, and to modify her as far as possible, so as to adapt her to prevailing methods of thought and feeling. It is her zealous but mistaken friends, who, guided by a short-sighted policy, and taking counsel of the world around them, seek, as they express it, to *liberalize* her, to bring her more into harmony with the spirit of the age, from whom we, as good Catholics, should always pray, *Libera nos, Domine!*[9]

---

7   See chapters 14 and 23, and Diane Montagna, "Two thousand years of error? Pope Francis moves closer to calling death penalty intrinsically evil," *LifeSiteNews*, March 1, 2019.

8   See chapter 40.

9   "Newman's Development of Christian Doctrine," *Brownson's Quarterly Review* 3.3 (July 1846).

39

Civilized Man Is Reverting to Barbarism ... and Catholic Leaders Are Not Calling Him Back

LifeSiteNews

APRIL 11, 2019

H ISTORY IS MADE BY FREE HUMAN BEINGS under the gaze of a sovereignly free God, so it does not follow a strict and settled pattern. The dark nights of human history, ages of invasion, warfare, plague, rebellion, can last much longer than any natural winter does, while long days of religious fervor and cultural flourishing can stretch on with preternatural beauty. In *all* cases, however, sooner or later, night succeeds day, and day succeeds night. We have here no abiding day, even as we have no endless night. Everlasting day is heaven's property; everlasting night, hell's.

C. S. Lewis wrote:

> One of the most dangerous errors is that civilization is automatically bound to increase and spread. The lesson of history is the opposite; civilization is a rarity, attained with difficulty and easily lost. The normal state of humanity is barbarism, just as the normal surface of the planet is salt water. Land looms large in our imagination and civilization in history books, only because sea and savagery are to us less interesting.[1]

Those conversant with modern history—in many ways epitomized, as Roberto de Mattei has argued, by the three symbolic dates 1517 (the start of the Protestant Revolt), 1717 (the founding of the first Masonic Lodge), and 1917 (the Bolshevik Revolution)[2]—can see an ever-lengthening, descending gloom covering the beauty of

---

1   "Our English Syllabus," in *Rehabilitations and Other Essays* (London: Oxford University Press, 1939), 82–83.
2   See "1517, 1717, 1917: Three Revolutions and Fatima," in *Love for the Papacy*, 157–79.

the Bride of Christ on Earth, as if to smother her at last.

The lights go out, one by one—be it from national apostasy as in Germany or England, from anticlerical revolutions and state-sponsored brutality as in France or Russia, from the choking comforts of a world hypnotized by technology, from wolves who shepherd and sheep who wander into the night. Finally, in the era of Vatican II, the Church entered a winter like none she has ever seen before.

I recently read: "In 1914 the Russian Church had 54,457 churches; the Communist persecution reduced this number to 6,800." The thought struck me: is not something like this true of the post-conciliar disaster, as well? The ill-starred *aggiornamento* (updating, bringing the Church up to date in the modern world) tore down sanctuaries and now boards up churches everywhere throughout the Western world. The transmission of the Faith has been diluted, contaminated, in many cases simply dropped. Above all, the worship of God has been altered almost past recognition except in those few churches that hold on to tradition. As historian Henry Sire puts it: "In today's climate, the many signs of irreverence that originated as abuses and were then promptly authorised, are taken for granted; and a generation brought up in ignorance of the Church's true prayer has been taught to regard Paul VI's creation as the norm."[3]

If most Catholics are still in the dark about the devastation that was wrought on liturgy, theology, spirituality, catechesis, *everything*, during and after the Second Vatican Council, who can blame them? Are they likely to hear about any of this in RCIA or from the pulpit? That is why those who take their faith seriously are understandably bewildered by what is happening in high speed under Pope Francis: they have no mental or spiritual framework within which to make sense out of it. How did we reach a moment when a pope of the Catholic Church would celebrate Luther and invite Lutherans to communion, sing the praises of "fraternity" to the applause of the Freemasons, and cut a deal subjecting the Church to the control of China's Communist Party? The spirits of 1517, 1717, and 1917 have descended on Vatican Hill and made themselves at home.

---

3 *Phoenix from the Ashes: The Making, Unmaking and Restoration of Catholic Tradition* (Kettering, OH: Angelico Press, 2015), 253.

Happily, the traditionalist critique of the current pontificate and of the entire trajectory that paved the way for it is becoming much better known.[4] Ever increasing numbers of Catholics are opening their eyes, dropping their faulty assumptions, preparing themselves for the great tribulation and purification ahead of us—indeed, already upon us.[5]

Let us be candid: we are in another Dark Ages, only this time it's much darker than the first run. And yet people think we are well off because we have technology and comfort. So what? That makes us techno-barbarians. We can cause more harm more quickly—and then follow it on the news or rehearse it as a video game.

This kind of unnatural Western way of life, including its ecclesiastical manifestations, cannot survive. It is contrary to all the laws of sound growth; it is stillborn. Where the Catholic Faith survives, it will be not in the realms of Cardinals Tobin, Cupich, or Marx. It will be in the many places, most of them humble and small, where the Faith is still believed and lived in earnest.

---

4   See "RIP, Vatican II Catholicism (1962–2018)," *OnePeterFive*, October 9, 2018.
5   See "For a Darkening Church, the Light Is Tradition," in Peter Kwasniewski, *Reclaiming Our Roman Catholic Birthright: The Genius and Timeliness of the Traditional Latin Mass* (Brooklyn, NY: Angelico Press, 2020), 311–18.

40

What Good is a Changing Catechism? Revisiting the Purpose and Limits of a Book†

Lecture for the Catholic Citizens of Illinois
Union League Club, Chicago
JUNE 14, 2019

W HAT IS A CATECHISM? HOW WOULD you answer that question?
    A standard dictionary definition runs like this: "a summary of the principles of Christian religion in the form of questions and answers, used for the instruction of Christians." Wikipedia, which as we all know is hit or miss, does a decent job: "A catechism (from Ancient Greek κατηχέω, to teach orally) is a summary or exposition of doctrine and serves as an introduction to the Sacraments" and for the "Christian religious teaching of children

---

† The text of this lecture was published at *Rorate Caeli* on June 15, 2019. The title could have been, alternatively: "The Death Penalty for the *Catechism*? A How-To Guide for Excluding a Text from the Catholic Tradition." Fortuitously, the lecture came at the end of an eventful week in Illinois and in Baltimore. On Wednesday, June 12, the state of Illinois disgraced itself by the passage of the most extreme pro-abortion legislation yet seen in the United States (see Calvin Freiburger, "Illinois gov signs extreme law repealing partial-birth abortion ban," *LifeSiteNews*, June 12, 2019). Ironically, those who celebrate the indiscriminate murder of innocent children are usually opposed to capital punishment for guilty criminals, and the reasoning is consistent: the unborn, not having consciousness of their own personal dignity, cannot defend themselves, so the strong may do away with them at pleasure; but adults, no matter how wicked, are recognized as autonomous individuals with inviolable dignity who must be given free room and board by the state for the remainder of their lives. Then, on Thursday, June 13, the United States bishops voted, by a huge majority—194 in favor, 8 against, 3 abstentions—to alter the text of the U. S. Catholic Catechism for Adults to bring it in line with Pope Francis's novel teaching on the death penalty (see Carol Zimmermann, "Bishops vote to revise U. S. catechism's capital punishment section," *National Catholic Reporter*, June 12, 2019). The revolution in moral teaching thus continues unabated.

and of adult converts. Catechisms are doctrinal manuals—often in the form of questions followed by answers to be memorized."[1]

It seems to me that this is the answer of history, of Church practice, and of what we might call "supernatural common sense." A catechism is a convenient guide to what the Church teaches; more than that, a guide to what she has always taught and will always teach. A good catechism is like a clean, smooth, untainted mirror that reflects the content of the Catholic Faith and nothing else.

A poor catechism—like the infamous 1966 *Dutch Catechism* that caused so much trouble after the Council—is, on the contrary, a cloudy, scratched, bent, or chipped mirror that does not lucidly reflect the Faith. Good catechisms preserve and pass on the teaching of Christ and His Church, while bad catechisms distort it, or one-sidedly exaggerate it, or muffle or silence it.

FRANCIS'S CHANGE TO THE *CATECHISM*

On August 2, 2018, the world learned that Pope Francis approved a change to the *Catechism of the Catholic Church* so that, whereas previously it admitted the legitimacy of capital punishment in principle while discouraging its use in practice, it would now exclude the legitimacy of any recourse to capital punishment, for any reason. The new text cites, as its only source, a speech given by the pope in October 2017 in which he stated that the death penalty is "*per se* contrary to the Gospel," which means it must be an intrinsically evil action. In a meeting with 850 religious sisters of the International Union of Superiors General this past May 10, he doubled down: "I said clearly that the death penalty is not acceptable—it's immoral. But, fifty years ago, no. Did the Church change? No. Moral conscience has developed." This is only one of many statements in which the pope or his Vatican staff have breezily invoked "development," as if this notion is automatically supposed to explain how we got from one position to its polar opposite.

Since the legitimacy of the death penalty will serve as my primary example today, I will start with an overview of the defense Christians have offered of it over the millennia, from the double

---

1   The reason we memorize things as children is that we expect them to come in handy for the rest of our lives. We don't anticipate the alphabet, the rules of grammar, or the circle of fifths changing on us by surprise.

vantage of reason and revelation.[2] Then, I will probe the question of what purpose a catechism serves, how the pope's action undermines this purpose, and finally, what we should do as Catholics.

NATURAL LAW DEFENSE

A natural law defense proceeds on the basis of four truths.

First, God has authority over life and death. This is a crucial premise that liberalism has almost knocked out of people's heads. Man has a right to life vis-à-vis his fellow men, but no such right to life vis-à-vis God, who is the author of all being and the source of all rights. God owes no man his life; it is a free gift. Moreover, human life is given with a purpose: to seek God and to be happy with Him. Therefore any man who turns against God by mortal sin has already forfeited his own life, and God with perfect justice

---

2 Those who wish to see a detailed argument should read Edward Feser and Joseph Bessette, *By Man Shall His Blood Be Shed: A Catholic Defense of Capital Punishment* (San Francisco: Ignatius Press, 2017). This work is not without its flaws, but by the end of it, one cannot escape the conclusion that the legitimacy of capital punishment is as deeply lodged in the bones and marrow of the Judeo-Christian tradition as the content of the Ten Commandments handed down to Moses on Mount Sinai, or the Beatitudes handed down by Our Lord to His disciples on the mountainside. Several fine articles have been published by *First Things*, among them J. Budziszewski's "Capital Punishment: The Case for Justice," back in August 2004; then, directly in response to Pope Francis, Michael Pakaluk's "Capital Punishment and the Sex Abuse Crisis," August 22, 2018; Ed Feser's "Pope Francis and Capital Punishment," August 3, 2018; and of course, on August 15, "An Appeal to the Cardinals of the Catholic Church," signed by 75 clergy and scholars, which contains this ringing paragraph: "Since it is a truth contained in the Word of God, and taught by the ordinary and universal magisterium of the Catholic Church, that criminals may lawfully be put to death by the civil power when this is necessary to preserve just order in civil society, and since the present Roman pontiff has now more than once publicly manifested his refusal to teach this doctrine, and has rather brought great confusion upon the Church by seeming to contradict it, and by inserting into the *Catechism of the Catholic Church* a paragraph which will cause and is already causing many people, both believers and non-believers, to suppose that the Church considers, contrary to the Word of God, that capital punishment is intrinsically evil, we call upon Your Eminences to advise His Holiness that it is his duty to put an end to this scandal, to withdraw this paragraph from the Catechism, and to teach the word of God unadulterated; and we state our conviction that this is a duty seriously binding upon yourselves, before God and before the Church."

could punish him with physical and spiritual death (i.e., damnation) at any moment. Scripture is clear that it is only God's "patience" and mercy that give us many second chances before we are finally summoned to our particular judgment.

Second, the State's authority derives from God's, as the Magisterium teaches consistently and unambiguously, especially in the encyclicals of Pope Leo XIII. Thus, when the State coerces or punishes, it does so by God's authority, not by its own merely human authority. Modern political philosophy, in the social contract theory, derives all political authority from the consent of the governed, and this ought to make the death penalty absolutely unacceptable. The social contract theorists find various ways to justify it anyhow, but this is irrelevant, since Catholics do not and cannot hold the social contract theory, but rather derive all human authority of any kind—spousal, parental, or civic—from God Himself.

Third, the State's first and only obligation is to preserve and promote the common good of its citizens, not the private good of its individual citizens. Some crimes are so opposed to the common good that society cannot flourish without these crimes being severely punished and, to the extent possible, eradicated from the body politic. Traditionally, murder was seen as so opposed to the basic good of society that it warranted death, without further discussion.

Lastly, punishment is primarily retributive, not corrective or instructive or dissuasive. That is, the point of punishing a criminal is not to ensure that he becomes better (although we may hope this result will follow, as it often has), or to educate him in morality (although he probably needs it), or to dissuade him or others from further crime (although again we expect and rely on this effect). No. The point is to punish the doing of moral evil with a physical evil that corresponds to the gravity of the damage done to the common good. As the ancient Greek philosophers put it, someone who abuses his freedom by taking away someone else's good deserves to have his freedom curtailed and to have some good taken away from him, up to and including the greatest physical good he has, his life in the flesh. If a crime is contrary to the very foundations of civil life, as murder is, the criminal deserves to be removed from civil life altogether. This may take the form of temporary exile, as when someone is incarcerated or sent away to a distant land, or permanent exile, that is, death.

THE TESTIMONY OF REVELATION

Can we say that this, too, is the teaching of divine revelation? Yes, without a doubt.

The Old Testament portrays God many, many times asking for the death of particular individuals at the hands of men, or requiring by law the death of certain kinds of sinners.[3] If Pope Francis were correct in saying that the death penalty is *per se* contrary to the Gospel, or that it is contrary to the dignity of the criminal, that would instantly result in Marcionism, that is, the heresy that the God of the New Covenant contradicts the God of the Old Covenant; it would require seeing the Bible in general to be erroneous because it never recognizes, indeed it contradicts, any absolute dignity in the human person that would be off limits even to God's just sentence. Or if the pope would not say this about God, he would say it about the state, thus denying unanimous Catholic teaching about the state receiving its authority from God and acting as His representative.

But not even the New Testament teaches what the pope of mercy seems to think it does. In the Gospel of John 19:11, we read that Jesus answered Pilate: "Thou couldst have no power at all against me, except it were given thee from above: therefore he that delivered me unto thee hath the greater sin." Here Jesus confirms, in words that have never given interpreters any trouble, that the power Pilate wields to have Him crucified has been given from above—in other words, the power of the civil authority to administer capital punishment comes from God, even when exercised by an imperial power in a usurped colony. Of course, Pilate's sentence is manifestly unjust, but Christ does not question that he has received from God—indeed, from Christ Himself standing before him!—the authority that belongs to any public office. It is nothing other than this divine origin of power that *requires* of civil officials a total conformity to the law of God as knowable by reason and bestowed by revelation.

---

3   When Jesus deflected the stoning of the woman caught in adultery, it was not because He knew she did not deserve it, but because He wished to reprieve her in His mercy and give her a second chance. Civil governors may also choose to reprieve criminals, but it cannot be a simple rule that every criminal guilty of capital crime must be reprieved. There is no basis for this in either divine law or natural law.

This truth is confirmed in the dialogue between Our Lord and the criminals on Golgotha, as recorded in the Gospel of Luke, 23:39–43:

> And one of those robbers who were hanged, blasphemed him, saying: If thou be the Christ, save thyself and us. But the other answering, rebuked him, saying: Neither dost thou fear God, seeing thou art condemned under the same condemnation? And we indeed justly, for we receive the due reward of our deeds; but this man hath done no evil. And he said to Jesus: Lord, remember me when thou shalt come into thy kingdom. And Jesus said to him: Amen I say to thee, this day thou shalt be with me in paradise.

Here we see that Christ did not confute the words of the "good thief," St. Dismas, who said about the death penalty: "we indeed *justly*, for we receive the *due reward* of our deeds." Then, this thief explained why it was a sin of Pilate and a greater sin for those who had delivered Jesus to Pilate: "this man hath done no evil," as if to say: "had he done evil, his punishment would be just, like ours." Then one beholds the manifestation of true mercy and justice by Christ, when he says: "Amen I say to thee, this day thou shalt be with me in paradise." This came after Dismas had said to his fellow criminal: "Neither dost thou fear God, seeing thou art condemned under the same condemnation?," and then to Jesus: "Lord, remember me when thou shalt come into thy kingdom." Justice for the criminal; mercy for the one who converts. Isn't this passage in Luke a luminously clear example of both justice and mercy in action?

THE WITNESS OF TRADITION

Is my reading of the Bible idiosyncratic, or is it what we find in the Catholic tradition? To answer that question, we cannot do better than to turn to our greatest theologian, St. Thomas Aquinas, who writes in his *Catechetical Instructions* of circa 1260:

> Some have held that the killing of man is prohibited altogether. They believe that judges in the civil courts, who condemn men to death according to the laws, are murderers. Against this, St. Augustine says that God by this commandment ["Thou shalt not kill"] does not take

away from *Himself* the right to kill. Thus, we read: "I will kill and I will make to live" (Deut. 32:39). It is, therefore, lawful for a judge to kill according to a mandate from God, since in this God operates, and every law is a command of God: "By Me kings reign, and lawgivers decree just things" (Prov. 8:15). And again: "For if thou dost that which is evil, fear; for he beareth not the sword in vain. Because he is God's minister" (Rom. 13:4). To Moses also it was said: "Wizards thou shalt not suffer to live" (Ex. 22:18). And thus that which is lawful to God is lawful for His ministers when they act by His mandate. It is evident that God, who is the Author of laws, has every right to inflict death on account of sin. For "the wages of sin is death" (Rom. 6:23). Neither does His minister sin in inflicting that punishment. The sense, therefore, of "Thou shalt not kill" is that one shall not kill by one's own authority.

Note that St. Thomas, in this typically compact, watertight argument, cites one of the heavyweight Fathers of the Church, St. Augustine, and half-a-dozen biblical texts.

Fair enough; but is St. Thomas to be taken as a reliable guide in this matter? After all, he was wrong about the Immaculate Conception, and a few others things, too. Well, the Church evidently thinks his arguments hold water, because in the *other* universal catechism published by a pope—the *Roman Catechism* of 1566, issued by Pope St. Pius V three years after the conclusion of the Council of Trent—we read the following rather bold appropriation of Thomistic reasoning:

> Another kind of lawful slaying belongs to the civil authorities, to whom is entrusted the power of life and death, by the legal and judicious exercise of which they punish the guilty and protect the innocent. The just use of this power, far from involving the crime of murder, is an act of paramount obedience to the commandment that prohibits murder. For the end of the commandment is the preservation and security of human life. Now the punishments inflicted by the civil authority, which is the legitimate avenger of crime, naturally tend to this end, since they give security to life by repressing outrage and violence. Hence these words of David: "In the morning I put to death all

the wicked of the land, that I might cut off all the workers
of iniquity from the city of the Lord" (Ps. 100:8).

We are living in a world in which the word "catechism" immediately brings to mind a single book: *The Catechism of the Catholic
Church* from 1992, revised in 1997.[4] As I just mentioned, however,
this was the second universal catechism of the Catholic Church. And
these two are not a solitary pair, like the Pillars of Hercules. There
were a host of national or regional catechisms published in every
language. Famous examples included the three catechisms published
by the Jesuit St. Peter Canisius in Germany in 1555 in its long form,
1556 in its short form, and 1558 in its medium-length form—the
Papa Bear, Baby Bear, and Mama Bear of German catechisms for
centuries to come. So popular were these books that the expression
"knowing your Canisius" became synonymous for "knowing your
faith."[5] Other very popular works included the *Baltimore Catechism*
of 1885, based on St. Robert Bellarmine's *Small Catechism* of 1614;
the *Douay Catechism* of 1649; and the "Penny Catechism" of Great
Britain from the start of the twentieth century. Such books were
translated into many non-European languages by the missionaries
who planted the standard of the Cross on every continent.

How many catechisms were published prior to the Second
Vatican Council, in all languages? Has anyone ever counted? Five
hundred? One thousand? Now think of it: nearly *every one* of these
catechisms would have stated that the death penalty is legitimate.[6]
Let me offer just a few examples from a wide array available online:
two from the sixteenth century, one from the seventeenth, one
from the nineteenth, and two from the twentieth.[7]

---

4   See www.scborromeo.org/ccc/updates.htm for a complete list of revisions.
5   See "A Brief History of Catechisms, and Peter Canisius," *Siris*, December
21, 2011, http://branemrys.blogspot.com/2011/12/brief-history-of-catechisms-
and-peter.html.
6   If the topic went unmentioned, it was owing to the brevity and simplicity of a given catechism, not to any disagreement on the part of its
authors with what was received as common doctrine. Indeed, in an age as
sensitive to ecumenical concerns as our own, it merits mentioning that the
vast majority of Protestant catechisms transmitted exactly the same doctrine
about capital punishment as Catholic ones did, and for obvious reasons: it
is not especially difficult to mount a defense of it.
7   For many examples of this point, see "Those Clarion Catechisms: Death
Penalty Far From 'Inadmissible,'" *Whispers of Restoration*, August 18, 2018.

An influential catechism published in 1567 by Fr. Laurence Vaux nicely connects the rationales for civil and ecclesiastical punishments:

> What is the fifth Commandment of God? Thou shalt not kill. That is to be understood: thou shalt not without just authority kill or hurt any man in body or in soul. And therefore both the Judge in the commonwealth does lawfully put offenders to death, or otherwise punish them bodily, and the Bishop does lawfully excommunicate wicked or disobedient persons, for the preservation of peace and tranquility in the commonwealth, and in the Church.

Fr. Henry Tuberville's *An Abridgement of Christian Doctrine* from 1649 asks: "Is it not lawful to kill in any cause?" and responds:

> Yes, in a just war, or when public justice requires it: "For the magistrate beareth not the sword without cause" (Rom. 13:4). As also in the blameless defence of our own, or our innocent neighbour's life, against an unjust invader.

The *Baltimore Catechism* of 1885 says, with admirable nuance:

> Human life may be lawfully taken (1) in self-defense, when we are unjustly attacked and have no other means of saving our own lives; (2) in a just war, when the safety or rights of the nation require it; (3) by the lawful execution of a criminal, fairly tried and found guilty of a crime punishable by death, when the preservation of law and order and the good of the community require such execution.

The beloved *Catechism of St. Pius X*, published in 1908, poses the question "Are there cases in which it is lawful to kill?" and replies:

> It is lawful to kill when fighting in a just war; when carrying out by order of the Supreme Authority a sentence of death in punishment of a crime; and, finally, in cases of necessary and lawful defense of one's own life against an unjust aggressor.

Canon Henry Cafferata's 1922 book *The Catechism, Simply Explained*, true to its title, simply explains the matter as follows:

The fifth Commandment forbids all wilful murder, fighting, quarrelling, and injurious words; and also scandal and bad example. Wilful murder is one of the sins crying to heaven for vengeance. Suicide, which is self-murder, is forbidden by this commandment. Also the direct deliberate killing of an unborn child. But it is not murder when the State executes a criminal; it has the right to do so. Nor is it murder when the State orders its armed forces to kill the enemy in a just war. And one may always kill in self-defence, when there is no alternative.

Believe me when I say that such examples could be multiplied all the day long. There is simply not the slightest bit of deviation in any of them from the common orthodox teaching.

Adding Aquinas and the *Roman Catechism*, what we are seeing here, in seven exemplary texts from a span of 700 years, is nothing less than a glowing example of the universal ordinary Magisterium of the Church—namely, the verbalization of that which is taught and believed "by everyone, always, and everywhere," displaying the three hallmarks of the Vincentian canon: antiquity, universality, and the consensus of authorities. As an online catechist reminds us:

> Because Christ committed to His Church a single, "defined body of doctrine, applicable to all times and all men," one should expect to peruse not only decades, but centuries of Catholic catechisms and theological manuals and discover harmonious agreement and unbroken continuity on all matters of faith and morals. And find it one can; for when Catholic bishops spread throughout the world and across time give unified voice to their teaching office in catechisms approved by them, this is an authentic expression of the *universal ordinary magisterium*, an organ of infallibility, and an effective antidote in our own time against the erroneous notion (long since condemned by the Church) that dogma can evolve.

EVALUATING POPE FRANCIS'S CHANGE

Along comes Francis, and by a stroke of the papal pen—I had almost said magic wand—suddenly falsifies hundreds of other catechisms on a point of no small significance. Think of it: contrary to every catechism from ancient times to the Counter-Reformation down to the era of John XXIII who convened the Second Vatican Council, the "new and improved" *Catechism* speaks alone.

This, I would argue, is a sign of dangerous megalomania—the evidence of a pope disconnected from his office and from reality. And this case is far from unique: every week, it seems, gives us another example of deviation from the common heritage of Christians. A breathtaking example of episcopal and papal arrogance was given to us quite recently by the bishops' conference of Italy, whose decision to change the wording of the Lord's Prayer was approved (as expected) by Francis—in spite of the fact that not a single theologian or scholar from ancient to modern times has disagreed even slightly about the meaning of the Greek text of the Lord's Prayer recorded in the New Testament, which is precisely what the Church herself has prayed in Greek, Latin, Slavonic, and every other language, for 2,000 years without interruption. In other words, the Italian bishops and the pope have changed the Our Father to say something that it simply does not say, and in doing so, they have implied one of two heretical positions: either Our Lord made a mistake and was wrong in saying what He did, in which case He is not God, or the evangelists made a mistake in reporting His most solemn utterance on prayer and attributed something false to Him, in which case the Gospel text is not inspired by the Holy Spirit and is, as a consequence, not infallible and inerrant. A similar point can be made about the Italian bishops' change to the opening words of the Gloria, which are taken from St. Luke's Gospel. They have distorted them past recognition. A true Christian does not dictate to God what He should say, but humbly accepts His word, not only when it is easy to understand, but also, and even more so, when it is difficult, challenging, perplexing, mysterious, or strange.

I turn again to the death penalty. Pope Francis went so far as to dismiss his papal predecessors, some of whom actively promoted capital punishment in the Papal States, as "having ignored the primacy of mercy over justice." Commenting on this astonishing statement, Fr. John Hunwicke said: "Dear dear dear. Pretty nasty, that. What silly fellows they must all have been to make such an elementary error. But Don't Worry. All, apparently, can be explained by 'development.'"[8] Never mind that in dismissing all of them at

---

8   "How and how speedily does the Teaching of the Church 'develop'?," *Fr Hunwicke's Mutual Enrichment*, December 18, 2018.

once, he is undermining his own authority. If all the earlier popes can be wrong, *a fortiori* Francis can be wrong—and, indeed, is far more likely to be wrong, with a witness of 265 against 1.[9]

The change introduced by Francis fundamentally misconstrues the nature and purpose of a catechism; indeed, it misconstrues the nature and purpose of papal authority. A catechism is not, and has never been seen as, an instrument for introducing novel doctrine or for pushing forward the so-called "development of doctrine." It is not an opportunity for dare-devil avant-garde speculative theology, or a trial balloon to see how the media or the masses will react, or a wedge to open up a "safe space" for further changes to doctrine or morality. Neither should it marginalize or silence unpopular truths by giving them short shrift or no shrift at all. A catechism's function is far humbler: to pass on, simply, accurately, and integrally, the *pre-existing* teaching of the Church.[10]

As Edward Feser recently wrote:

> What Catholics who are concerned about the revision to the Catechism want to know, specifically, is whether the revision is meant to teach that capital punishment is always and intrinsically evil, and not just ill-advised under current circumstances. If that is indeed what is being taught, then that would be a direct contradiction of Scripture, the Fathers and Doctors of the Church, and all previous popes, and thus would not be a true development of doctrine but a reversal or corruption of doctrine. *Calling* something a "development" doesn't *make* it a development, otherwise the Church could reverse any teaching at all—concerning the Trinity, the Resurrection, you name it—and simply label it a "development" reflecting a "dynamic tradition," etc. The great Catholic theorists of the development of doctrine, such as St. Vincent of Lérins and Blessed John Henry Newman, are

---

9   See Diane Montagna, "Pope Francis: Former popes ignored mercy in using 'inhuman' death penalty," *LifeSiteNews*, December 17, 2018.

10   In other words, a catechism is a witness to the universal and ordinary Magisterium of the Church taught by all the bishops throughout the world over time (not just at the present moment) as well as to the extraordinary Magisterium consisting of *de fide* definitions of dogma by councils or popes.

always very clear that a genuine development can never contradict past teaching.[11]

The false understanding of "development of doctrine," in the name of which today's churchmen contradict the plain meaning of Scripture as received by the unbroken tradition of the Church, was in fact condemned in Pope Pius IX's *Syllabus of Errors* under the following thesis: "Divine revelation is imperfect, and therefore subject to a continual and indefinite progress, corresponding to the advancement of human reason."[12] This notion of endless "progress" always hides a form of relativism: we can never actually attain certainty of anything at any time, since we must await the latest deliverances of theologians or politicians who, in some mysterious shamanistic way, have access to the elusive "truth" called for by the "signs of the times."

I think we can dig deeper into what is going on here. The death penalty vexes progressives and liberals because it reminds them of the existence of objective truths and absolute norms on which both justice and mercy are necessarily based; it reminds them of the final judgment each of us must undergo before the God of the Decalogue and the Beatitudes, the God who has revealed Himself in and through the "scandal of the particular": in the Incarnation, in the Blessed Virgin Mary, in the Holy Eucharist and the other sacraments, in the organic development of the liturgy. To face this most personal God, and to be judged according to His absolute and particular truth, is the unspoken nightmare from which liberals are running away in every direction, even at the cost of contradicting reason, sanity, history, reality itself. In this way, they have already chosen hell, although they do not yet realize it, since hell is the place of irrationality, insanity, meaningless repetition, and banishment from the God who *is* the most real and contains all reality in Himself.

---

11   See Dorothy Cummings McLean, "Pope's new teaching on death penalty appears in revised theological commentary on catechism," *LifeSiteNews*, June 5, 2019.

12   Recall Francis speaking to the International Union of Superiors General of Woman Religious about how much can change in fifty years. What else happened fifty years ago? *Humanae Vitae*. One can see where all this is going. It isn't even necessary for Francis to connect the dots himself; he knows that others will do so. He need only supply the inch so that others may take the mile.

As Joseph Ratzinger pointed out some decades ago, hell is already breaking into this world and annexing portions of it, as people increasingly abandon the protection of the Holy Cross, the name of Jesus, the sacraments and sacramentals, the sacred liturgy. We might say that Satan has established colonial governors in, just to name three of his colonies, the United Nations, the European Union, and the Democratic Party.

WHAT IS THE VALUE OF THE "NEW" *CATECHISM*?

Francis's change to the *Catechism* of John Paul II prompts another train of thought. What, after all, *is* the value of this very catechism?

Years ago, it was pointed out to me that the *Catechism* omits mention of the New Testament teaching on the headship of the husband in marriage—despite the fact that this teaching is given *multiple times* in the New Testament, with a clarity greater than that of many other doctrines we typically consider crystal-clear, and despite the fact that the doctrine was often repeated by the Magisterium, at least up through Pius XI's classic encyclical *Casti Connubii*, where it was given a winsome interpretation: the wife is the heart of the family, as the husband is its head (with all of the responsibilities each of these roles entails!), and the wife owes him lawful and rational obedience, even as he owes her the highest respect, devotion, and love. Why was this aspect of Christian teaching on marriage omitted in what was purported to be a trustworthy guide to the Catholic Faith? Oh, feminism and things like that. How do we know? Because the *Catechism* dances around the question, cites NT texts *adjacent to* the "offensive" ones, and does all that it can to avoid bringing up the subject.[13] In short, it is embarrassed about a truth revealed by God, because that

---

13   The *Catechism of the Catholic Church* avoids teaching the subordination of wives to husbands, replacing it with a novel doctrine of mutual subordination (see n. 1642, but also nn. 369–72, 1616, and 1659, eloquent in their omissions); for commentary, see Michael Haynes, *A Catechism of Errors: A Critique of the Principal Errors of the Catechism of the Catholic Church* (Fitzwilliam, NH: Loreto Publications, 2021), 80–83. In contrast, the *Roman Catechism* unambiguously transmits the teaching of Scripture on this point: see the *Catechism of the Council of Trent for Parish Priests*, trans. John A. McHugh and Charles J. Callan (Rockford, IL: TAN Books and Publishers, 1982), 339, 346, 352. For important precisions about the use and abuse of catechisms, see Aaron Seng, "Weaponized Catechisms," *Crisis Magazine*, March 16, 2022.

truth fails to harmonize with the Zeitgeist, the spirit of the age.

Should this bother us? Absolutely. If we discover only *one* important teaching that is missing from a catechism *by design* and not by editorial oversight, then *in principle* the reliability of this catechism is called into question. It is seen to be under the curse of political correctness *to some extent*—how much would be difficult to say without exhaustive study, but the seed of doubt is already planted. We start to feel that this guide may not, after all, be entirely trustworthy.

If I might digress for a moment: the same thing can be said of the omission of 1 Corinthians 11:27-29 from the missal of Paul VI and its multi-year lectionary. In these verses the Apostle states the following:

> Therefore whosoever shall eat this bread, or drink of the chalice of the Lord unworthily, shall be guilty of the Body and of the Blood of the Lord. But let a man prove himself; and so let him eat of that bread, and drink of the chalice. For he that eateth and drinketh unworthily, eateth and drinketh judgment to himself, not discerning the Body of the Lord.

This passage—the clearest text in the Bible warning against unworthy or sacrilegious Eucharistic communion, a problem that has exponentially increased in the decades since the Council—was deliberately omitted from the new liturgy, even though it had always been prominently present in the traditional Latin Mass, for as far back as we have records of the Church's worship. Similarly, the omission of many psalm verses from the Liturgy of the Hours means that whoever follows these liturgical books no longer prays the Psalter as given by God.[14] Such omissions, against the backdrop of a hitherto uninterrupted practice, call into question the value and legitimacy of the entire projects to which they pertain. At this point in my life, knowing what I do, I cannot trust the new lectionary or the new Liturgy of the Hours to give me an accurate formation in the Catholic Faith as received and professed by the Church from the time of her founding to the time of the Second Vatican Council. The *lex orandi* or law of praying was deeply

---

14　See "The Omission of 'Difficult' Psalms and the Spreading-Thin of the Psalter," *Rorate Caeli*, November 15, 2016.

modified, which means the *lex credendi* or law of believing has also been modified. The problems we are dealing with in catechesis are exactly paralleled by the problems we are dealing with in liturgy. It is all a single package deal, and the sooner Catholics realize this, the sooner they will stop pretending that they can have their cake and eat it, too—that they can entrust their minds to the Novus Ordo liturgy, while remaining, in the words of the Roman Canon, "orthodox believers and professors of the Catholic and apostolic Faith."

To return to the *Catechism* of 1992, and the problem of tinkeritis: we remember how there were already changes to the new *Catechism* almost before its ink was dry. The second edition, published in Latin in 1997, featured a few substantive changes, including one already on the death penalty to reflect the liberal European manner in which John Paul II was thinking about it. Another change, on homosexual inclinations, was admittedly a significant improvement—and yet one wonders why the original editorial team, headed by Christoph Schönborn, later Archbishop of Vienna, would have expressed the point so badly to begin with. This doesn't inspire confidence in the competence of the drafters. Indeed, in the case of Cardinal Schönborn, whom I admired and spent time with in the period between 1999 and 2006, we have seen a gradual decline into progressivism and outright heresy, especially on the subject of sexual ethics.

THE "CHURCH OF TOMORROW"

Since at least *Dignitatis Humanae*, there's been a tendency to portray doctrine as malleable, according to the whims of the reigning pontiff or the consensus of academic theologians. Back in the day, conservative Catholics tried to do this with social doctrine when they refused to accept John Paul II's critique of certain aspects of modern-day capitalism in *Centesimus Annus* and other documents. Now, under Francis, it's the liberals' turn in the limelight, railing against the death penalty, but there's been a general tendency for just about every modern school of Catholic thought to play this game. The ultimate source of this tendency is poor theology and even poorer philosophy—a refusal to acknowledge, on the one hand, that truth is a correspondence between thought and reality and, on the other, that the content of our faith is divinely revealed to us and is not subject to a process of mutation and evolution, no matter how many centuries we spend pondering its inexhaustible truth.

A friend recounted to me how a devotee of Hans Urs von Balthasar, a dazzling synthesizer of orthodoxy and modernism who could deceive even the elect, once told him that Balthasar's concept of what Our Lord did during His time in the grave on Holy Saturday couldn't get into the *Catechism* right now, because it hadn't been "received" yet, but in time it *might*. According to this notion of revelation, a theologian gets a brilliant idea; it catches on with other theologians; and after a time, lo and behold!, we have *a new doctrine*. Or perhaps just a "deeper grasp" of a doctrine, albeit one that actually contradicts just about everything held on the subject until now. One is reminded of the eulogy pronounced upon Teilhard de Chardin by one of his disciples, Henri Rambaud: "He was already thinking then what the Church did not yet know she would be thinking shortly.... Instead of being in agreement with the Church of today, he is in agreement with the Church of tomorrow."[15]

If any of this were true, then *nothing* in the Faith would ever be certain; our house would be built on shifting sand, not solid rock. We know this to be false, because all twenty ecumenical councils prior to the *sui generis* experiment of Vatican II solemnly declared, in the name of God, binding dogmas of truth and condemnations of error. One who walks down the path of novelty is not deepening our collective grasp of truth, but simply departing from the Catholic Faith. As the ancient "Athanasian" Creed thunders: *Quicumque vult salvus esse, ante omnia opus est, ut teneat catholicam fidem: quam nisi quisque integram inviolatamque servaverit, absque dubio in aeternum peribit.* "Whoever wishes to be saved must, above all, keep the Catholic faith; for unless a person keeps this faith whole and entire, he will undoubtedly be lost forever."

As good as much of it is, the new *Catechism of the Catholic Church* is not the "be-all and end-all" that many make it out to be. One would have felt ashamed to admit such misgivings back in the misty-eyed days of its promulgation when, after decades of doctrinal chaos and almost no guidance from Rome at the catechetical level, the *Catechism* came forth like Lazarus from the tomb. And

---

15   From Gerard Verschuuren, *The Myth of an Anti-Science Church: Galileo, Darwin, Teilhard, Hawking, Dawkins* (Brooklyn: Angelico Press, 2018), 120; see chapter 62 below.

perhaps it *was* something of a miracle in the early nineties. Even so, the well-respected Jesuit Fr. John Hardon (1914–2000)—himself an author of copious catechetical materials, and by no means a "traditionalist" in the sense in which that term is used today—wrote a detailed critique of certain formulations in the working draft of the new *Catechism* that he considered ambiguous, incomplete, misleading, or erroneous. While many of the problems were fixed, others remained.[16]

Other "catechism shenanigans" include Benedict XVI's strategic deployment of the shorter *Compendium of the Catechism* to make up for defects in the larger one, and the multi-lingual release of a hipster youth catechism or "YouCat" that continues the process of dumbing-down the Faith that began with the first translations of the liturgy into the vernacular.

SEEKING GUIDANCE FROM BETTER SOURCES

What Pope Francis has done will backfire, like the *hubris* of the protagonist in an ancient Greek tragedy. For he has given us a new and, I would say, pressing invitation to close the modern *Catechism* and place it on the upper shelf, and to reach instead for the *Roman Catechism*, the *Baltimore Catechism*, or dozens of other books that,

---

16   See "On Doctrinal and Moral Disorders Abiding in the Church: Father John A. Hardon's 1990 Commentaries on the 'Revised Draft' of the Catholic Catechism," prepared and elaborated by Robert Hickson, in *Christian Order*, January and February 2016, and placed on the internet at Rorate Caeli, April 11–12, 2022. For example, the *Catechism* does not unambiguously teach that, because the old covenant with Israel has been fulfilled in Christ as the new covenant in His blood, the Jews are no longer God's "chosen people," but should be regarded as called to faith in Christ and baptism, even as all other unbelievers are; or that Christ enjoyed the beatific vision throughout His earthly life, including in His most bitter Passion. The first draft of the *Catechism*, ca. 1991, was much more explicit about Christ's direct vision of God during His earthly life than the final version. See CCC 151, 473, and 478, from all of which, and from their footnoted sources, one may deduce the doctrine. Fr. Georges de Nantes' *Book of Accusation*, which claims to find twelve heresies in the *Catechism*, is far from sound on all points, but it does raise a few potent criticisms: http://crc-internet.org/further-information/liber-accusationis/against-ccc/. The SSPX's Fr. Michel Simoulin has also presented cogent objections: see his four-part article "Is the New Catechism Catholic?," https://sspx.org/en/new-catechism-catholic; cf. http://archives.sspx.org/SSPX_FAQs/q14_new_catechism.htm.

sidestepping political correctness, are more accurate guides to what the Church has believed and taught in her 2,000-year pilgrimage.[17] In his Apostolic Constitution *Fidei Depositum* of October 11, 1992, Pope John Paul II declared his new *Catechism* "a sure norm for teaching the faith and thus a valid and legitimate instrument for ecclesial communion." Recent abuses of papal authority are pushing us (helpfully, I would say) to recognize that the "sure norm" in catechesis is not one single book, especially not a book that has trouble walking in a straight line, but rather the collective unanimous witness of centuries of catechisms. The uniform testimony of a host of traditional Catholic catechisms is an undimmed light amid the doctrinal darkness now besetting the Church in an age dominated by secularism, liberalism, and relativism.

What the confusion of our day requires, and what the much-touted dignity of man deserves, is not the new and improved Catholicism of the ever-newer *Catechism*, but the illuminating Faith of our fathers, "the faith which was once for all delivered to the saints" (Jude 1:3). May the Most Holy Trinity have mercy on us and deliver us from the tyranny of novelty.

---

17   As we read at *Whispers of Restoration*, "RESOURCE: Traditional Catholic Catechisms [Updated]," July 9, 2018: "For the average Catholic seeking to learn this Faith and hand it on to others in an error-plagued age, few things will bear this out [viz., every articulation of the Faith must exhibit discernible continuity in all its propositions with those preceding] like the reading of traditional catechisms. The continuity found in such study is both clear and compelling, and little wonder; for it illustrates the teaching of the universal ordinary magisterium."

41

How U.S. Bishops' Vote on Death Penalty in Catechism Contradicts Word of God

LifeSiteNews

JUNE 25, 2019

THE VAST MAJORITY OF U.S. BISHOPS VOTED on June 13, 2019 to rewrite the *United States Catholic Catechism for Adults* to bring it into line with the novelty introduced by Francis into the *Catechism of the Catholic Church*.[1] Pope Francis espouses the error that capital punishment is illegitimate in principle, a claim that can be true only if it is intrinsically immoral—which Francis has indicated he believes when he called it *"per se* contrary to the Gospel" (October 11, 2017) and "immoral" (May 10, 2019).

In this way, the U. S. bishops showed themselves a collective chameleon turning white from clinging so closely to the papal habit, rather than standing on their own feet as successors of the apostles, handing down the consistent teaching of the Church over the past two millennia.

A particular irony of the day of the vote has been lost on those who have commented thus far. The Novus Ordo Mass readings for June 13, as given by the USCCB on its website, included as the First Reading a passage from 2 Corinthians.[2] The Lectionary tells us the source: 2 Cor. 3:15–4:1, 3-6. Note that little comma. The liturgical reform in the 1960s was careful to excise verse 2 of chapter 4 from the Lectionary. And guess what that skipped verse is. I will put it in boldface:

> Brothers and sisters:
> To this day, whenever Moses is read, a veil lies over the hearts of the children of Israel, but whenever a person turns to the Lord the veil is removed.

---

1   See Zimmermann, "Bishops vote to revise U. S. catechism."
2   See https://bible.usccb.org/bible/readings/061319.cfm.

Now the Lord is the Spirit and where the Spirit of the Lord is, there is freedom.

All of us, gazing with unveiled face on the glory of the Lord, are being transformed into the same image from glory to glory, as from the Lord who is the Spirit.

Therefore, since we have this ministry through the mercy shown us, we are not discouraged.

Rather, we have renounced shameful, hidden things; not acting deceitfully or falsifying the word of God, but by the open declaration of the truth we commend ourselves to everyone's conscience in the sight of God.

And even though our Gospel is veiled, it is veiled for those who are perishing, in whose case the god of this age has blinded the minds of the unbelievers, so that they may not see the light of the Gospel of the glory of Christ, who is the image of God.

For we do not preach ourselves but Jesus Christ as Lord, and ourselves as your slaves for the sake of Jesus.

For God who said, *Let light shine out of darkness,* has shone in our hearts to bring to light the knowledge of the glory of God on the face of Jesus Christ.

Another translation (RSV) of the missing verse reads: "We have renounced disgraceful, underhanded ways; we refuse to practice cunning or to tamper with God's word, but by the open statement of the truth we would commend ourselves to every man's conscience in the sight of God."

A friend who saw this lacuna wrote to me: "I'm in the market for an irony meter, because mine just broke."

In a first layer of irony, we have a verse in which St. Paul protests that he will not act deceitfully or falsify God's word, that he will not practice cunning or tamper with this word—and the liturgical reformers surgically remove it, as if to make a virtuosic display of their own willingness to do exactly what St. Paul would never dare to do. This, we know, is not the only time this sort of game is played in the new Lectionary.[3]

---

[3]   See Peter Kwasniewski, "The Reform of the Lectionary" in *Liturgy in the Twenty-First Century: Contemporary Issues and Perspectives,* ed. Alcuin Reid (New York: Bloomsbury T&T Clark, 2016), 287–320; idem, "Not Just More Scripture, But Different Scripture," Foreword to Matthew Hazell, ed., *Index*

In a second layer of irony, we have the U.S. bishops voting to change the country's national catechism to a position that contradicts the revealed Word of God—refusing, that is, to make an "open declaration of truth... in the sight of God." This verse, which amounts to a promise before God *not* to falsify His revelation, was conveniently missing on the day when these bishops could not have made such a promise without committing perjury. The new and improved Lectionary in that sense ran interference for the new and improved Catechism. The veil over the hearts of the children of Israel that prevents them from grasping the meaning of the Law seems to be a veil that continues into the present for those who would reject the tradition of biblical interpretation on the death penalty that has been common to Catholics and even to most non-Catholic Christians. The "god of this age"—a god that wears many masks, including the European-style social liberalism so favored by Francis—"has blinded the minds of the unbelievers," that is, of the believers who no longer believe as their forefathers did.

Bishop Robert Barron thinks he can get around the problem by saying this vote was not a vote on the death penalty *as such*, but merely on what the catechism should say at this time.[4] Sorry, that won't cut it. The catechism is supposed to teach us what is true according to the Faith. If it speaks in such a way as to lead most readers into thinking that the death penalty is intrinsically immoral, *always* unjust, then it has failed as a catechism and indeed has become a cause of separation from the Catholic Faith instead of communion in it.

As the "Appeal to the Cardinals of the Catholic Church," signed by 75 clergy and scholars, said back on August 15, 2018, in words that ring out as truthfully today as they did last summer:

> Since it is a truth contained in the Word of God, and taught by the ordinary and universal magisterium of the Catholic Church, that criminals may lawfully be put to death by the civil power when this is necessary to

---

Lectionum: A Comparative Table of Readings for the Ordinary and Extraordinary Forms of the Roman Rite (n.p.: Lectionary Study Press, 2016), vii–xxix. These two pieces are available online as well.

4   See Lisa Bourne, "US bishops follow Pope in calling death penalty 'inadmissible,' admit they don't know what it means," *LifeSiteNews*, June 21, 2019.

preserve just order in civil society, and since the present Roman pontiff has now more than once publicly manifested his refusal to teach this doctrine, and has rather brought great confusion upon the Church by seeming to contradict it, and by inserting into the *Catechism of the Catholic Church* a paragraph which will cause and is already causing many people, both believers and non-believers, to suppose that the Church considers, contrary to the Word of God, that capital punishment is intrinsically evil, we call upon Your Eminences to advise His Holiness that it is his duty to put an end to this scandal, to withdraw this paragraph from the Catechism, and to teach the word of God unadulterated; and we state our conviction that this is a duty seriously binding upon yourselves, before God and before the Church.[5]

---

5   Published at *First Things*, August 15, 2018; reprinted in Lamont and Pierantoni, *Defending the Faith*, 161-65.

42

Centuries Ago, Popes Warned of Modern Church Crises as If They Were Alive Today

LifeSiteNews
JUNE 27, 2019

THE JUNE 10, 2019, RELEASE OF THE "DEC-laration of the truths relating to some of the most common errors in the life of the Church of our time"[1] signed by Cardinal Burke, Bishop Schneider, and several other bishops—a veritable "New Syllabus of Errors," or perhaps "Syllabus of New Errors"—put me in mind of the great papal magisterial documents of centuries past, when reigning pontiffs knew the difference between truth and falsehood, knew how to exalt the former and condemn the latter, and possessed sufficient courage and charity to spread these judgments far and wide among the clergy and faithful. I found myself digging back into my files of papal encyclicals, and was, as usual, impressed by my rediscoveries. Today I will share two of them.

How many have heard of Pope Pius VIII (Francesco Saverio Maria Felice Castiglioni, 1761–1830)? His reign was short, less than two years, but his encyclical letter *Traditi Humilitati*, published almost exactly 190 years ago, resounds with penetrating insight and fervor. Here he might as well be speaking about Abu Dhabi and the working document of the Amazon Synod:

> Among these heresies belongs that foul contrivance of the sophists of this age who do not admit any difference among the different professions of faith and who think that the portal of eternal salvation opens for all from any religion.... Against these experienced sophists the people must be taught that the profession of the Catholic faith is uniquely true.

---

1   Diane Montagna, "Cdl Burke, Bp Schneider issue 'declaration of truths' to correct rampant 'doctrinal confusion' in Church," *LifeSiteNews*, June 10, 2019.

He urges the bishops of the world:

> Be very careful in choosing the seminarians, since the salvation of the people principally depends on good pastors. Nothing contributes more to the ruin of souls than impious, weak, or uninformed clerics.

As if anticipating trouble, Pius VIII cuts through the darkness unleashed by *Amoris Laetitia*:

> We also want you to imbue your flock with reverence for the sanctity of marriage so that they may never do anything to detract from the dignity of this sacrament. They should do nothing that might be unbecoming to this spotless union nor anything that might cause doubt about the perpetuity of the bond of matrimony.... [T]he union of marriage signifies the perpetual and sublime union of Christ with His Church; as a result, the close union of husband and wife is a sacrament, that is, a sacred sign of the immortal love of Christ for His spouse.

In words reminiscent of St. Catherine of Siena, the pope urges his brother bishops to prove their zeal when the flock is in danger due to modern errors and revolutions:

> Shall We hold back Our voice when the Christian cause is in such great need? Shall We be restrained by human arguments? Shall We suffer in silence the rending of the seamless robe of Christ the Savior, which even the soldiers who crucified Him did not dare to rend? Let it never happen that We be found lacking in zealous pastoral care for Our flock, beset as it is by serious dangers. We know you will do even more than We ask, and that you will cherish, augment, and defend the faith by means of teachings, counsel, work, and zeal.

A still earlier pope, Clement XIII (Carlo della Torre di Rezzonico, 1693–1769), dilated on the duties of bishops in his encyclical *Christianae Reipublicae* of 1766. Having railed against licentious books as well as the empty philosophy of Enlightenment thinkers, Clement reminds the bishops that their function is to defend the foundations of the Church, watch over the *depositum fidei*, and expose the wolves who are ravaging the fields:

It is principally your duty to stand as a wall so that no foundation can be laid other than the one that is already laid. Watch over the most holy deposit of faith to whose protection you committed yourselves on oath at your solemn consecration. Reveal to the faithful the wolves which are demolishing the Lord's vineyard. They should be warned not to allow themselves to be ensnared by the splendid writing of certain authors, that they may halt the diffusion of error by cunning and wicked men. In a word, they should detest books which contain elements shocking to the reader; which are contrary to faith, religion, and good morals; and which lack an atmosphere of Christian virtue. We manifest to you Our great happiness in this matter that most of you, following the apostolic customs and energetically defending the laws of the Church, have shown yourselves zealous and watchful in order to avert this pestilence and have not allowed the simple people to sleep soundly with serpents.

In short, Clement XIII is condemning the sort of authors praised by Pope Francis, such as Walter Kasper,[2] Fritz Lobinger,[3] Teilhard de Chardin,[4] Francesca Pardi,[5] and Stephen Walford.[6] In keeping with his name, Pope Clement, truly the merciful one, is warning us, as all good pastors have done, never to exchange novelties for established doctrine, temporary experiments for time-tested spirituality, dubious lifestyles for sound Christian morals.

We sorely need a Clement XV, a Pius XIII, a Gregory XVII, or a Leo XIV, emerging from a future conclave, to issue that long-overdue Syllabus of New Errors, to establish an Oath against Neo-Modernism, and to restore the liturgical tradition of the Roman Church. The healing of our tragic situation will require

---

2   See David Gibson, "Cardinal Kasper is the 'pope's theologian,'" *National Catholic Reporter*, June 3, 2014.

3   See Julia Meloni, "The Amazon Synod's Long Game Is More Radical Than You Think," *OnePeterFive*, June 19, 2019.

4   The influence of Teilhard on *Laudato Si'* is obvious: see, inter alia, numbers 77, 80, 81, and 83, with its footnote 53.

5   See Rosie Scammell, "Pope Francis sends letter praising gay children's book," *The Guardian*, August 28, 2015.

6   See Steven O'Reilly, "Pope Francis, the Open Letter, and the Pesky Preface," *OnePeterFive*, May 6, 2019.

nothing less than several such popes, as did the reforms after the Council of Trent. *Deus, in adjutorium nostrum intende: Domine, ad adjuvandum nos festina.*

43

Why Honoring Francis as the Pope Means Showing Concern for His Errors

LifeSiteNews
JULY 4, 2019

W ITH SO MANY POPES IN THE CHURCH'S history who are duly venerated as saints, it would be inconvenient to celebrate special Masses for all of them. Accordingly, the traditional Roman calendar wisely set aside a particular day—July 4th, as it turns out—for the Commemoration of All Holy Popes, with its own Mass Propers, starting with the Introit "Congregate illi sanctos."

I will not try to force a symbolic connection between this July 4th observance and the much more familiar Fourth of July celebrations in the United States of America, especially given that the Commemoration of All Holy Popes has fallen on different dates at different times. Nevertheless, the two occasions do have something crucial in common: each is an expression of the virtue of *pietas* or tender devotion to one's father or fatherland.[1]

When the Open Letter accusing Pope Francis of heresy was first released on April 30, many commentators accused the signatories of rejecting the pope or failing to hold him in proper esteem.[2] Nothing could be further from the truth. If we rejected his claim to the papacy, as some do, there would be no grounds for complaint, since he could not then be guilty of abusing his office, as a madman who thinks himself the emperor of China is not really guilty of international crimes. If we failed to hold him in proper esteem, we would not care so acutely about what he is doing and saying; one does not bother with a person one holds in contempt, or about whose fate one cares nothing.

---

1   See Timothy Flanders, "Is Patriotism a Virtue?," *OnePeterFive*, July 3, 2019.
2   See Lamont and Pierantoni, *Defending the Faith*, for the Open Letter (127–49) and various reactions in favor of or against it.

In reality, it is *because* he is the pope that we cry out against his errors; it is because we reverence him that we decry his abuse of power. An anarchist throws a bomb at the target of his hatred, but a Catholic raises his voice in prayer and protest for a shepherd gone astray, who is loved with a charity that seeks out remedies, natural and supernatural.

I know some of the signatories personally, and I am friends with many others who concur with the content of this Open Letter. Not a single one of us fails to pray for Pope Francis. He is the common father of Christians—whether worthily discharging his paternal office or not—and we owe him our urgent and oft-repeated prayers to God.

The Institute of Christ the King Sovereign Priest exemplifies this correct attitude. Almost every day of the Church's year, the Institute's canons add the *Commemoratio pro Papa* to the orations of the Mass. This old custom, abolished (like much else) in the middle of the twentieth century, is well worth reestablishing. Indeed, can we fail to notice that the most precipitous decline in papal orthodoxy began right around the time of the abandonment of this custom? It's as if the Vatican officials in charge of the liturgy had said to God: "With all due respect, the popes don't need Your help as much anymore." And God said: "Okay, let's see how they manage with less of it."

The orations read as follows:

> *Collect.* O God, the shepherd and ruler of all the faithful, look down favorably upon Thy servant Francis, whom Thou hast willed to appoint pastor over Thy Church; grant, we beseech Thee, that he may benefit both by word and example those over whom he is set, and thus attain unto life eternal, together with the flock entrusted to his care. Through our Lord...

> *Secret.* We beseech Thee, O Lord, that Thou mayest be appeased by the gifts we offer, and govern by Thy continual protection Thy servant Francis, whom Thou hast willed to appoint as pastor over Thy Church. Through our Lord...

> *Postcommunion.* May the reception of this divine sacrament protect us, we beseech Thee, O Lord, and ever save and

defend Thy servant Francis, whom Thou hast willed to appoint as pastor over Thy Church, together with the flock committed to his care. Through our Lord . . .

The Institute's restoration of this custom is admirable. They understand that Pope Francis will be pope only for a short time; he is the 266th in order from St. Peter, and, however painfully the years drag on, there will someday be a 267th, a 268th, and so forth, until Christ returns in glory to judge the living and the dead. Accordingly, the attitude we have towards the *papacy* should remain highly respectful. When Our Lord sees fit to come to the aid of His Church by providing a better shepherd, we need to have retained all along the right dispositions towards the Sovereign Pontiff. We cannot let our righteous and reasonable anger about Bergoglio, who passes like a shadow, contaminate our grateful and prayerful relationship to the office that abides.

How different is this terrifying example of neo-ultramontanism: a "Prayer for the Pope" disseminated by the movement Regnum Christi, associated with the scandal-haunted Legionaries of Christ, who owed part of their great success to John Paul II's blind endorsement of Marcial Maciel and the latter's cultivation of a robotic obedience among his rank and file:

> Christ Jesus, King and Lord of the Church, in your presence I renew my unconditional loyalty to your Vicar on earth, the Pope. In him you have chosen to show us the safe and sure path that we must follow in the midst of confusion, uneasiness, and unrest. I firmly believe that through him you govern, teach, and sanctify us; with him as our shepherd, we form the true Church: one, holy, catholic, and apostolic. Grant me the grace to love, live, and spread faithfully our Holy Father's teachings. Watch over his life, enlighten his mind, strengthen his spirit, defend him from calumny and evil. Calm the erosive winds of infidelity and disobedience. Hear our prayer and keep your Church united around him, firm in its belief and action, that it may truly be the instrument of your redemption. Amen.[3]

Seen with squinted eyes, this prayer *could* be given an orthodox interpretation, but when we read it in light of the milieu out of

---

3   Text at www.regnumchristi.org/en/pray/.

which it comes, and consider the stubborn refusal to acknowledge the reality of papal errors characteristic of "conservative" movements, we cannot but regard it as the epitome of a certain extreme, that of papolatry, which is as false as its contrary, Protestant antipapalism. The golden mean of virtue, so beautifully expressed in the traditional Roman orations *pro Papa*, lies in a reverent adherence to the pope as the transmitter of the deposit of faith and of the Catholic tradition that precedes and governs him, even as he presides over and rules the body of the faithful.

44

Why Pope Francis's New Document on Scripture Gives Reasons for Concern

LifeSiteNews
OCTOBER 8, 2019

O N SEPTEMBER 30, THE FEAST OF ST. Jerome, Pope Francis released the text of a motu proprio entitled *Aperuit Illis*, instituting the so-called "Sunday of the Word of God."

This motu proprio was oddly timed, appearing right before the creation of new cardinals and the start of the controversial Synod on the Amazon Region. Given the circumstances, one might be forgiven for thinking the motu proprio was meant to be overlooked or undervalued. There has been almost no commentary on it. A few conservatives thought it sufficient to say: "This document is orthodox in content, therefore we can breathe easily. No *Amoris Laetitia* moment has occurred. Potential bullet dodged."

Such an approach is understandable but problematic. Those who remain at the level of the "truth of the text" in an abstract sense are ignoring the *context* for this intervention. Why *this* document, and why *right now*? Was there some pressing crisis or dispute Pope Francis stepped in to resolve? Errors on Scripture have been rife for the past fifty years and more, and previous popes have responded more adequately to them than this brief document does. For far too long, conservatives have been isolating each papal act and X-raying it for its truth value, not recognizing that we have allowed ourselves to be reduced to a pathetic caricature of Catholicism if the best we can say of a papal act is that it does not contradict the Deposit of Faith!

Instead, we must look at cumulative patterns and tendencies in order to understand how each piece fits in: not just text, but context. Unfortunately, as with most of Pope Francis's "conservative" statements, it is much more likely that *Aperuit Illis* is part of a calculated strategy to keep the conservatives on board as long as possible, using them for the ultimate triumph of papal progressivism.

Perhaps the most striking thing about this motu proprio is the astonishing cynicism of the timing of it, coming right before the start of a synod that represents, in its planning and already in its execution, a standing insult to the Word of God (both written and incarnate). Pope Francis is throwing a bone to the conservatives, who will fawn all over this motu proprio because it's basically orthodox and even quotes Church Fathers—as if the Vatican cares at all nowadays about continuity with tradition. Anyone who has studied the past six years of this pontificate can see the classic signs of a clever propaganda move: keep clueless people guessing as to your real intentions and beliefs, by taking two steps to the left, then one step to the right. If only the remaining conservatives would wake up and see the bigger picture, they would recognize that they're being "had." And then we could get on with the work of rebuilding authentic Catholicism with such ingredients as the ancient one-year lectionary that has been read in the Church, in one form or another, for 1,500 years.

Nevertheless, *Aperuit Illis* is not a document without problems, and these we need to understand in order to fit this latest piece into the puzzle.

The motu proprio drives a new wedge between the traditional worship of the Church and the modern papal rite by instituting yet another feast (of sorts) in the Novus Ordo calendar: "the Sunday of the Word of God," to take place on the Third Sunday of Ordinary Time. Each Sunday is already, and has always been, a day of the Word of God, inasmuch as the Bible is proclaimed and the Word Incarnate, whom the Bible announces, comes to be present on our altars. This new observance is either superfluous or moving in a different direction from the Catholic understanding of Scripture in the liturgy. As Gregory DiPippo explains, the goods the pope says he wants are already present in the Church's tradition—something the pope acts as if he doesn't know (and maybe he doesn't!).[1]

Some might object in the pope's favor that the Catholic liturgy has always added feasts over the centuries to celebrate this or that particular mystery (e.g., Corpus Christi). In reality, however, the Christian liturgy exists to celebrate the mysteries of Christ and His

---

1   "Putting *Aperuit Illis* Into Practice," *New Liturgical Movement*, October 1, 2019.

saints. From this point of view, a generic exhortation to celebrate "the Word of God" in the sense of Scripture is regressive, since the Church already celebrates the Word of God made flesh on March 25 and December 25, and the Word of God permeating the Church on Pentecost and its entire season. In fact, since the motu proprio emphasizes the role of the Holy Spirit in reading and assimilating Scripture, the pope ought to have admitted that the Green Sundays deserve to be called once again, as they had been for over fifteen centuries, "Sundays after Pentecost," which reminds the Church of the intimate bond among Christ, His Word, and His Spirit of Love and Truth, rather than "Sundays of Ordinary Time."

The Mass is not a Scripture study à la Protestant Bible services, but a sacrificial offering in which readings occupy a preparatory and subservient role, as "verbal incense" offered in the presence of God, lifting the people to praise Him for His mighty deeds of deliverance.[2] This latreutic function of Scripture is very clear in the ancient liturgies both Eastern and Western, but quite obscured in the Novus Ordo.[3]

Although it often names its Sundays after Gospel pericopes, the Byzantine church would never have a "Sunday of the Word of God" in the sense in which it is defined in *Aperuit Illis*, which has nothing to do with liturgical tradition, with icons or mysteries in the life of Christ. Those who love the Word of God want to venerate it *in the ways that traditional liturgies already venerate it*. The Tridentine Mass gives far greater ceremonial weight and honor to the proclamation of Scripture than the Novus Ordo does. My own love of *lectio divina* has come from and been nourished by an ever deeper experience of the traditional Latin liturgy, which meditatively weaves passages of Scripture together in a manner that is comparable to *lectio divina* as practiced by a true master of Scripture like St. Bernard of Clairvaux.

One of the most harmful aspects of the Novus Ordo is its cult of the "new and improved." A shining example is the new calendar, by which centuries of deeply rooted customs and devotions in the Church were swept away. The traditional liturgy shows great

2   See "Why the 'Word of God' for Catholics is not only the Bible, but more importantly, Jesus Himself," *LifeSiteNews*, August 29, 2019.
3   See "Against Vernacular Readings in the Traditional Mass," *New Liturgical Movement*, October 18, 2021.

stability over many centuries, and the new feasts grow organically from within it. This "Sunday of the Word of God," on the contrary, looks like another "I woke up this morning and had a good idea" sort of thing. And how vague it all is—not like the sharply defined feast of Christ the King, which was originally instituted in relation to the feast of All Saints.[4] One result of the new motu proprio is indisputable: it helps us to see more clearly that the whole conception of what a feast is and how it is to be celebrated is different in the old missal and in the new. If the pope really wanted Scripture to be exalted among Christians, the best way of doing that would be to ensure *the proper celebration of the liturgy in which Scripture is embedded.* Offering the Mass worthily, reverently, and beautifully does more to lift the faithful's appreciation of and reverence toward the written Word of God than any amount of preaching, or artificial and piecemeal spotlights like "enthroning the Gospel book" (when, at the same liturgy, non-vested lay people will just walk up out of the nave and read a vernacular text at the ambo, which kills any sacrality that that moment might have had). As Fr. Zuhlsdorf likes to say, "a rising tide lifts all boats." Make the liturgy great again, and the Bible will rise with it. If the liturgy is dumbed down, superficial, horizontal, the perception of the Bible will sink with it.

Along these lines, the document praises postconciliar lector praxis, in spite of the fact that it has been a powerful force for the Protestantizing of Catholic perceptions of both Scripture and liturgy.[5] Moreover, the role of lector, which is a legitimate liturgical function (albeit historically reserved to those who had received at least the minor order of lector), is placed alongside the fabricated and much abused function of "extraordinary ministers of holy communion," which has greatly contributed to the lessening of belief in and reverence for the Blessed Sacrament.[6]

---

4   See "Should the Feast of Christ the King Be Celebrated in October or November?," *Rorate Caeli*, October 22, 2014; the feast was subsequently modernized by Paul VI into a Teilhardian celebration of "Christ the King of the Universe": see idem, "Between Christ the King and 'We Have No King But Caesar,'" *OnePeterFive*, October 25, 2020.

5   See "How Typical Lector Praxis Transmits a Pelagian and Protestant Message," *New Liturgical Movement*, January 15, 2018.

6   See "Time to End the Ordinary Use of 'Extraordinary Ministers,'" in Kwasniewski, *Holy Bread*, 147–58.

In this way, *Aperuit Illis* lends support to abusive liturgical praxis, shoring up one unnecessary and untraditional lay ministry by means of another. The "progressives" in the Church have long been agitating for female-instituted lectors and acolytes (as further steps toward deaconesses and priestesses), and when the moment arrives, you can be sure that *Aperuit Illis* will be footnoted as a "magisterial" precedent.[7]

Then there is a simple psychological point. If anyone seriously thinks setting aside a Sunday in which clergy will ramble on from the pulpit about Scripture—as they already mostly do, Sunday after Sunday, thanks to a mechanical application of the idea that preaching should always be based on the readings—will increase Catholics' appreciation for the Bible, he is more to be pitied than censured. What would really make a difference in the life of the Church is if the pope himself *obeyed* the Word of God in his teaching and life, defending the doctrine of Christ and fighting corruption in the ranks, especially in the Vatican. Instead, he contradicts the Word of God and not only dines with corrupt clergy, but promotes them in their corruption.

It is therefore not a little alarming when Francis, in *Aperuit Illis*, quotes Benedict XVI that "the letter [of Scripture] needs to be transcended" (n. 15). One immediately thinks not of medieval exegesis, but of Modernism. For indeed, Pope Francis has become an expert in "transcending the letter" of Scripture—although perhaps the verb "transgressing" would be more appropriate in this connection.[8]

For the Church Fathers, the "letter" of Scripture, its historical or first-level meaning, is inspired and inerrant and always true, although it *also* opens out onto spiritual meanings—allegorical, moral, and anagogical—i.e., pointing to the mystery of Christ, telling us how we are to live today in imitation of Him, and illuminating our final destiny in Heaven with Him. When we see the spiritual meaning of a passage, we do not transcend its letter by leaving it behind; we see into the letter more deeply. In contrast, proponents of the "new paradigm" advocate "transcending the letter" when it comes

---

7 This in fact occurred by means of the motu proprio *Spiritus Domini* of January 10, 2021. For an extended critique, see Kwasniewski, *Ministers of Christ*, esp. ch. 6: "Lay Ministries Obscure Both the Laity's Calling and the Clergy's."
8 See chapter 7.

to things like commandments and prohibitions. For example, we have to transcend the absolute prohibition of adultery to find the *real* meaning, which is that we have to "love one another." That's the only thing God had in mind, see? No one should be left without expressions of affection, to which everyone has a right. So the transcendental meaning is, adultery is okay as long as the partners "love" one another. "Love is love," after all.

When I shared my misgivings about the motu proprio with a priest, he said to me: "Would you criticize this document if it had come from Benedict XVI?"—the implication being that I am criticizing it only because it comes from Francis. That is simply not true. I would say the same things regardless of who the author was. The bare orthodoxy of a document, its avoidance of gross and explicit heresy, is not the only consideration in the world, and in many ways, practically, *not even the most important.* For example, one could have a liturgy that does not contradict Catholic faith and morals but nevertheless damages the spiritual lives of the faithful by being impoverished in its expression of Catholicism, riddled with options, horizontal, and anthropocentric. The fact that a liturgy is free from error does not, in and of itself, make it beneficial for building up the life of the Church. Orthodoxy isn't enough; one needs an adequate *expression* of orthodoxy, in continuity with tradition, and girt about with unassailable reverence.

Returning to my point of departure—namely, that we have to consider how *Aperuit Illis* fits into the Bergoglian pattern—I would like to paraphrase the poignant words of a friend:

> The motu proprio follows a trend: celebrate something in order to denigrate and forget it. The Year of the Priest: a year where more priests than ever before are thrown under the bus by their bishops. The Year of Mercy, to remind everyone that those guilty of clericalism can't be saved and that there's no mercy for traditionally-minded Catholics. Synodality, to express that you have no voice; only the Pope, Coccopalmerio, Coccopalmerio's boyfriend, and his friends do. Issue a document to "end all abuses" before tolerating or spurring on more of them. Canonize John Paul II and then forget about his teaching in *Familiaris Consortio.* Canonize Paul VI and dismiss *Humanae Vitae.* Canonize John Henry Newman and solemnly distort

his views on the development of doctrine and why the Catholic Church is the one true Church. Now, with *Aperuit Illis*, celebrate the Word of God—so as to ignore the Word of God.

We are witnessing here the consummately Machiavellian application of the old expression *promoveatur ut amoveatur*, let him/her/it be promoted so that he/she/it may be removed or shunted away. Surpassing the Jewish leaders excoriated by Christ (cf. Lk. 11:47), Pope Francis, the canonizer of John Paul II, Paul VI, and John Henry Newman, both kills the prophets *and* builds them splendid tombs.

45
Feast of the Divine Maternity— or of Papa Roncalli?

Rorate Caeli
OCTOBER 11, 2019

TODAY, OCTOBER 11, IS A PERFECT ILLUS-tration of the basic problem of the Catholic Church in the twentieth century.

In 1931, Pope Pius XI instituted on October 11 the feast of the Divine Maternity of the Blessed Virgin Mary, to commemorate the 1500th anniversary of the Council of Ephesus, which had bestowed on her the glorious title *Theotokos* or God-bearing-One. This feast was placed on October 11. Thus, it's not an ancient feastday (as neither was Christ the King, instituted by the same pope), but fits into that slow and loving process of amplification by which the traditional liturgy has been enriched over twenty centuries with ever-new facets of devotion.

Pope John XXIII comes along and decides to open the Second Vatican Council on October 11, *precisely because* it was the feast of the Divine Motherhood of Our Lady.

Fast-forward to after the Council: Bugnini's *Consilium* decides to abolish the feast and to conflate it with January 1st, which had been the Octave of Christmas and the Circumcision of Christ, but which would now be styled "the Solemnity of Mary Mother of God." Lots of busy scissors and paste...

And then along comes Pope Francis, who canonizes John XXIII and declares that October 11 will be—*his* feastday.

Hey presto!, October 11 has shifted from honoring the deepest mystery of the Virgin Mary—her being the *Theotokos*—to honoring Vatican II's architect as elevated by the Council's mutant progeny, Jorge Bergoglio. As Ratzinger said in a different context, we now celebrate ourselves and our achievements rather than the mightiest works of God.

This is the kind of thing I had in mind when I maintained that the modern Church is characterized by a Nietzschean "transvaluation of all values."[1]

It also seems a haunting coincidence (but there are no coincidences under Divine Providence) that Pope Francis has been reported this week by Scalfari to have denied the divinity of Our Lord Jesus Christ, making Bergoglio a sort of Nestorian (at best), with Our Lady being demoted to *Christotokos*, Christ-bearer, as she is for Protestants who refuse her the august title "Mother of God." Neither the pope nor the Vatican is willing to confront Scalfari for egregious lies or misrepresentations or amnesia; instead, the usual non-denial denial has been issued. Unlike his predecessor Pius XI, who cared enough about the dogmatic formulation of Ephesus to institute a feast in commemoration of its principal definition, the current pope said two days ago, in a homily painfully reminiscent of the anti-theological mentality of the 1970s: "Do I love God or dogmatic formulations?"

The silver lining on this otherwise dark cloud is that, in spite of everything that has transpired, despite all the wickedness in high places, October 11 continues to this day to be celebrated as the feast of the Divine Maternity, in all communities and parishes that avail themselves of the traditional *Missale Romanum*. The feast has not perished; it has merely been eclipsed, and it will return in splendor to illuminate the Church after this night of self-celebration has passed.

---

1   See "The New Synthesis of All Heresies: On Nietzschean Catholicism," *OnePeterFive*, May 16, 2018.

46

Famous Modern Jesuits Totally Disagree with Jesuit Pope on Importance of Dogma

LifeSiteNews

OCTOBER 17, 2019

AS REPORTED EARLIER AT THIS SITE, POPE Francis in his weekly general audience of October 9 made the following remark: "Do I belong to the universal Church—with the good and the bad, all of us—or do I hold a selective ideology? Do I love God or dogmatic formulations?"[1]

Apart from the false opposition and sentimentality implicit in the second question, more reminiscent of the Woodstock "summer of love" than of Christian charity for God and neighbor based on faith in divine revelation, I would like to point out that the pope is departing here from the spirit of approval for dogmatic formulations entertained by notable members of his own order— modern intellectuals whom it is customary and indeed fashionable to praise. Francis is an outlier even among his own.

Thus, Fr. Pierre Rousselot, S.J. (1878–1915) wrote:

> A passionate love for the absolute Mind naturally engenders a love of dogma. The truth of Faith is the basis of our religion, and dogma serves to express the object of our religion. Were religion nothing more than a human product, and dogma merely the expression of human reactions to the facts of dogma, it would be the merest folly to sacrifice human happiness or human life for the sake of a dogma. But dogma has truth, it is more true even than science, and the object of dogma is above and beyond man. Likewise, sins against dogma are the most grievous of all, and errors concerning ideas are more dangerous than those concerning men. Take away dogma

---

1   See Doug Mainwaring, "Pope Francis: 'Do I love God or dogmatic formulations?'" *LifeSiteNews*, October 9, 2019.

and you take God away; to touch dogma is to touch God. To sin against dogma is to sin against God.[2]

We have to ask the reason for these startling claims. With a human person, what he is, who he is, what his qualities are, and his thoughts and acts of will—all these differ from one another. There is a substantial unity but much accidental diversity within it. So attacking a man's ideas or choices is not the same as attacking the man himself, his human nature, or his personal dignity. With God, it is quite otherwise. God, His nature, His personality, His ideas, His volitions, His truth, and His love, are all *identical with Himself*; He is absolutely one. It would be impossible, therefore, to love God without equally loving all that is true in Him and about Him. God *is* truth. For this reason, adherence to dogma is inseparable from adherence to God; one's willingness to embrace dogma is a concrete measure of one's love for Him. We express our love for God by adhering to His truth, and we adhere to His truth because we love Him.

Fr. Emile Mersch, S. J. (1890–1940), with similar enthusiasm for the God-given gift of intellect and the inherent nobility of the truth, speaks of virtues and vices in the use of faith-illuminated understanding:

> [D]ogma tells [Christians]: "Think! Think with all your power, with all your love, with all your loyalty; think as a man ought to think when he is thinking with God." But when God entrusted His truth to their intellects, in answer to their need for understanding, did He not impose on them an obligation to seek it out? In uniting Himself to them in the incarnate Word, did He not wish to give them a new knowledge, and hence to awaken in them a new understanding, that would be worthy of Him who helps them to achieve it and also worthy of the children of light? When God comes to dwell in the intellect as truth, does He intend the intellect to be saved without its cooperation? When He lodges His truth in the mind, is not the withholding of a desire to know it equivalent to casting it out from the soul? Is not lack of interest in comprehending that truth a sin of omission, is it

---

2   *The Intellectualism of St. Thomas Aquinas* (London: Sheed & Ward, 1935), 221.

not contempt and blasphemy, analogous, in the order of knowing, to indifference regarding good and neutrality regarding duty in the order of volition? A faith that renounces understanding renounces life.[3]

Mersch goes on to say:

The same Christ resides in dogmatic pronouncements, in the official teaching authority [of the Church], and in the life of grace...for the Truth is Christ.... Christianity lives on truth.[4]

As if to further develop the point made by his confrères Rousselot and Mersch, influential Patrologist Fr. Henri de Lubac, S. J. (1896–1991) had this to say about heresy:

If heretics no longer horrify us today, as they once did our forefathers, is it certain that it is because there is more charity in our hearts? Or would it not too often be, perhaps, without our daring to say so, because the bone of contention, that is to say, the very substance of our faith, no longer interests us? Men of too familiar and too passive a faith, perhaps for us dogmas are no longer the Mystery on which we live, the Mystery which is to be accomplished in us. Consequently then, heresy no longer shocks us; at least, it no longer convulses us like something trying to tear the soul of our souls away from us... And that is why we have no trouble in being kind to heretics, and no repugnance in rubbing shoulders with them... It is not always charity, alas, which has grown greater, or which has become more enlightened: it is often faith, the taste for the things of eternity, which has grown less.[5]

Fr. Piet Fransen, S. J. (1913–1983), a Belgian theologian and historian, specified that his favoritism for the existentialist approach did not make of him a relativist:

If the Son of God came amongst us, and spoke to us in the name of the Father in our human words, our human

---

3   *The Theology of the Mystical Body*, trans. Cyril Vollert, S. J. (St. Louis: B. Herder, 1951), 14–15.
4   Mersch, 19.
5   *Paradoxes of Faith* (San Francisco: Ignatius Press, 1987), 226–27.

symbols and images, and if he entrusted his own truth to his Church, a human institution, even if it was founded by God, and united as his body and bride with Christ himself, this act of redemption which was at the same time an act of revelation of the thoughts and the truths of God about himself and about man, gives us not only the possibility, but also the duty to think about those truths, to defend them against possible deformations, to translate them into other languages for other times and cultures .... I do believe strongly in right and wrong, in truth and falsehood, in orthodoxy and heresy. I think that theology, as soon as it despairs of obtaining the truth, is no longer a Christian theology.[6]

A more recent Jesuit, Fr. Avery Dulles, S. J. (1918–2008), staunchly defends dogmatic teaching:

The Church as a divine oracle is commissioned to bear authoritative witness to God's revelation in Christ.... Its authoritative teaching imposes a certain obligation on members of the Church to believe. Unlike civil societies, the Church is a society of faith. Its members are united by professing the same body of revealed truth, expressed in creeds and dogmas. To reject the faith of the community is to exclude oneself from the Church as a society. The teaching of the Magisterium therefore has an obligatory force resembling that of a law or precept.... Having received the word of God, the Church has an inalienable responsibility to hand it on, explain it, and defend it against errors.[7]

Such authors and quotations could be multiplied, but there is no need for that. What we can see is that the pope's regrettable habit of indulging in false oppositions—dogma against love, theory against practice, principles against reality, tradition against progress, and many other pairs—is not only repugnant to the instinct of the faithful and their "supernatural common sense"

---

6   *Intelligent Theology* (Chicago: Franciscan Herald Press, 1969), vol. 1, 14–15; 34.
7   *Magisterium: Teacher and Guardian of the Faith* (Naples, FL: Sapientia Press, 2007), 2–4.

(as Roberto de Mattei puts it), but also out of alignment with the best thinking of modern Jesuits on the absolute value of rational and dogmatic truth and the serious peril of embracing or surrendering to error, which cuts us off from God and salvation as effectively as moral turpitude or hatred for our neighbor does.

47

How to Properly Use Righteous Anger about the Amazon Synod

LifeSiteNews

NOVEMBER 5, 2019

A FRIEND AND FORMER STUDENT OF MINE sent an email to me recently that will surely resonate with many who have been dismayed, scandalized, and horrified by the paganism, syncretism, and contempt for the Catholic religion on full display during last month's Synod in Rome. With his permission, I share below the email and my reply.

Dear Dr. Kwasniewski:

I'm relieved. For some reason, I'm happy that the evil everyone has suspected all along and warned against is finally rearing its head—though it is far nastier than I thought it would be. To me, the disaster of the Amazon Synod has completely and forcefully established the failure of Vatican II, exposed the modernist influence preceding Vatican II, put a floodlight on the abuses of the current and more recent popes, and stripped bare the lukewarm, pathetic, bright-lipstick-wearing-and-hand-sanitizing-before-distributing-communion-in-the-hand kind of Catholicism that has been around since before I was born. Any compromises I was willing to make either with other people or *even in myself* are totally banished. Here is the polarizing point I've been longing for. Do you think it's appropriate to feel relief along with great sadness?

A different kind of question: Why do you suppose a vague pantheism has gained so much appeal in our times, becoming the most common opponent of Christianity—more popular than atheism, agnosticism, or even downright satanism?

The big question: What do we do? Pray, obviously, and shuck any vestiges of non-traditional Catholicism in our lives. But I kind of want to *fight*. For some reason, I see this Pachamama demon as an antithesis of the Virgin Mary. Mother Earth vs. Mother Mary, or a generic cult of "fertility" vs. the veneration of the Theotokos. That makes me so angry. It makes me so angry that our pope, our bishops, and our cardinals are disrespecting our Mother so blatantly and viciously. It makes me so angry that I want to take the wooden idols and smash them to pieces before hurling them into the Tiber, this time for good. How can I turn that anger to constructive purposes?

Here was my reply.

You have expressed to perfection the way we are all feeling. It is a worldwide phenomenon, and we can indeed be thankful for the clarity with which the evil of modernism (with all of the other -isms that precede or follow it) is being exposed on the stage of the Vatican. My own "polarizing point" already occurred long ago, when I studied how the Novus Ordo came into existence and how much the tradition of the Church was despised during and after Vatican II. Everything that is happening now is an extrapolation of this fundamental sin against tradition. Once you reject your identity, you can become anything—or nothing.[1]

The reason for pantheism's appeal is not hard to see: in spite of its falsehood, it mingles in enough truth to appeal to the human mind, which has an instinctive apprehension of divinity. Atheism, in that sense, is always artificial and forced; it runs against the grain of our conscience and our experience. But Christian theism is much more radical and demanding than pantheism, because one has to profess one's faith in a God utterly transcendent and at the same time fearfully intimate (since His immediate presence to all things is caused by His very transcendence).[2] Pantheism lets a person be "cool" with "religious stuff" while keeping the true God at arm's length. It adds a religious veneer to an essentially secular lifestyle.

Anger always has to be channeled into thoughtful and focused efforts; otherwise, it disperses itself wastefully and harmfully. I

---

1   See "Augustine: patron saint of identity crisis," *LifeSiteNews*, August 27, 2019.

2   See "How the theism of Aquinas differs from 'theism' in the marketplace of ideas," *LifeSiteNews*, September 19, 2019.

have spoken a little bit elsewhere about what laity can do,[3] but it boils down to a few things.

1) Don't give a red cent to any bishop or priest who does not publicly and expressly preach the orthodox Catholic faith and condemn the errors going on in the Church and at the Vatican. Their most basic job, after offering sacrifice, is to preach the truth, in season, out of season, reproving, rebuking, exhorting (cf. 2 Tim. 4:2). If a bishop or priest is not doing this, he's like a parent who neglects or abuses his children and who therefore deserves to lose their affection, their support, and their collaboration—even if not their prayers for his conversion. If we have any extra money, we should give it to reliable traditional religious orders and apostolates, which are the hope of the future.

2) Pray and fast more seriously. We are doing battle with evil spirits: "For our wrestling is not against flesh and blood; but against principalities and powers, against the rulers of the world of this darkness, against the spirits of wickedness in the high places" (Eph. 6:12), and about such demons, Our Lord says: "This kind can go out by nothing, but by prayer and fasting" (Mk. 9:28). All of us—myself included!—tend to talk a lot and wring our hands, but when push comes to shove, how often do we sign up for holy hours, or skip meals, or abstain from meat or alcoholic beverages or TV or other creature comforts, or pray 15 decades of the rosary, or get up for an early morning Latin Mass? Like Jesus, of whom Scripture says, "He began to *do* and to teach" (cf. Acts 1:1), we have to begin with *doing*.

3) Keep studying the Faith, and know it very well. Only in this way can we marvel at it, give thanks for it, live it, discuss it with others and debate its opponents, and pass it on to the next generation. This is no small thing: there is so much ignorance, error, and wishful thinking out there that an accurate knowledge of the Faith, and especially of the liturgy, is rarely to be met with. Books like Mosebach's *Heresy of Formlessness* and my *Noble Beauty, Transcendent Holiness*; books like the Canons and Decrees of the Council of Trent, the Catechism of Trent, and Ludwig Ott's *Fundamentals of Catholic Dogma*—and I would add Bishop Schneider's new book, *Christus Vincit*—these ought to be in front of our eyes

---

3 See "Five ways Catholic laity can powerfully influence Church for good from within," *LifeSiteNews*, November 8, 2018.

for some period of time each day. Extrapolating from this, one could think about starting a book group, or inviting people periodically to one's home or apartment for readings and discussions. It is the age of the laity: we are the ones doing the heavy lifting at this point in terms of evangelization, catechesis, theology, and liturgical renewal.

4) We should pray about joining ourselves more closely to a traditional community, be it as an oblate of a Benedictine monastery,[4] the Confraternity of St. Peter (Priestly Fraternity of St. Peter), the Society of the Sacred Heart (Institute of Christ the King Sovereign Priest), or some other, in order to share in the spiritual riches of that community and have a more orderly rule of life to follow.

5) This may seem an odd bit of advice, but it is the advice of many saints: *practice giving thanks.* Thank God each day for making you a Christian and a Catholic. Thank Him for leading you away from ignorance, error, and sin. Thank Him for giving you a hunger for the truth, a desire for the good, eyes and ears for the beautiful. Thank Him for leading you to Catholic tradition, to a good education, and to good friends. Thank Him for exposing evils and stirring up resistance. Thank Him even for your feelings of anger, sadness, dismay, and perplexity, which keep us from being lukewarm and comfortable. The more we acknowledge and rejoice in His gifts to us, the more we are drawn through the hardships of this time to spiritual and eternal goods that will never fade.

I agree with Roberto de Mattei that we must have, or recover, a "militant conception" of Christian life:[5] we are soldiers fighting for Christ the King, even if all we are doing at the moment is faithfully discharging a desk job or nursing a baby. We will not be passive, indifferent, lazy, taking whatever nonsense the hierarchs of the Church decide to dump on us; we will resist, respectfully but firmly, and insist on the true Faith.

---

4   See "Even if you can't be a monk, you can still benefit from monastic life. Here's how," *LifeSiteNews,* July 28, 2020.
5   See my lecture "Christian Militancy in the Prayer of the Church," *OnePeterFive,* March 16, 2022, in the course of which de Mattei is quoted several times.

48

A Theological Review of the Amazon Synod†

Lecture in Houston, Texas
NOVEMBER 24, 2019

CATHOLICS THE WORLD OVER HAVE BEEN disturbed, demoralized, scandalized, and galvanized by the Amazon Synod. As Br. André-Marie observed:

> The recently concluded Amazon Synod was at least as horrifying as expected: on display were idolatry, syncretism, indifferentism, feminism, modernism, radical environmentalism, and liberation theology, a much more terrifying combination than anything Stephen King or John Carpenter could imagine.[1]

A complete theological analysis of this Synod would take many lectures, not just one, so I will have to be selective and brief. My talk today will have four parts. First, I will discuss the violations of the first Commandment that took place at the Vatican. This will segue into part 2, on the concept of inculturation. Then part 3 will take up the proposal to abolish mandatory clerical celibacy, and part 4, the proposal to ordain female deacons or deaconesses.

---

† This lecture was given on Sunday, November 24, 2019, in Houston, Texas; the text was published at *OnePeterFive* on December 4, 2019. A video has been prepared that includes Vatican footage and photography, so that whenever I mention or comment on some event, such as the Pachamama rituals in the Vatican Garden, the prostrations, the blessing of the idol, the giving of the black ring, the procession into the Synod hall, the bowl placed on the altar, etc., it is shown as it appeared on Vatican News, in *L'Osservatore Romano*, etc. It's a tremendous tool for teaching about the evils of the Synod. The video may be found by searching YouTube for "Kwasniewski Amazon Synod."

---

1 "The Antichurch of the Pseudomissionaries, and How It Came to Be," *Catholicism.org*, October 31, 2019; he provides links to back up each of these claims. See also Douglas Farrow, "The Amazon Synod is a Sign of the Times," *First Things*, October 17, 2019.

IDOLATRY

I imagine that the first thing on everyone's mind is the commission of sins of idolatry that punctuated the Synod. The Ten Commandments are listed in order of importance. Think about what that means: having false gods is a sin worse than adultery or murder. For this reason I did not hesitate to add my signature to the signatures of a hundred other scholars and pastors on the recent "Protest against Pope Francis's Sacrilegious Acts," dated November 9 and released November 12. [2] Before continuing, we must define a key term. "Pachamama" is a South American fertility goddess or divinity, venerated for centuries by pagans, by poorly evangelized or ill-catechized Christians, and, more recently, by some New Age cults. [3]

The protest lists the following sacrilegious acts:

• On October 4, Pope Francis attended an act of idolatrous worship of Pachamama.

• He allowed this worship to take place in the Vatican Gardens, desecrating the vicinity of the graves of the martyrs and of the church of the Apostle Peter.

• He participated in this act of idolatrous worship by blessing a wooden image of Pachamama.

• On October 7, the idol of Pachamama was placed in front of the main altar at St. Peter's and then carried in procession to the Synod Hall. Pope Francis said prayers in a ceremony involving this image and then joined in this procession.

• When wooden images of this pagan deity were removed from the church of Santa Maria in Traspontina, where they had been sacrilegiously placed, and thrown into the Tiber by Catholics outraged by this profanation of the church, Pope Francis, on October 25, apologized for their removal and another wooden image of Pachamama was returned to the church. Thus, a new profanation was initiated.

---

2   For the text and signatories, see Lamont and Pierantoni, *Defending the Faith*, 167–76.

3   While some hyperpapalists dispute these claims, it is easy to find abundant verification of them in popular and literary materials from South America. In an age of eclecticism, syncretism, and ecotourism, it is not at all surprising that pagan beliefs and superstitions would not only extend their influence past historic boundaries but also be deliberately revived by post-Christians and neo-pagans.

- On October 27, in the closing Mass for the synod, he accepted a bowl used in the idolatrous worship of Pachamama and placed it directly on the altar.

Some commentators have dismissed the charges of idolatry and sacrilege, arguing that the wooden figures were not idols; that they were not being venerated as gods or spirits or forces of nature; and even that they were meant to represent the Virgin Mary (however offensively portrayed). But these arguments do not hold up to critical scrutiny.[4]

Vatican officials repeatedly clarified that the pregnant female wooden figure was *not* intended to be an Amazonian representation of the Blessed Mother. At a news conference on October 16, Father Giacomo Costa, a Vatican communications official for the Synod, stated: "It is not the Virgin Mary... It is an indigenous woman who represents life,... [and is] neither pagan nor sacred." Paolo Ruffini, prefect of the Vatican Communications Dicastery, said, "Fundamentally, it represents life... life through a woman."[5] Finally, Pope Francis himself referred to these wooden images as being of "Pachamama," i.e., definitely not the Blessed Virgin Mary.

Fr. Costa's claim that the image is "neither pagan *nor sacred*" needs to be evaluated in the light of the recorded fact that in the Vatican gardens, and later in Santa Maria in Traspontina, the Pachamama images were integrated into religious ceremonies.[6] The

---

4   In the next several paragraphs I am relying on argumentation provided by Fr. Brian Harrison, whose help I gratefully acknowledge.

5   The foregoing information is from Catholic News Agency journalist Hannah Brockhaus, whose report is reproduced in the *National Catholic Register*, October 27–November 9, 2019, p. 7, under the heading, "Vatican Official: Carved Figure at Amazon Synod Is Not the Virgin Mary."

6   A canon lawyer has pointed out that, since, according to a verse in the Psalms, "all the gods of the gentiles are demons," it follows that simply *displaying* pagan idols and offerings is a tacit invocation of demons. For this reason, Fr. Zuhlsdorf is surely right to say that much of the Vatican requires exorcism at this point. "The real scandal here is that Pope Francis is implicitly asserting in yesterday's statement [October 25, 2019] that pagan idols can be exposed in a place of honor in a Catholic Church, provided that they are displayed 'without idolatrous intentions,' or even worse, that it is possible to split such a display of manifestly pagan idols in a place of honor in a Catholic Church from the tacit invocation of demons that they per se constitute." See anon., "Full transcript of the Pope's comments on pagan 'Pachamama' statues," *LifeSiteNews*, October 25, 2019; Maike Hickson,

female shamaness can be seen on video raising hands before the twin Pachamama figurines, kneeling, and prostrating herself, face to the ground.[7] (It has been pointed out that even if the image *were* of the Blessed Virgin, such a gesture would be reprehensible as superstition, since Catholic tradition sees prostration as a mark of adoration, which is reserved for God alone.) The shamaness then presented one of the images to Pope Francis, who blessed the proffered wooden image with the sign of the cross. All this disproves Fr. Costa's claim that the Pachamama figurines are not seen as "sacred" by their devotees. And it renders ridiculous the claim that carrying Pachamama into a church in procession is not morally different from a sports team taking their banner (a purely secular object) into a church during Mass.

Since the Pachamama images do *not* represent the true God, the Blessed Mother, or any other Christian saint, the religious acts involving them stand condemned by Catholic teaching. The section entitled "idolatry" in the *Catechism of the Catholic Church* teaches in n. 2112 that the First Commandment, in condemning polytheism, "requires man neither to believe in, nor to venerate, other divinities than the one true God." Note how the *Catechism* uses the more general words "venerate" and "divinities," rather than "adore" and "gods": the Church is setting the bar relatively *low* as to what constitutes idolatry. While the prostrations she received strongly suggest *latria* or adoration, it is beyond dispute that Pachamama was at least *venerated* in these papally-patronized ceremonies. The *Catechism*'s language also renders irrelevant the heated debate over whether Pachamama, in the current Amazonian (as distinct from Incan) usage, is truly seen as a "goddess" or not. For the word "divinities" is broader than "god" and "goddess." It covers also the animistic and/or pantheistic belief that certain objects and places are intrinsically sacred, numinous, holy, and to be religiously revered. The religious honor given to Pachamama in Rome and elsewhere makes it clear that "she," or the "Earth

---

"Swiss bishop: It is a 'scandal' that the Pope 'defends those rituals inside the Vatican Gardens,'" *LifeSiteNews*, October 26, 2019.

7   She herself made clear that the rituals were for Mother Earth and Creator Father: see Diane Montagna, "Amazonian woman who led Vatican tree-planting ceremony reveals its pagan significance," *LifeSiteNews*, November 8, 2019.

Mother" represented by her images, is seen by her devotees as a "divinity" of some sort—and certainly not "the one true God."[8] The female cult leader spoke explicitly of the "divinity" or "divine" quality inherent in the Amazonian soil that she reverently brought up in a black bowl, which was placed by papal *fiat* on the high altar during the final Synod Mass.[9]

Finally, the next paragraph of the *Catechism*, n. 2113, speaks of "idolatry" in quite general terms as being constituted by *falsos paganismi cultus* ("false pagan worship"). Since the Pachamama religious rites carried out in Rome were clearly not monotheistic (i.e., Christian, Jewish, or Muslim), it follows that they were pagan. The fact that Jesus, Mary, or a Christian saint or two may be venerated alongside traditional tribal divinities, which is technically known as "syncretism," would not *stop* such cults from being pagan. Hindus and some other pagans are often happy enough to include Jesus as one god among others in their various pantheons, as indeed the ancient Romans were willing to do.

Steven Mosher, famous for his decades-long work exposing the evils of China's policies on abortion and their violent treatment of the Catholic Church, adds these important details:

> The ritual [on October 4] was presented as a "tree-planting ceremony" celebrating St. Francis of Assisi's love of nature, but this was just a smokescreen. During the course of the ritual, Pope Francis received and blessed a Pachamama idol and was given a pagan necklace, an offering of soil to Pachamama, and a Tucum ring. The Tucum ring is a black wooden ring made from an Amazonian palm tree. It is often taken to symbolize a commitment to Liberation Theology, a Marxist distortion of the Faith that emphasizes

---

8   Officials at the Synod clearly stated: "We have already repeated several times here that those statues represented life, fertility, mother earth" (see "Prefect for Communication comments on theft of statues from Rome church," *Vatican News*, October 21, 2019). But Catholics do not bow to representations of life, fertility, and mother earth, nor carry them in procession. We carry Our Lord, the Way, the Truth, and the Life, in procession on Corpus Christi; we carry Our Lady—unambiguously depicted as the Virgin Mary, Mother of God—in procession, to honor specifically her and her role in salvation history.

9   See Montagna, "Amazonian woman who led Vatican tree-planting ceremony reveals its pagan significance."

liberation from poverty over liberation from sin.[10] But in shamanistic Pachamama rituals, such as the one conducted in the Vatican gardens, it has a deeper and darker meaning. Here, a gourd rattle and occult spells were used to direct demonic energy to the Tucum, which comes to represent a spiritual marriage with the "earth goddess" (or, in fact, demon, since as Scripture teaches, "all the gods of the nations are demons"). In the Vatican News video recording the ritual, the shamaness can be seen empowering the Tucum with occult spells and her gourd rattle beginning at the 11-minute mark. She then approaches the pope and puts the black ring on what appears to be the ring finger of his left hand at just before the 13-minute mark.[11]

Mosher's report grows darker still when he discusses the significance of the bowl of soil with several plants bearing red flowers that was carried into the closing Synod Mass by a woman in Amazonian tribal dress.[12] It is customary in South America to mix the soil in such an offering bowl with the blood of a sacrificed animal or, in older times, blood of sacrificed children.[13] Mosher continues:

---

10   Internal reference: see Courtney Mares, "Amazon Synod: Ecological ritual performed in Vatican gardens for pope's tree planting ceremony," *Catholic News Agency*, October 4, 2019.

11   See Steven Mosher, "All Catholics must act to atone for Vatican idolatry during Amazon Synod," *LifeSiteNews*, November 8, 2019. Another critic of the event wrote to me in an email: "It is the inclusion of darkness into the light of Christ, and that in a formal way. It is the old occultist view that God needs evil to fulfill himself, that light and darkness belong together, that Lucifer gains back his position that he lost in Paradise."

12   This closing Mass fell on the "Thirtieth Sunday of Ordinary Time" in the calendar of the modern rite, but it was the feast of Christ the King in the traditional Roman calendar.

13   As Paolo Pasqualucci writes in a private correspondence: "By the way, in the past, also human sacrifices were offered to the deities representing vegetation, fertility, etc. (Pachamama for the Inca, Toci for the Aztecs, etc.) because they embodied the terrible forces of nature that had to be continuously placated by the offerings of animal and especially human flesh to their idols. But this aspect of these ancient cults is of course kept completely hidden, nowadays. Archaeologists discovered at Huanchaquito-Las Llamas the skeletons of over 140 children aged 5–14 and 200 young llamas ritually sacrificed to avert hurricanes. The children's faces were smeared with red cinnabar-based pigment before their chests were cut open to remove their hearts."

> Such a Pachamama offering is intended as an act of reparation to the "earth goddess" for the "sins" that human beings have committed against "her" by taking from "her" the fruits of the earth—animal, vegetable, and mineral. In other words, it is the exact pagan imitation of the body and blood of Jesus Christ that are daily offered up on the altars of hundreds of thousands of churches during the Holy Sacrifice of the Mass in reparation for the sins of the world. Such a pagan Pachamama offering has no place in a Catholic church, and yet not only was it brought into St. Peter's at the very head of the procession, but it was placed on the high altar itself.

Placing anything extraneous on the altar like this is forbidden by the *General Instruction of the Roman Missal* that governs the Novus Ordo. Evidently, the Successor of Peter was very intent that the soil offering be placed upon the altar above the tomb of St. Peter.

All of this has nothing to do with so-called "inculturation"; it is *syncretism*, the deliberate blending of pagan and Christian worship,[14] which has been fought against by the Church and her missionaries for twenty centuries. Missionaries do not take a pagan idol and dress it up like the Blessed Virgin Mary; they tend rather to burn and destroy idols, as we frequently read about in the lives of the saints.

At one point a Vatican talking head said that there was "no idolatrous intention" in the prostration before an Amazonian idol. A key author of the Synod's working document, Fr. Paulo Suess, said it doesn't matter if a pagan rite took place, because it would still be the worship of God.[15] There you have it: the apotheosis of the view that externals don't matter! It literally doesn't matter if you are bowing before a pagan statue, so long as your intention is good and vaguely religious. A Catholic blogger, Father Angelo Sotelo, stated: "There's been no comment or assertion from the Amazonians that they intended to adore an idol. Only when people state that they are intending to commit the sin of idolatry should they be accused of that in public." On this, Fr. Brian Harrison comments:

---

14   See Phillip Campbell, "What People Don't Understand About Syncretism," *Unam Sanctam Catholicam*, November 30, 2019.

15   See Maike Hickson, "If 'pagan' rites are part of Amazon synod, they're still 'worship of God': synod working doc writer," *LifeSiteNews*, October 23, 2019.

Is it not obvious that setting the bar *that* high for the sin of idolatry would define this offence against the First Commandment out of existence? (We could thus rid the world of idolaters by the stroke of a pen, just as some seek to reduce sexual abuse of minors overnight by simply lowering the legal age of consent, thereby redefining "minor.") What idolater has ever "*stated* that [he/she was] intending to commit the *sin of idolatry*"?

Brian McCall, editor of *Catholic Family News*, points out:

If the mere lack of idolatrous intent makes bowing before a pagan statue unobjectionable, then thousands of early Christian martyrs died in vain. All they needed to do is go through the actions of offering a pinch of incense to pagan gods but with the intent of saving their lives and *not* with the intent of false worship. Suggesting that to any Christian worth his salt in the first three centuries would have earned laughter, if not something more painful. This is basic moral theology: while a *bad* intention can make a good action morally wrong, the converse is not true: a good intention cannot transform an objectively evil action—in this case, worship offered to an image of a false god—into something objectively good. This is an old Modernist trick they used with dogma. As St. Pius X points out in *Pascendi*, when the Modernists are caught saying something contrary to the Faith, they reply: But I didn't *mean* it in that way.

This brings me to my next point. Let us assume, for the sake of argument, that no idolatry actually took place at the Vatican in October. This hypothesis would not make the slightest difference in the judgment that must be passed on the events. Scripture teaches that we are to avoid not only evil actions, but also the *appearance* of evil—any actions that may reasonably cause scandal to others. St. Paul explains in 1 Corinthians 8 that even if a certain idol is "nothing," we would need to refrain from eating meat sacrificed to it if there was any danger of leading a brother astray. I recently completed a diocesan "safe environment training course," which kept insisting on the principle that we must take into account not only what we do, but the *appearance to others* of what we do, the perceptions that may arise in others' minds. The slogan was: "Intent is not relevant; *impact* is what matters."

Obviously, we can't avoid *all* misinterpretation of our actions and motives. But we *can* avoid things that are likely to look bad to most people or that might, at a given point in time, be especially likely to be perceived as bad. Let me offer an example. If a married man and one of his female colleagues from work have to go on a business trip together, it would be sinful for them to share a hotel room or a hotel suite, even if there were separate beds or bedrooms. People who got wind of it might jump to false conclusions based on a realistic notion of fallen human nature. So, too, with the Pachamama affair. Carrying in procession and bowing down before the image of a naked woman with a bulging belly, prominent breasts, face paint, and a savage expression, an image that does not look in any way Christian, unquestionably gives the *appearance* of idolatry, and when there is a well-known pagan cult of Pachamama in parts of South America, the picture is complete. *It does not matter* whether anyone intended idolatry; it is enough that the appearance was manifestly given, and the perception of it widespread. Sadly, we know that one of the favorite tactics of Protestant preachers in South America is to accuse the Catholic Church of idolatry, and the Amazon Synod has just provided them with a lifetime supply of new ammunition for their proselytizing efforts.[16]

There are other indications we are dealing with syncretistic idolatry. On September 1 in the Cathedral of Lima, Peru, a Mass was opened with the hymn: "Mother Earth, Pachamama, we've come to sing to you." The celebrant of Mass was the Pope Francis-appointed Archbishop Carlos Gustavo Castillo Mattasoglio. The hymn includes these words: "Pachamama, good mother, destroyed,

---

16   Pope Francis and his allies will have to answer before God for many thousands of defections from the Church that will have resulted from the Amazon Synod alone. As Bishop Schneider said: "In front of the eyes of the entire world, and in the presence of the Pope, there were conducted clear acts of religious adoration of symbols and statues of the pagan, indigenous, South-American religions, the so-called 'Pachamama.' Such conduct of the highest Church authority, which does not only not forbid the symbols of pagan religions and their worship, but, rather, even justifies them, causes a great damage for the salvation of souls, because thereby the First Commandment is being undermined and in practical terms is being rescinded." See Dorothy Cummings McLean, "Vatican communications chief denies Amazon Synod guests prostrated themselves before wooden statues," *LifeSiteNews*, October 25, 2019.

without love, with your soil mistreated, and rivers muddy already, there are no more forests, there are cities with cement and solitude. Forgive me, Mother, for my carelessness, Mother Earth, I must convert."[17] Moreover, a group connected with the Italian Bishops' Conference, even before the Synod, published an Incan prayer to Pachamama that reads (in part):

> Pachamama of these places,
> drink and eat this offering at will,
> so that this land may be fruitful.
> Pachamama, good mother
> Be propitious! Be propitious! . . .
> We ask you from you:
> give us everything.
> Be propitious! Be propitious![18]

Bishop Erwin Kräutler, a key figure in the Synod, stated on October 30 that the Pachamama statues were "a form of expression of the indigenous people," which could be "integrated into our [Catholic] liturgy. And if it is for many a divinity, then it is an attack upon the soul of a people to throw them into the Tiber."[19] This is an astonishing pair of statements, for while admitting that many still perceive and treat Pachamama as a divinity, he nonetheless advocates integrating it into the proposed Amazonian rite of Mass as a valuable symbol. I don't know whether to marvel more at the blasphemy or at the sheer intellectual incoherence. Symbols matter; they *mean* something. Symbols are not haphazard things that can be interpreted any which way we want.

Should we be surprised that all this is happening? In a way, yes, and in a way, no. We are reaping the rotten fruit of fifty years of Karl Rahner's theory of the "anonymous Christian," the *nouvelle*

---

17 All this is available in video and audio online: see "Demon Pachamama Adored in Lima Cathedral," published October 30 at Gloria.TV. Fr. Mitch Pacwa, in a widely-viewed program on EWTN, mentions from his firsthand experience in Peru that there are Peruvians in the mountains who venerate and make offerings to Pachamama. See "Scripture and Tradition with Fr. Mitch Pacwa," November 5, 2019, on YouTube.

18 See "For your 'You can't make this up!' file. Italian Bishops publish 'Pachamama Prayer' in booklet," *Fr. Z's Blog*, October 31, 2019.

19 See Maike Hickson, "Key Amazon Synod organizer calls for Pachamama to be 'integrated' into Catholic liturgy," *LifeSiteNews*, November 1, 2019.

théologie's conflation of the natural and supernatural orders, liberation theology's idea of the world as divine revelation and of secular society and human culture as equal or superior to the Church, and many other popular postconciliar errors, including what Fr. Serafino Lanzetta calls "eco-religion."[20] Paolo Pasqualucci notes:

> The *Instrumentum Laboris* for the Amazonian Synod promoted the so-called "teología india" as a means to enrich Catholic theology, starting with the introduction of a dual notion of God, male and female at the same time (God-father and God-mother, where the "mother" would be mother-nature, in a sort of cosmic sense—Pachamama). This dual deity is to be honored by introducing ancient Meso-american and South-american rites into the liturgical rites of the Catholic Church.[21]

This brings me to the second theme of my talk: inculturation.

INCULTURATION[22]

In recent decades, there has been a great confusion about the concept of inculturation. We can see this confusion rising again to the surface in the notorious *Instrumentum Laboris* or working document that was released prior to the Amazon Synod and criticized by bishops and theologians across the world.[23]

Inculturation has been taken by its modern proponents to mean that the Catholic faith and its practice should be changed to conform

---

20   He writes: "It was clear from the beginning that the Amazon Synod would present a new eco-religion linked to the Earth—Mother Earth, a symbol of pronounced femininity and a source of inspiration and prophecy for our time which would give the Church its 'true' face, an 'Amazonian' face. It was a face that was revealed, in fact, in the carved fertility fetish." See Fr. Serafino M. Lanzetta, "Why Catholics honoring Pachamama is a result of apostasy," *LifeSiteNews*, November 1, 2019.

21   In private correspondence.

22   This section incorporates almost verbatim the article "Why Amazon Synod working doc's notion of 'inculturation' is a false approach," *LifeSiteNews*, June 20, 2019.

23   Two translations are available: Edward Pentin's "Unofficial English Translation of Pan-Amazonian Synod Instrumentum Laboris," at Scribd. com, and the Vatican's official version at http://secretariat.synod.va/content/sinodoamazonico/en/documents/pan-amazon-synod--the-working-document-for-the-synod-of-bishops.html.

to an indigenous culture, and should assimilate that culture's own religious beliefs and practices. In other words, Catholicism is seen as raw material and the alien culture as an agent of transformation. The *Instrumentum Laboris* tells us, for example: "In function of a 'healthy decentralization' of the Church (cf. *Evangelii Gaudium* 16), the [Amazonian] communities ask the Episcopal Conferences to adapt the Eucharistic ritual to their cultures" (126d); and, citing Francis again: "We must be bold enough to discover new signs and new symbols, new flesh to embody and communicate the word, and different forms of beauty which are valued in different cultural settings" (IL 124). The document continues with a strangely authoritarian passage, culminating in Marxist utopian language:

> The celebration of the faith *must* be carried out in an inculturated way so that it may be an expression of one's own religious experience and a bond of communion in the celebrating community. An inculturated liturgy will also be a sounding board for the struggles and aspirations of the communities and a transforming impulse towards a "land without evil." (125)

How will such liturgies look? The document tells us:

> It is suggested that the celebrations should be festive, with their own music and dances, using indigenous languages and clothing, in communion with nature and with the community.... We are asked to overcome the rigidity of a discipline that excludes and alienates, and practice a pastoral sensitivity that accompanies and integrates.

The language of "communion with nature and with the community" is naturalistic and horizontal, at loggerheads with the supernatural and vertical character of the revealed religion of Christ and its cultic action: the formal, objective, solemn, public worship known as the sacred liturgy. We note also a radical departure from the unanimous teaching of all the popes, including John Paul II and Benedict XVI, who underlined, with Vatican II, that the traditional music of the Faith, Gregorian chant and polyphony, should be given the foremost place[24]—as indeed the first missionaries

---

24   See "Is 'Contemporary' Church Music a Good Example of Inculturation?," *OnePeterFive*, May 11, 2016.

who planted the Cross on the soil of Central and South America themselves did, training natives to be musicians and composers of superb quality.[25]

The "inculturation" described in the working document and reiterated in the Synod's final document is a false approach, rooted in religious indifferentism, dogmatic relativism, and liturgical experimentalism. Ironically, if acted upon, this approach would not inspire new currents of culture in the Amazon, but merely colonize non-Europeans with the modern European angst of ex-Christian self-loathing—a hatred directed uniquely at Europe's own past and the Church's own traditions.

In reality, it is pagan cultures that are in need of conversion and elevation. Any elements taken from these cultures, duly purged of sin and error, will stand as matter to the "form" imparted by the life-giving Catholic Faith. It is the Church that is the agent, form, and goal in any true inculturation, while the recipient culture is the matter that receives the form from the agent for the sake of salvation in Christ.[26] Many cultures benefited from the *Missale Romanum* in its integrity and fullness. The Japanese and Chinese, to take two important examples, initially welcomed the beauty and majesty of the traditional Latin liturgy as celebrated by the missionaries, seeing in it a sublime expression of a divinely-revealed religion, powerfully conveyed in ceremonies and texts. Hostile cultures have been overcome by the persistent witness of a religion more definite, more coherent, and more beautiful than any of fallen mankind's false religions.

In any case, it is never necessary to seek *as a goal* the taking of elements of a heathen culture and the incorporating of them into

---

25   The recordings of the San Antonio Vocal Arts Ensemble (SAVAE) explore this marvelous repertoire.

26   This, in sharp contrast to the attitude of Brazilian Cardinal Claudio Hummes—the pope's "good friend" who inspired his historic choice of name (see "'I Want A Church Which Is Poor, And For The Poor!'—To the Press, Francis Talks His Name," *Whispers in the Loggia*, March 16, 2013)—who stated: "[The expression] 'new paths for the Church' also means deepening the process of inculturation and interculturality. And for this it is important that the original peoples make the church 'their own' ... thus *the process of inculturation is up to them.*" And again: "Being temporary"—and hence outsiders—the cardinal-designate added that "missionaries must accept a secondary role and give priority to the protagonism proper to the evangelized indigenous community."

the sacred culture. If there are elements worthy of elevation into the sacral domain, this will happen slowly, subtly, with discernment. Running after these elements in a kind of desperate hunt for relevancy is doomed to failure; it is a kind of prostitution to the present age and its malevolent prince. A so-called "Amazonian rite," manufactured by committee and imposed by episcopal fiat, is contrary to the laws of organic liturgical development and the primacy of the Gospel over all cultures to which it arrives. Inculturation as it has been understood and practiced by liturgical revolutionaries is one more ploy of Satan to destabilize and denature the Church of God, to water down her distinctiveness, to poison and pollute her divine *cultus* and human culture.

Things that are *really* true, good, and beautiful in a native people and their civilization will line up in front of the doors of the church and beg admission; they will sue for peace, and beg pardon, and offer themselves like lambs for the sacrifice. Then we may take them up in our arms and make of them vehicles of grace. But not in any other way. As St. Augustine says: "He that believes not, is truly demoniac, blind, and dumb; and he that has not understanding of the faith, nor confesses, nor gives praise to God, is subject to the devil."[27] The Church does not go to the blind and dumb to ask for advice on how she should worship or what she should believe; she does not go to subjects of the devil, in desperate need of baptism, and beg them for a seat at Belial's table. The great Jesuit, Dominican, and Franciscan missionaries brought the Catholic faith in all the splendor of its abiding truth, and by that light, they converted nations and baptized all that was noble and good in their people.

The *Instrumentum Laboris*, however, bluntly sets aside traditional views of evangelization, salvation, and sanctification:

> An insincere stance of openness to the other, as well as a corporatist attitude, which reserves salvation exclusively to one's own creed, is destructive of the same creed. In the parable of the Good Samaritan, Jesus explained this to the inquiring lawyer. Love lived in any religion pleases God. "Through an exchange of gifts, the Spirit can lead us ever more fully into truth and goodness."

---

27 Cited by St. Thomas Aquinas, *Catena aurea* on Matthew 12:24.

In this remarkable text, Christians are said to be "insincere" if they are not so "open to the other" that they will admit that their Christianity is lacking some truth or goodness that the non-Christians can offer instead. Moreover, the *de fide* dogma *extra ecclesiam nulla salus,* outside the Church there is no salvation, is dismissed as a "corporatist attitude" destructive of one's own creed, in spite of the fact that no one can be saved who does not belong to the Church and who does not confess, either explicitly or implicitly, that salvation is in Jesus Christ alone. The document then fatuously asserts that "love lived in any religion pleases God," although the New Testament makes it clear that only the love poured into our hearts by the Holy Spirit, which we call *charity,* is the love of God that pleases Him.

Perhaps the most startling error in the *Instrumentum Laboris* and in the Synod discussions is the idea of the *world* as a more complete divine revelation than that found in the *lex orandi* and *lex credendi* of Christianity:

> In the Amazon, life is inserted into, linked with, and integrated in territory. This vital and nourishing physical space provides the possibility, sustenance, and limit of life. Furthermore, we can say that the Amazon—or another indigenous or communal territory—is not only an *ubi* or a where (a geographical space), but also a *quid* or a what, a place of meaning for faith or the experience of God in history. Thus territory is a theological place where faith is lived, and also *a particular source of God's revelation: epiphanic places* where the reserve of life and wisdom for the planet is manifest, a life and wisdom that speaks of God. In the Amazon, the "caresses of God" become manifest and *become incarnate in history* (cf. LS 84, "Soil, water, mountains: everything is, as it were, a caress of God").[28]

In an interview with Ross Douthat published on November 9, Raymond Cardinal Burke observes:

> What was proposed in the working document...is an apostasy from the Catholic faith. A denial of the unicity and universality of the redemptive incarnation of our Lord Jesus' saving work.... I mean the idea that Jesus' grace is one element in the cosmos—but it's the cosmos,

---

28   *Instrumentum Laboris* 19.

the world, that is the ultimate revelation. And therefore, even in going to a region like the pan-Amazon region, you wouldn't be concerned to preach the gospel because you recognize there already the revelation of God. This is a falling away from the Christian faith.[29]

I view the Synod as representing the repudiation of Pope Benedict XVI's *Regensburg Address*, in which he explained why the program of "dehellenization" is contrary to the wisdom and Providence of God.[30] The call for dehellenization is based on the claim that a "pure" original form of Christianity was compromised or even perverted by the intertwining of Greek culture and philosophical thought with the original *kerygma* or proclamation of the Good News. The program can be traced back to the Protestant Reformers of the sixteenth century who argued that after the conversion of the Emperor Constantine, Christianity, which was intended to be a domestic, familial religion of breaking bread and giving thanks for the holiness of everyday life, was distorted into an imperial, sacerdotal, hierarchical, patriarchal, dogmatic religion that eventually exalted asceticism, monasticism, and strict sexual morality.

The dehellenizers want to remove Christianity from its Jewish, Greek, Roman, and European cultural matrix and to "Africanize" or "Asianize" or "Amazonify" it. They want to make it a vehicle for the divine self-expression inherent in every people and culture, which of course is not what anyone ever thought the Christian faith was or was supposed to be. Our religion comes to us from God decisively intervening in human history and giving us the message and means of salvation, to the Author of which every culture, like every individual, must bend the knee in a process of conversion. It is man who must submit to the truth from on high—submit in faith, in baptism, in ecclesial order, in liturgy. It is not the *truth* that must submit to man and reflect his inner aspirations or feelings or ideas. This latter view was espoused by the Modernists of the nineteenth and early twentieth centuries, and by their latter-day disciples, including Pope Francis. We should not be surprised that

29 "Cardinal Burke: 'I'm Called the Enemy of the Pope, Which I Am Not,'" *New York Times*, November 9, 2019.
30 Many other documents of the Magisterium have also opposed versions of this program, e.g., John Paul II in his encyclical *Fides et Ratio* and Paul VI in his encyclical *Mysterium Fidei*.

he has espoused so many heresies, dozens of them: for Modernism itself was defined by St. Pius X as "the synthesis of all heresies."[31]

Thus we can see the Amazon Synod as a moment of accelerated dechristianization, an inversion and perversion of the Catholic religion.

CLERICAL CELIBACY

Also much in the news for many months has been the subtle attack of the Modernists against the ancient discipline of clerical celibacy. It is important to understand that this attack has nothing to do with a shortage of clergy. There has *always* been a shortage of clergy in missionary territories, but no one prior to our decadent age has ever thought that abolishing celibacy was the right solution. Rather, the Church has obeyed Christ by redoubling her prayers to the Lord of the harvest, asking Him to send more workers into the vineyard, and by purifying herself of corruption so that she may be found worthy of having her prayers answered.

We also know, as Bishop Athanasius Schneider says in his outstanding book *Christus Vincit*, that there have been heroic Christians in all ages who have persevered in spite of sacramental deprivation, because they had been taught the Faith and they remained true to it. He cites especially the example of Japanese Catholics who held on to the orthodox faith for more than 200 years without clergy or recourse to any sacraments besides baptism. When French missionaries reestablished contact with these Christians, they "were amazed to find that they knew the Apostles' Creed and many prayers, including the Our Father, the Hail Mary and the [other prayers of the] rosary, in both Japanese and Latin."[32] Frankly, this is a better track record than the local churches in almost any country after the Second Vatican Council, in spite of a comparative abundance of bishops and priests. So, in order to understand the attack against mandatory celibacy, we must look deeper than the excuses of its proponents.

---

31   The *Instrumentum Laboris* is a textbook example of Modernism, and another low-water mark in an already disgraced pontificate. For further commentary, see Roberto de Mattei, "The Amazonian Church of Pope Francis," *Rorate Caeli*, June 20, 2019, and Meloni, "Amazon Synod's Long Game."
32   See Roy Peachey, "Saints, authors and prime ministers: The dramatic story of Japanese Catholicism," *Catholic Herald* (UK), November 14, 2019.

The devil hates priestly celibacy because, like consecrated virginity, it is a charism and way of life *most intrinsically opposed* to the pride that brought about Lucifer's fall. The devil desired to receive beatitude as a reward for his own natural greatness, not as a pure gift of grace undeserved by any creature. He desired to be the "firstborn son" who received the homage of inferior creation—perhaps even to be a mediator between the human race and its Creator. When God revealed that He would enter into friendship with rational animals (so vastly inferior to the angels) and grant them beatitude; that his own Word would become flesh; that this Word-made-flesh would raise up the human race by suffering and dying for it—Lucifer would have none of it. His love of self turned inward. In his pride, he said: *Non serviam*, I will not serve God, I will not serve such a God, I will not serve such a plan. Lucifer rejected the supernatural in favor of the natural.

The man or woman who chooses virginity or celibacy for the kingdom of God is doing the opposite: setting aside the natural in favor of the supernatural. The virgin or celibate is relinquishing that which is most natural to the human being—to live in partnership with another of the opposite sex, finding in this community a friendship and fruitfulness intended for man from the beginning, written into his very bodily nature. Just as nothing is more natural to man than marriage, nothing is more suitable to expressing the primacy of God over creation than relinquishing it for His sake, in a supreme testimony to the sufficiency of His love, a offering of one's entire self to Him in love. The life of a celibate is a holocaust in imitation of Jesus Christ, the Lamb of God, who gave all of Himself to His bride, the Church. As the Word became flesh for our sakes, the consecrated soul makes of his or her own flesh a living word of total consent and surrender to God. The celibate is the supreme human sign of God's radically self-emptying redemptive love—and thus the complete antithesis of Lucifer's self-absorption.

Now, as the saints pray without ceasing and generate prayer in others, so the devil, who is a liar and the father of lies (Jn. 8:44), lies without ceasing, and fathers ever more lies in his victims. He persuades people to think that celibacy or virginity is a denigration of marriage, that those who promote this higher state and calling are casting aspersions on the order of creation, the goodness of nature, the beauty of married love. He presents himself, at times, as a *defender* of these things, but only in a distorted way, as Martin Luther was. The devil wants the exclusive commitment of priests and religious to the Lord and His people to be diluted or abandoned, so that, stripped of the clothing of grace, they can follow him to the emptiness and frustration of eternally denuded nature. Most of all, he sows the lie that man cannot be fulfilled apart from sexual experience and expression—that humans are maimed and impoverished if they do not enjoy intimate conjunction with another.

How subtle the strategy of Satan is! The ultimate poverty for man is, in reality, *to live without God,* to live without knowledge of or desire for eternal communion with Him in heaven. Since the priesthood and the religious life are both directly ordered to living out and proclaiming the reality and primacy of the Kingdom of Heaven, it is *crucial* for the well-being of mankind that priests and religious be clear signs of our ultimate destiny—for in heaven, as Our Lord teaches, there is neither marrying nor giving in marriage. The one all-sufficient marriage in heaven is the perfect union of Christ and His Church.

The devil's strategy is multifaceted. He works to undermine the covenant of marriage, which is the sacramental sign of the indissoluble, fruitful union of Christ and His Church. The contemporary war against marriage is also, indeed more deeply, a war against the nuptial union of Christ and the Church—a vain but frenzied effort to erase from the minds of men any memory of this glorious union consummated on the Cross. Satan works to undermine the Most Holy Eucharist, which is the sign and cause of our communion with Christ, our highest sharing in His self-oblation on the Cross. He works to undermine the priesthood and religious life, which exemplify and bring about in this world the ordering of all creation, through Christ, to the Father, who is the beginning and end of all things. The common element in all of these attacks is the devil's fury that anyone or anything *natural* should ever be subordinated to that which is *supernatural*—that a faithful, radical self-sacrifice should be the path of salvation and blessedness.

False teachings on marriage and the "relaxation" of the required discipline of clerical celibacy are two flanks of a single army laying siege to the City of God on earth. Any word, any action against the sanctity of marriage, the good of the family, or the exalted vocations of clerical and religious life finds its origin in the General of this army, whom St. Ignatius of Loyola called "the Enemy of mankind."

I wish now to confront head-on the claim that both Modernists and Eastern Christians will often make (although for quite different reasons), namely, that clerical celibacy is "just a disciplinary matter," something that depends only on Church authority and could be easily changed. This is not true. Celibacy is one of the crown jewels of Latin Christianity; the roots of it are found in many passages of the New Testament and confirmed by abundant testimonies from the Church Fathers.

Marriage is not *absolutely* incompatible with holy orders, since the power of order is a supernatural gift that may be conferred on any apt man by the laying on of hands. However, marriage is *relatively* incompatible with holy orders, which explains why from apostolic times on, there is a steady effort to enforce perpetual continence among the clergy. The Christian East bears witness to this connection in three ways: first, they hold monastic or consecrated life as the highest vocation; second, bishops may be chosen only from celibates; and third, even married clergy must abstain from marital relations the day before the offering of the Divine Liturgy, which is one of the reasons why a daily Eucharistic liturgy is rare in the East outside of monasteries or cathedrals.

In truth, celibacy is *profoundly fitting* to the clerical state; and fittingness, in the Catholic tradition, is often the highest and strongest argument for what we believe and what we do. For example, we say that it was *fitting* for the Son of God to empty Himself of the radiance of glory and become a lowly man in the likeness of sinful human flesh; we say that it was *fitting* for Him to die upon the Cross in atonement for our sins; we say that it was *fitting* for Christ to found a visible Church with visible and efficacious signs of grace. For these sublime truths, there are no strictly *necessary* arguments; there are only arguments from how beautiful it is that God should be this way or act this way. In short, the greatest mysteries of our Faith are said to be true because we can see that they harmonize with who God is and how He works. It is no different with celibacy: it is fitting that the one who follows the virginal Christ who gave His entire life as a pleasing offering to God should imitate Him in exactly this way.

The Amazon Synod's recommendation, therefore, strikes at the Catholic Church's *imitatio Christi*, her adherence to biblical teaching and patristic witness, and her fidelity to a consistent Magisterium from the earliest times until now. This novelty of the Synod must be rejected without qualification.

MINISTRIES FOR WOMEN

All traditional Eucharistic liturgies, whether of the Christian East or of the Christian West, are hierarchically structured: the roles of bishop, priest, deacon, subdeacon, lector, acolyte, and so forth are clearly delineated. Only men serve in these roles, since they are all modes of exercising Christ's royal priesthood in the flesh.[33] The faithful in attendance also have their role, which is not to be confused with the roles of any of the ministers. Moreover, all traditional liturgies are designed for and make expressive use of buildings in which the sanctuary, representing the Holy of Holies and the Church Triumphant, is clearly separated from the nave, representing this world and the Church Militant. Only certain individuals, correctly vested, may enter into the sanctuary during the liturgy. Christian theology is thus articulated in the architecture itself, especially through the use of barriers, doors, and images of saints.

There are scattered indications throughout Church history of an office that was known as "deaconess." Sometimes this term meant a deacon's wife; at other times, it means widows who received a special blessing for their pastoral work. They are mentioned in Origen, Clement of Alexandria, and John Chrysostom, among others. Their purpose was to assist with the pastoral care of women: women being baptized by full immersion; uncatechized women needing instruction or sick women needing visitation. They apparently served at times as ushers. In the Western church, however, they became less and less needed as baptism moved away from full immersion and society became more generally Christian. They appear less and less in historical records until they vanish from sight around the start of the second millennium.

What *is* clear is that deaconesses never exercised a properly liturgical ministry—one involved with the administration of the

33 That is, Christ is a priest and a servant not in His divinity, but according to His humanity.

sacraments, especially the offering of the Holy Sacrifice of the Mass. Thus, to talk today of "deacons" and "deaconesses" in the same breath is simply to equivocate, like speaking of the canons of a cathedral and the Roman Canon. The word in Greek simply means "servant," and surely, both men and women were *serving* in various capacities. But just as the practice of giving communion in the hand died out over a thousand years ago, so did the practice of employing deaconesses; and it is one more example of false antiquarianism to try to bring them back in a totally different context.

It is unquestionably the introduction of the Novus Ordo, which was itself a product of false antiquarianism, that has created the current push for women's liturgical ministries.[34] The new rite of Mass is horizontal and democratic in its manner of practice: the hierarchical offices are either canceled out or confused, the distinction between clergy and laity is blurred, the roles of men and women are mingled in a way only imaginable after the Sexual Revolution, and instead of the verticality of simultaneous action directed to God, there is linear, modular, sequential liturgy in service of audience-oriented rationalism. The symbolism of separation and articulation inside the church building is not respected by the rite or its rubrics. In such an environment, there is no convincing reason to exclude women from ministries, because the entire concept of liturgy has been disconnected from tradition, homogenized, and harnessed to utilitarian and social functions, not symbolic and theological ones.

There are some functions for which any Catholic can substitute in a pinch, such as making responses from the pews at Mass if a proper acolyte or a vested male altar server is not present. But we can say with historical and theological certainty that there are certain offices that can be conferred upon and exercised by men alone. The diaconate that is part of Holy Orders is one such office, as the Magisterium has always held—a teaching supported by a mountain of scholarship and two independent Vatican studies.

It is surely not unreasonable to think that the demons tacitly invoked throughout the Synod, before it, and after it were

---

34 For the current confusion, we have Paul VI and John Paul II to blame, since the former abolished the minor orders and the latter permitted female altar servers. For more discussion of all the points taken up in this section, see my book *Ministers of Christ.*

assiduously at work to push forward the ecclesiastical Sexual Revolution consisting in the ever-greater conflation or denial of the distinctive roles of men and women in the Church and the denigration of the gift of perpetual continence. In this way the Vatican regime sets itself against both creation at the beginning, represented by the procreative duality of sexes, and re-creation in Christ, represented by the Virgin Birth and the virginal Eternal High Priest.

CONCLUSION

Looking back over this disastrous Amazon Synod, from which we will be suffering radioactive fallout for many years, the question arises: What can we do in these circumstances? What are we supposed to do? The answer is simply this: we must counteract the apostasy in the Church by adoring the one true God, Father, Son, and Holy Ghost, as devoutly and fervently as we can; we must hold fast to the one and only Catholic Faith received from tradition, and never abandon it under any pressures or threats whatsoever. We should increase our Mass attendance and rosaries; renew our consecration to the Blessed Virgin Mary; do penance and make reparation, especially by fasting and going to Eucharistic Adoration. When the apostles could not cast out a certain demon, the Lord said to them: "This kind does not come out except by prayer and fasting" (Mt. 17:21). Are we not confronting the work of demons—no longer acting in secret, but openly?

We have to approach the state of the Church today with *Christian realism*. This is a realism that recognizes the way things really are, judging from obvious signs of the times.

The Gospel of John says of Judas: "He therefore having received the morsel, went out immediately. And it was night" (Jn. 13:30). Not long after, Our Lord said to His enemies in the Garden of Gethsemane: "But this is your hour, and the power of darkness" (Lk. 22:53). For us, it is night; it is the hour of the Judases, the high priests, scribes, and soldiers of the temple; the power of darkness reigns.

But *Christian* realism is also supernatural realism, one that is shot through with hope and confidence. We recognize that God Himself has permitted this darkness, since nothing escapes His will, and that He is and always will be in charge, as Christ while sleeping in the boat remained in charge of the storm. When God permits evil, He does so in order to raise up saints and to expose the works of darkness for their ugliness. As long as any convenient compromise between the Church and the world remains hidden, it endures; but when the ugliness of this compromise becomes visible, then its doom is upon it. Every period of crisis in the history of the Church has yielded to a subsequent period of peace and light, thanks to the trustful prayers and strenuous efforts of the saints. Such periods of peace and light are and will always be relative and temporary in this vale of tears; "we have here no abiding city but we seek one that is to come" (Heb. 13:14).

Fr. Zuhlsdorf issued this rousing call to arms:

> We are in *The Fight of Our Lives....* *[B]attle isn't pretty.* Just as a soldier in the state of grace who does his duty knows that even in battle he is in the "safest" place he can be, so too we know that we members of the Church in the state of grace are in the safest place we could be, even though corruption and infidelity and disgusting things are going on at every level. Since the Church is of *divine* origin, there is no place else we should ever want to be. We can be sad sometimes at the results of the battle. We can be afraid sometimes in the midst of the battle. But let us not waiver in our trust in Christ's promises. Heaven is our reward, not worldly security, even in the Church. The Lord is my strength and shield and my trusting heart exults in Him and with song I will give Him thanks even for the terrible battle it falls to me to fight...
>
> Moreover, Rome is only Rome. The "Vatican" is only the Vatican. Curial structures are not of divine origin. Christ promised nothing to the Roman Curia. He made no guarantees that the Faith would be preserved in the Curia. "Put not your trust in princes: In the children of men, in whom there is no salvation." Stick to the true and the proven. Stick to *traditional* sources for the review of the content of your Catholic Faith. Remember too that the content of your Faith is not just stuff to be read and memorized, but is also a Person with whom you have a relationship. Stick to Christ. Use the sacraments well. Review your own state in life and, having determined

your duties and obligations, carry them out faithfully and with singularity of purpose.[35]

Supernatural realism also recognizes that the Church on earth is only the outer shell, so to speak, of the Mystical Body of Christ. Understandably, we are caught up in what is happening around us on earth, but we must never forget that the Church triumphant in heaven is far greater than the Church militant on earth. It is populated with countless angels and with saints who have passed beyond the trials of this world to an eternal blessedness that can never be lost. The heavenly liturgy is indescribably glorious and beautiful, the friendships of the saints overflowing with joy. Nothing and no one can touch this Kingdom of God, this kingdom of unending peace and never-darkening light, where Christ the King reigns as absolute monarch over perfectly free and willing subjects.

This is the Catholic Church, first and foremost. We on earth are united to it by our baptism, and if we remain faithful, we will find ourselves there after death, no matter *what* happens in this messy world. To me, this is a great consolation, because it helps me to think twice before I say something like: "the Church is crumbling before our eyes" or "the Church is being destroyed." No. Parts of the Church on earth are apostatizing, because those who still live in this mortal life can change for the worse; but the Church of Christ in its now-existing perfection is immortal, spotless, beyond the reach of sin or the devil—and we are members of that same Church, sustained by its prayers, enveloped in its grace, drawn onward by its glory. The gates of hell cannot prevail.

---

35   See "Wherein Fr. Z maps weird things, connects dots, rants a lot, and offers an ACTION ITEM!," *Fr. Z's Blog*, November 9, 2019.

49

Remembering the Pope
Who Suppressed the Jesuits
and Hosted Mozart

LifeSiteNews
DECEMBER 12, 2019

A S I'VE HAD OCCASION TO POINT OUT before,[1] we can learn a great deal by going back to earlier papal encyclicals—expressions, all of them, of the ordinary Magisterium of the Church—and seeing how these successors of Peter, conscious of the spiritual mission they had received, taught "as having authority," and not like scribes or Pharisees (cf. Mt. 7:29), whose latter-day imitators strain at plastics and climate change while neglecting larger matters of justice.

To the charge that looking back to the teaching of earlier popes and using their clearer words to call into question the vacillations and venoms of today is somehow to set up a fantasy Church of the past against the actual Church of the present shows a fundamental misunderstanding of the way Catholicism works. As a constitutive element of their religion, Catholics maintain that the consistent teaching of the popes over the centuries is, in and of itself, a testimony to the correct understanding of Divine Revelation, and that this understanding can be recognized and grasped by men of good will. The latest pope is therefore not the sole arbiter of the content of the Christian faith or possessed of a power to dismiss or reinvent the entire Magisterium of his papal predecessors, but rather bound to follow in the same doctrine, the same meaning, the same intention. In other words, he is merely a *successor* of a line of popes, not *superior* to this line in its entirety, and that means the value of his teaching depends on its being in harmony with this collective witness. Put simply: Each later pope stands on the shoulders of earlier popes; were he not to do so, he would exclude himself from their company as a renegade.

---

1   See chapter 42.

Giovanni Vincenzo Antonio Ganganelli (1705–1774) became pope in May of 1769 and took the name Clement XIV. Two historical facts, one great in its implications, the other small and charming, are associated with his reign.

In a move universally condemned by subsequent historians of the papacy, he suppressed the Society of Jesus in 1773, which, all the same, continued to exist in Prussia and Russia and would eventually be restored in 1814 by Pope Pius VII. More recent commentators have wryly remarked that the suppression came approximately two centuries too early; if only this papal act had waited for the postconciliar period, it might have found a *theological* justification!

In 1770, Pope Clement hosted the 14-year-old child prodigy Wolfgang Amadeus Mozart and his father Leopold. In his visit to Rome, Wolfgang had heard a performance of Allegri's *Miserere*, the music of which was, at that time, forbidden to be possessed by anyone outside the Sistine Chapel. Undeterred, the young composer wrote out the work in its entirety after having heard it once and, instead of receiving a rebuke, was rewarded by Clement with the Order of the Golden Spur.

In any case, Clement XIV is on my mind because today marks the 250th anniversary of his inaugural encyclical *Cum Summi*, published December 12, 1769. We should pay heed to the timeless wisdom contained in his words, which in many ways come across as fresher and more pertinent to our current situation than any of the documents published so far by the current incumbent of the See of Peter. Nor should we be surprised at this: for the wisdom that guides true Christians is always timely, whereas the fashionable causes *du jour* bear the disposable imprint of their Zeitgeist.

Addressing first his brother bishops, he reminds them of their primary duties, and the nature of the challenges facing the Church in the modern world:

> Together we must all labor for the health and safety of the church, so that, without blemish or strain, it may flourish. With God's help we can accomplish this if each of you is enkindled by as strong a zeal for his flock as possible and if your one concern be to remove from his flock all contagion of evil and pitfalls of error and to strengthen it diligently with all the aids of sound doctrine and holiness.

If ever those in charge of the Lord's vineyard should be concerned about the salvation of souls, they must be so in this age especially. For many ideas aimed at weakening religion arise almost daily. When men are enticed by novelty and led on by an eagerness for alien knowledge, they come together more eagerly for this very purpose and more willingly embrace it. Wherefore, We lament that the destruction of souls is propagated more widely each day. Accordingly, you must work all the harder and exercise diligence and authority to repel this audacity and insanity which stalks even divine and most holy matters. Be confident that you will accomplish this by the simplicity of sound doctrine and by the Word of God which penetrates more than any two-edged sword.

You will easily be able to contain the attack of enemies and blunt their weapons when in all your sermons you preach and present Jesus Christ crucified. By His own laws and institutions He founded and reenforced this holy city which is His Church. To it he entrusted, as it were, the deposit of faith in Him to be preserved piously and without contamination. He wished it to be the bulwark of His teaching and truth against which the gates of hell would never prevail. We, therefore, the overseers and guardians of this holy city, must preserve the magnificent heritage of Our laws and faith which has been passed down intact to Us; We must transmit it pure and sound to our successors. If We direct all our actions to this norm found in Sacred Scripture and, moreover, cling to the footsteps of our ancestors, We will be best equipped to avoid whatever could weaken and destroy the faith of the Christian people and loosen in any way the unity of the Church. Whatever pertains to religious worship, to moral training, to right living can be found in the twofold instrument of Scripture and Tradition. From this source we learn the depth of mysteries and the duties of piety, honesty, justice, and humanity.

"We, the overseers and guardians of this holy city, must preserve the magnificent heritage of Our laws and faith which has been passed down intact to Us; We must transmit it pure and sound to our successors." Could any more perfect expression be found of the Catholic's commitment to sound doctrine and a holy life, in adherence to received tradition?

Living in the heyday of the Enlightenment and its increasingly violent attacks against the Catholic Church and the *ancien régime*— attacks that would coalesce and burst forth into violence in the French Revolution only twenty years later—Pope Clement goes on to remind the bishops of the inherent connection between right religion and good civil order. Note that the latter category includes the right to execute criminals:

> From no other source than these laws of true religion do we recognize more clearly the established rights of citizens and society. Accordingly, no one has ever attacked the divine sanctions of Christ without likewise disturbing public tranquility, without lessening obedience owed to rulers, and without rendering everything unsafe and uncertain. For there is a strong bond between divine and human rights; therefore those who realize that rulers are protected by the authority of the Christian law obey them, venerate their authority, and protect and cherish their dignity.... They are ministers of God and not without reason do they carry the sword as vindicators in wrath on him who does wrong; moreover they are beloved sons and patrons of the Church, whose part it is to cherish it like a parent and protect its interest and rights.

In his concluding remarks, Pope Clement XIV, having urged the bishops to seek holiness, charity, and humility in all things in imitation of Christ, reminds them of the force of their example:

> If once you are inflamed with this desire, then this same ardor will spread among all your people. Indeed the force and authority of the pastor for moving the spirits of his flock is truly marvelous. For when they recognize that all his thoughts and actions are conformed to this model of true virtue, when they see in him nothing harsh, nothing arrogant, and nothing exalted, but rather charity, meekness, and humility, then truly they will feel themselves drawn most keenly to imitate these qualities. Moreover, when they see him paying no attention to private gain, instead serving the advantage of everyone else, coming to the aid of the needy with his resources, of the afflicted with his

consolation, of the ignorant with his teaching, of all men with his service, advice, and piety, even preferring their salvation to his life, they will listen to his voice as he teaches, exhorts, implores, and even blames and reproves in a most loving manner. For if pastors are hampered by private interests and prefer worldly things to heavenly, how can they rouse others to love of God and mutual kindness? If they seek after wealth, pleasure, honors, how can they rouse others to the contempt of human things? If they are puffed up with pride and arrogance, how can they rouse others to meekness and humility?

Therefore, since you have taken upon yourselves the office of instructing souls in the knowledge of Jesus Christ, you must adhere to his holiness, innocence, and gentleness. Consider, too, that your proper business is to instruct the people in this fashion, and that by carrying out this task correctly will come all your praise and good fortune, from neglecting it, your calamity and turpitude. Therefore, seek only those riches that come from gaining souls for Christ. Seek only that glory which comes from promoting divine worship, from adding to the beauty of the house of God, and from extirpating vice and promoting virtue.

What a stirring program is here placed before the eyes of the bishops! His proper business is to instruct the people in sound doctrine, true piety, and upright morals. He must put worldly affairs and standards aside; immortal souls are the wealth he seeks, and for their benefit he prioritizes divine worship, "adding to the beauty of the house of God." Oh, and they should uproot vices (sodomy may not be mentioned expressly, but, *pace* James Martin, S. J., it certainly qualifies as one of the most serious vices, according to the teaching of St. Paul, who enjoys greater authority than any Jesuit). The contrast between this "pastoral plan," announced by Christ Jesus in His plenary sessions with the apostles, and the one that bishops have tended to adopt after the Second Vatican Council leaves one positively speechless. Could anyone refute the truth of Clement's encyclical? From 250 years ago, his voice returns to us with redoubled urgency.

50

Pope Francis's Hermeneutic of Anti-Continuity

The Remnant

DECEMBER 22, 2019

POPE FRANCIS'S CHRISTMAS ADDRESS OF December 21—the traditional feast of the doubting apostle Thomas and, this year, the Ember Saturday of Advent—is exactly the antithesis of the famous "hermeneutic of continuity" address delivered by Pope Benedict XVI on December 22, 2005. In that speech, Ratzinger (successfully or unsuccessfully) tried to reconnect the postconciliar experiment with the 3,000-year history of the Church as God's Israel.

Francis is saying, in effect: "Nope, not gonna happen. In fact, we need to ramp up the modernization efforts and leave behind that stale, rigid old past. If we want to keep Christianity, we have to change everything."

After a groanworthy citation of the Jesuits' favorite out-of-context line from Cardinal Newman—"here below, to live is to change, and to be perfect is to have changed often"—Francis continues:

> The history of God's people—the history of the Church— has always been marked by new beginnings, displace- ments and changes. This journey, of course, is not just geographical, but above all symbolic: it is a summons to discover the movement of the heart, which, paradoxically, has to set out in order to remain, to change in order to be faithful.... All of this has particular importance for our time, because what we are experiencing is not simply an epoch of changes, but an epochal change. We find ourselves living at a time when change is no longer linear, but epochal. It entails decisions that rapidly transform our ways of living, of relating to one another, of communicating and thinking, of how different generations relate to one another and how we understand and experience faith and science. Often we approach change as if were a matter

216

of simply putting on new clothes, but remaining exactly as we were before. I think of the enigmatic expression found in a famous Italian novel: "If we want everything to stay the same, then everything has to change" (*The Leopard* by Giuseppe Tomasi di Lampedusa).

He insists that he is not talking about incidental or accidental change:

> Seen in this light, change takes on a very different aspect: from something marginal, incidental or merely external, it would become something more human and more Christian. Change would still take place, but beginning with man as its center: an anthropological conversion.

In view of the rhetoric of transhumanism and LGBTQ activism, to talk about an "anthropological conversion" is pretty scary stuff. What else could it mean but a change in how we understand man himself, and how we preach and minister to him? In such words we see how faithfully Francis is following the agenda of the revolutionary faction at Vatican II who considered modernity a period unique in history, cut off from the past and requiring for Modern Man a new liturgy, a new catechesis, a new theology—in short, a new Church.

As I tried to wrap my mind around this address, I came to the conclusion that the key to understanding Francis is to see that he confuses the traditional concepts of spiritual oldness (sinfulness) and newness (renewal by the grace of Christ) with, respectively, tradition and change, and therefore with rigidity and flexibility, legalism and life in the Spirit. So while the Church sees in Christ the New Adam and prays at Christmas to be renewed by His newness so that the oldness of sin may be purged from us—a process of lifelong conversion for which the Church's very tradition, developed under the guidance of Divine Providence, offers powerful assistance—Francis instead sees in *tradition* the Old Adam and the Pharisee, and in *evolutionary creativity* the New Adam and the man of the Gospel.

The pope continues:

> Appealing to memory is not the same as being anchored in self-preservation, but instead to evoke the life and vitality of an ongoing process. Memory is not static, but

dynamic. By its very nature, it implies movement. Nor
is tradition static; it too is dynamic, as that great man
[Gustav Mahler] used to say: tradition is the guarantee
of the future and not a container of ashes.

Note how he misquotes Mahler, who actually said something
deeper and more beautiful: "Tradition is not the worship of ashes,
but the preservation of fire." That is, Mahler sees the content of
tradition as a powerful fire to be preserved, while Francis sees it
as a prop for future novelty.

Having stated that modern people are no longer Christian, he
cries out:

> In big cities, we need other "maps," other paradigms, which
> can help us reposition our ways of thinking and our atti-
> tudes. Brothers and sisters, Christendom no longer exists!

Yes, Your Holiness: many believing Catholics would agree that
we need a paradigm shift, to get us away from the worn-out strategy of the past five decades since the Council, which has failed
mightily in keeping the Catholic world Catholic. We might try—I
know it's a daring concept—restoring our tradition! Experiments
have shown that it attracts the youth, you know. We also recognize
that Christendom has fallen—but those who are Catholic should
aim to rebuild it, rather than accepting its demise in the nihilistic
spirit of a *fait accompli*. After all, Christendom is nothing but the
Faith fully lived out, fully incarnated in culture.

> Humanity, then, is the key for interpreting the reform.
> Humanity calls and challenges us; in a word, it summons
> us to go forth and not fear change.

This is classic Montini language from the 1960s and 1970s: taking
humanity generically as the point of reference, rather than the
God-Man Jesus Christ and His revelation.

> Linked to this difficult historical process there is always
> the temptation to fall back on the past (also by employing
> new formulations), because it is more reassuring, familiar,
> and, to be sure, less conflictual. This too is part of the
> process and risk of setting in motion significant changes.
> Here, there is a need to be wary of the temptation to
> rigidity. A rigidity born of the fear of change, which ends

up erecting fences and obstacles on the terrain of the common good, turning it into a minefield of incomprehension and hatred. Let us always remember that behind every form of rigidity lies some kind of imbalance. Rigidity and imbalance feed one another in a vicious circle. And today this temptation to rigidity has become very real.

With the foregoing we have arrived at vintage Bergoglio, a text where his fingerprints are most apparent. As any student of Church history knows, reform movements in the Church have *always* looked to the past for inspiration and models. Rejuvenation has come from rediscovering buried treasures or revitalizing better practices than the ones to which our present-day mediocrity has reduced us. But not for this pope: looking to our heritage and our saints is, for him, a sign of fear and hatred.

I'm reading a very interesting manuscript now by a British philosopher, and this footnote really made me pause:

> It is significant that effectively the same dispute about the origin of the Word occurs in both Muslim and in Christian history: on the one hand, whether the Koran is merely *created* or exists eternally as an *uncreated* expression of what God requires of us, and on the other, whether the Son is truly of God's substance or only the first (perhaps) of all created things. In both spheres, the notion that it was "created" was preferred by rulers, as it suggested both that the Word as it had been previously declared might turn out to be obsolete, and—by analogy—that their own arbitrary commands were valid. [1]

Think about this for a moment. Both Christian and Muslim rulers wanted the divine Word (however differently they understood it) to be something created, so that it could be improved on or surpassed or suppressed by their own dictates. Believers, on the other hand, confessed the divinity of the Word, its immutability, and its normativity that stood above every ruler.

I'm not a big interreligious dialogue kind of guy, but this insight into history has more than a little relevance to Pope Francis. His not-really-denied comments to Scalfari, his semi-Arian

---

1   Stephen R. L. Clark, *Can We Believe in People? Human Significance in an Interconnected Cosmos* (Brooklyn, NY: Angelico Press, 2020), 194, n8.

meanderings in homilies, his willingness to contradict the teaching of the New Testament on adultery and capital punishment (et cetera), all indicate that he regards the Word as a creature, over which, in theory, the papacy has authority. The Christmas address today provides further scaffolding: change is potentially limitless, because there is nothing immutable ("rigid") in Christianity that cannot be changed.

Could anyone need more evidence that the Church is being ruled by someone who is barely, or not at all, Catholic? He wouldn't even make a good Muslim. At the end of the address, the pope, no longer hiding his cards, quotes one of the arch-progressives of the era:

> Cardinal Martini, in his last interview, a few days before his death, said something that should make us think: "The Church is two hundred years behind the times. Why is she not shaken up? Are we afraid? Fear, instead of courage?"

How interesting, Your Eminence and Your Holiness. Two hundred years prior to Martini's death in 2012 was 1812, a time we can still readily associate with the French Revolution and its long aftermath that cast a stygian shadow over Europe and the world. It was the heyday of Enlightenment rationalism and liberalism, soon to yield to the age of scientific positivism and materialism. If the Church were really and truly behind *these* times, it would be a mark of divine blessing and protection. If the Church ever "catches up" to them, we will know that Our Lord's prophecy has been fulfilled: "When the Son of Man returns, will he find faith on earth?"

This is a fate of which we *ought* to be afraid, because it would mean the loss of our souls. "Fear ye not them that kill the body, and are not able to kill the soul: but rather fear him that can destroy both soul and body in hell" (Mt. 10:28). This is the holy fear for which the pope has no room, even as the innkeepers had no room for the humble Virgin and her God-fearing spouse St. Joseph.

51
Querida Amazonia:
Syncretizing Smoke and
German-tinted Mirrors

The Remnant

FEBRUARY 18, 2020

T HE REACTIONS TO THE POST-SYNODAL
Apostolic Exhortation *Querida Amazonia* (February 2,
2020)—I had almost written Post-Sinusoidal Apostolic
Expectoration—have once again exhibited all the features of an
ecclesiastical Rorschach inkblot test. In spite of the document's
hailing from the man whom we might as well agree to call Pope
Lío (as in ¡Hagan lío!), conservatives of the *First Things* variety have
breathed a collective sigh of relief: "Peter has spoken through
Lío!"[1] The pope did not, after all, push through married priests
and female deacons, as everyone had feared! The Germans are
collectively wringing their hands in an anguish of disappoint-
ment. Liberals in the Anglosphere are incredulous that the God
of surprises did not deign to use their darling as a mouthpiece
for the Zeitgeist.

For a traditional Catholic, all is as it should be, right? Not so fast.

A powerful article published anonymously on February 13 at
Whispers of Restoration, "Of the Monster in Rome, and the Curious
Case of the Cataphrygiae; or, Does Right Worship Exist?," argues
that several ominous paragraphs of the Exhortation have gone
almost completely unremarked. Here are some excerpts from
those paragraphs:

> Let us not be quick to describe as superstition or paganism
> certain religious practices that arise spontaneously from the
> life of peoples . . . It is possible to take up an indigenous
> symbol in some way, without necessarily considering it as
> idolatry. A myth charged with spiritual meaning can be used
> to advantage and not always considered a pagan error. . . .

---

1   See R. R. Reno, "Francis Stands Firm," *First Things,* February 13, 2020.

[W]e can take up into the liturgy many elements proper
to the experience of indigenous peoples in their contact
with nature, and respect native forms of expression in song,
dance, rituals, gestures, and symbols. The Second Vatican
Council called for this effort to inculturate the liturgy
among indigenous peoples; over fifty years have passed
and we still have far to go along these lines. (*QA* 78–79, 82)

The *Whispers* author then comments:

The failure to give clear instantiations of these ideas is
a textbook "Vatican II time-bomb" approach; but if this
isn't also a redescription of the moral object in principle,
one wonders what would be. It reduces to the claim that
the First Commandment has no objective moral content.
Pagan elements in Catholic worship? Sure, bring 'em on.

It was the introduction of the Novus Ordo in 1969 that put the
official papal stamp of approval on the idea of liturgy as a permanent workshop of change, accommodation, inculturation, and open-
ended participation—to be defined as meaning whatever those in
charge want it to mean. This conclusion follows from the colossal
temerity of their repudiation of longstanding ecclesial tradition
formed and practiced by saints as a guarantee of right worship:

From its earliest days, this liturgical devolution has needed
to allow in principle for the legitimacy of all manner of
non-Catholic worship elements, because the fundamental
doctrines informing divine worship as a moral act had
already been subsumed, *ipso facto*, by the very promulgation
of this New Mass.... Being a departure from the objective
liturgical tradition ... the NO is not a tree grown in the
garden of the Most Holy, tended with humility and pious
devotion over centuries of organic growth; it is a thing
manufactured in a lab, the "banal fabrication" (said then-
Cardinal Ratzinger) of disjointed committees, collaborating
with heretics and purportedly "seeking to engage modern
man." It is an alien (or, more accurately, a Frankenstein's
monster), unmoored from the broader homeland that is
the governing context of Sacred Tradition. Thus the NO
cannot be theologically analyzed as a ritual action apart
from the notion of perpetual innovation—this is because

the Novus Ordo *is* liturgical innovation—"incarnate," as it were, in missal form.

Because of its rupturous autonomy, the Novus Ordo, while it *can* be done in a controlled environment with personal piety and "by the books" (at least in their current configuration), always remains a kind of template for worship that must be filled out each time anew, depending on who's in charge and who else is involved. Amorphous, it takes on the flavor of its surroundings; one might compare it to tofu. It is like the shifting sand on which Our Lord told us not to build our house. And it was *designed* to be that way for the sake of promoting the people's participation "above all else" (cf. *Sacrosanctum Concilium* n. 14), as the *Whispers* author continues:

> This fundamental shift in principle was and remains the lynchpin of the entire sacrilegious fiasco in the bosom of the Church today: for, rather than first asking "Do our rites pay maximum reverence to the All-Holy God?," a radically new path lay open to making of supreme importance the question: "Do our rites garner maximum participation from the community?" Rather than "How does *God* want us to worship Him?" the revolutionary first asks: "How do *we* want to worship God?"

Thus, whereas the traditional Latin Mass is like an unsinkable ship, perfectly built, strong, well-armed for spiritual combat, sailing effortlessly, of beautiful design through and through, the Novus Ordo is like a ship that's always leaking and being bailed out to stay afloat. This is wearisome business and helps us to understand why priests who attempt to "improve" the Novus Ordo get so easily discouraged, worn out, or bitter about the trials they face. Sisyphus had an easier time of it, since at least the rock he was pushing was something definite. Try pushing Jell-O uphill again and again.

Those who dismiss the axiom "save the liturgy, save the world" as romanticism are fooling themselves. It's a concrete matter of putting first things first: if you don't have the first, the secondaries will never line up properly. When you have the first in place, the secondaries will *always* follow. You know: something about the First Commandment... We could dust off the Book of Exodus:

> When my angel goes before you, and brings you in to
> the Amorites, and the Hittites, and the Perizzites, and
> the Canaanites, the Hivites, and the Jebusites [N.B.: the
> Pachamama worshipers could be understood here by the
> imaginative—PK] and I blot them out, you shall not bow
> down to their gods, nor serve them, nor do according to
> their works, but you shall utterly overthrow them and
> break their pillars in pieces. You shall serve the Lord
> your God, and I will bless your bread and your water;
> and I will take sickness away from the midst of you. (Ex.
> 23:23-25; cf. Deut. 30:16)

I encourage readers to visit *Whispers of Restoration* and read the rest
of the treatment, which analyzes the reformed liturgy in terms of
three moral categories: impiety, sacrilege, and superstition.

As far as *Querida Amazonia* is concerned, we see an endorsement not of an Amazonian rite *per se*, but of the mentality that
has desacralized and paganized the Novus Ordo for the past fifty
years. We can be fairly certain by this time that the Novus Ordo
will not die of natural causes; no major heresy ever has. It will
continue secreting multitudinous odd efflorescences until it is cut
down and burned, or at least quietly shuffled away in practice.

The Exhortation, therefore, is a textbook example of a reverse
bait-and-switch tactic, where customers were warned of something
horribly wrong with the product, and then reassured in the event by
something that *looked* pretty acceptable in comparison. A no-name
commenter online perfectly expressed the psychological device:

> A far greater error has been smuggled in unopposed [in
> the new Exhortation]. Inculturation, indigenous spiritu-
> ality, and the affirmation that worship of pagan deities
> is not idolatry are all in there and nobody gives a rat's
> ass about it. It is *Amoris Laetitia* all over again. Everybody
> was so relieved that homosexual unions did not receive a
> blessing that nobody now talks about the fact that public
> permanent adulterers are receiving Holy Communion in
> dioceses all over the world.

That's the method: syncretizing smoke and German-tinted mirrors. Turn people's attention over there and they won't notice what's
right in front of their faces. Why are so many falling for this classic

feint? It's a feint. It's part of the long game.[2] In chess, sometimes one is content to give up a piece to lure one's opponent into a trap.

When *Amoris Laetitia* came out, faithful Catholics across the world wrestled anxiously with its departure from Divine Revelation and settled dogma. Where's that debate now? The *dubia* were never answered. The Buenos Aires guidelines were jammed through in the *Acta Apostolicae Sedis*. Many bishops, showing themselves to be a new breed of Amorites, have quietly put into place communion for the divorced and "remarried." At least on the ground level, this battle is mostly over, and Bergoglio won a messy victory. The war, of course, is not over—not until the end of time.

The roughly dozen books that document Francis's criminality and heresy have provided countless examples of the many Machiavellian ways in which the Church of Kasper will be achieved. It is disheartening, to say the least, to see the calming influence of this Exhortation—or really, any of the pope's stray Catholic words or deeds—lull to sleep those who should know better, after almost seven years of psychological warfare.

***

LET ME OFFER AN EXAMPLE FROM *QUERIDA AMAZONia* of how we must keep our thinking caps on and pay close attention to the dropping of hints. One might be tempted to whiz right past the following paragraph:

> Let us awaken our God-given aesthetic and contemplative sense that so often we let languish. Let us remember that "if someone has not learned to stop and admire something beautiful, we should not be surprised if he or she treats everything as an object to be used and abused without scruple." On the other hand, if we enter into communion with the forest, our voices will easily blend with its own and become a prayer: "as we rest in the shade of an ancient eucalyptus, our prayer for light joins in the song of the eternal foliage" [note 76]. This interior conversion will enable us to weep for the Amazon region and to join in its cry to the Lord. (n. 56)

***

2   See Fr. Frank Unterhalt, "Priest: Pope's Amazon exhortation is 'Trojan horse' for female ministry, married priests," *LifeSiteNews*, February 14, 2020.

The first thing that made me scratch my head was the reference to the "ancient eucalyptus," a tree native to Australia, not to the Amazon region. So I took a look at note 76. "SUI YUN, *Cantos para el mendigo y el rey*, Wiesbaden, 2000."

Admittedly not as impressive as the earthshaking footnotes of *Amoris Laetitia*, this obscure reference piques one's literary curiosity all the same. Papal footnotes do seem to do a surprising amount of heavy lifting nowadays. I might draw attention to footnote 18 of the pope's Christmas address of December 21, 2019—an address on which I published an initial analysis on December 22:[3]

> Saint Paul VI, some fifty years ago, when presenting the new Roman Missal to the faithful, recalled the correspondence between the law of prayer (*lex orandi*) and the law of faith (*lex credendi*), and described the Missal as "a demonstration of fidelity and vitality." He concluded by saying: "So let us not speak of a 'new Mass', but rather of 'a new age [*nuova epoca*] in the life of the Church'" (General Audience, 19 November 1969). Analogously, we might also say in this case: not a new Roman Curia, but rather a new age [*nuova epoca*].

To my knowledge, this is the sole reference Pope Francis made in 2019 to the 50th anniversary of the going into effect of the *Novus Ordo Missae* promulgated by his predecessor. His comments are cryptic: Paul VI presented a *new* Roman Missal, yet it is not a "new Mass" but instead ushers in a "new age." If the *lex orandi* determines the *lex credendi*, and the Missal by which the *lex orandi* is established is "new," it follows that the *lex credendi* will be new as well. That he can then compare the liturgical transition to the upcoming massive overhaul of the Curia, after which it will barely resemble what it has been for many centuries, is extremely telling and suggestive.[4] For, as Giovanni Filoramo writes: "The New Age heralds the advent of a new post-Christian era, characterized by the 'exit from God,' in the sense of a faith no longer revolving around the personal and exclusive God of the Judeo-Christian tradition."[5]

---

3 See the preceding chapter.
4 See chapter 61.
5 "La *New Age* preannuncia l'avvento di una *nuova epoca* postcristiana, caratterizzata dall'«uscita da Dio», nel senso di una fede non piu ruotante intorno al Dio personale ed esclusivo della tradizione giudaico-cristiana."

Returning to *Querida Amazonia*: the line about "our prayer for light joins in the song of the eternal foliage" of the eucalyptus comes from a collection of poems written by a Chinese woman who lived in Peru, in the Amazonian region, and who later moved to California. Her real name is Katie Wong Loo. She started publishing pantheistic poems with nostalgic reflections on the Amazon in California in the 1970's under the pseudonym Sui Yun.[6] It cannot escape the notice of the careful reader that the book cited was published in Wiesbaden—that is, in Germany. Looking it up, I see that it is a bilingual edition: *Cantos para el mendigo y el rey/Gesänge für den Bettler und den König.* Is it not exceedingly probable that this reference to an obscure Sino-Peruvian poet came from a German source involved in drafting the Exhortation?

A little further research turned up information on the poetess in the book *Sinophone Studies: A Critical Reader,* edited by Shu-mei Shih, Chien-hsin Tsai, and Brian Bernards (Columbia University Press, 2013). From the description offered, her poetry sounds pantheistic, humanistic, and relativistic. A sample line: "The primitive from the civilized / The humble from the aristocrat / The positive from the negative / All these coordinate in the making of One whole." Shih, Tsai, and Bernards comment: "Therefore, the ultimate answers are to be found in the magical powers of nature and in its unity" (417). Sui Yun's second collection of poems, from 1983, is significantly entitled: *Rosa fálica* [phallic rose], in which "the prevalent topics are eroticism and love" (ibid.). Victor Manuel "Tucho" Fernández, author of *Heal Me With Your Mouth: The Art of Kissing* and partial ghostwriter of several of Pope Francis's documents (including chapter 8 of *Amoris Laetitia*),[7] would surely find delectation in her work.

The use of "eucalyptus" by a highly educated Sino-Peruvian poet is certainly not a mistake or an accident. Eucalyptus trees were introduced in post-colonial South America as a capitalist cash crop against which many NGOs have been actively protesting for decades, citing exploitation of the land and various problems

Millenarismo e new age: apocalisse e religiosita alternativa (Bari: Dedalo, 1999), 84.

6   See "Dos poetas amazónicas: Sui Yun y Ana Varela," *sol negro,* May 14, 2008; http://sol-negro.blogspot.com/2008/05/dos-poetas-amaznicas-sui-yun-y-ana.html.

7   See Christopher Ferrara, "'Tucho' Spills the Beans," *The Remnant,* June 14, 2016.

caused by the introduction of the foreign trees (how ironic is *that* for this Exhortation?). Since the eucalyptus tree is anything but ancient in South America, it is obvious that "ancient eucalyptus" (in the line "as we rest in the shade of an ancient eucalyptus, our prayer for light joins in the song of the eternal foliage") must bear a symbolic meaning. Sui Yun is drawing on the literal meaning of the word in its truly *ancient* Greco-Roman context. The Greek *eu* means good and *kalyptos* means covered, hidden, or veiled. One could relate the meaning of *kalyptos* to the meaning of *mysterion*, a hidden or secret thing (which is then rendered in Latin as *sacramentum*). *Eu-kalyptos* as "good mystery" makes the word pregnant with meaning. The Amazon does indeed have a ubiquitous "plant sacrament": *ayahuasca*.

At least one Catholic religious sister—"Sister Jaguar"—is well acquainted with what she calls the "sacrament" of *ayahuasca*; her story is told in a short documentary.[8] This "sacrament" is absolutely central to Amazonian spirituality, and anyone even minimally acquainted with the subject knows it. I can't prove it, but I would assume that the potted plant thing that was processed up and placed on the high altar of St. Peter's by Pope Francis contained some of the plants used for making *ayahuasca*. Why not? As the sacred plants of this Amazonian spiritual "tradition," they would be the most fitting choice for such a votive offering.

Many Germans make pilgrimage to the Amazon just to partake of *ayahuasca* in authentic ceremonies. How many bishops have? Who knows... But the spirituality surrounding it is pantheism. Mother Earth as the All-Spirit comes to people and reveals the mysteries of oneness to those who partake. The experience often has a very dark side as well, with the feeling of immanent death.

A reliable study by the National Center for Biotechnology Information includes descriptions of the spiritual aspects connected with the use of *ayahuasca*.[9] The article recounts how its use was pressed in the US Supreme Court, and the SCOTUS ruled that, in spite of its being a Schedule 1 controlled substance, its use for

---

8   www.sisterjaguarsjourney.com/filmviewer2/.
9   Jonathan Hamill, Jaime Hallak, Serdar M. Dursun, and Glen Bakera, "Ayahuasca: Psychological and Physiologic Effects, Pharmacology and Potential Uses in Addiction and Mental Illness," *Current Neuropharmacology*, February 2019, 17(2): 108–28; doi: 10.2174/1570159X16666180125095902.

religious purposes (that is, as a "sacrament") is legal in the US. Perhaps our next ecumenical dialogue needs to begin at once with the "Soul Quest Ayahuasca Church of Mother Earth."[10] You can now go and legally receive the sacrament of *ayahuasca* and encounter Pachamama directly for yourself. I wish this were a parody—but it's not. All of this stuff is right out in the open.

There is more. The Greek *kalyptos* is also used in Gnosticism to name one of three gods in a kind of Gnostic trinity as a threefold path to enlightenment: *Kalyptos, Protophanes, Autogenes*.[11] *Kalyptos*, whose name means "concealing," is a god who paradoxically *reveals* things that are hidden. It is a part of the Gnostic idea of revealing hidden mysteries, which also may be a part of Sui Yun's mysticism. (This, importantly, is precisely what *ayahuasca*, the "plant sacrament," is said to do: reveal hidden mysteries.) *That* line from *that* poem and *that* writer were specially chosen. As with the Gnostics of old, the "initiated" will see and know the meaning, hidden in plain sight.

---

10   www.ayahuascachurches.org/.
11   See John D. Turner, "The Gnostic Threefold Path to Enlightenment: The Ascent of Mind and the Descent of Wisdom," *Novum Testamentum* 22.4 (1980): 324–51. For examples: "Kalyptos" appears 32 times in the Gnostic text "Zostrianos" (http://gnosis.org/naghamm/zostr.html), and four times in the Gnostic text "Allogenes" (http://gnosis.org/naghamm/allogene.html).

How Francis is Attempting to Complete the Destruction of the Church Begun by Paul VI†

The Remnant

MARCH 13, 2020

I T HAS BECOME FASHIONABLE TO SAY THAT Pope Francis is not a liturgical revolutionary. It's true that he did not rush at the traditional rites of the Church with jackhammer and dynamite the way Paul VI did, leaving a pile of rubble and a sign marked (with mordant irony) "Renewal." But in his own more devious way, he has made a series of strategic moves that seek to canonize the revolution and immobilize the opposition.

Since the religious are the heart of the Church, any lasting renewal must come from religious orders; therefore Francis has made it his special care to obstruct their progress. The attack on the religious life so far has had three prongs.

1. The suppression of the Franciscan Friars of the Immaculate. Imagine if the popes in the thirteenth century had chosen *not* to support Francis and Dominic. That's what happened this time under Bergoglio. One of the most vibrant and growing orders in the Church was quashed because it had rediscovered and embraced the traditional liturgy. This was meant as a shot across the bow: "You existing orders, do not imagine you can take up again the old Mass. If you do, you know what fate awaits you. Those of you who are being permitted to use the old Mass, be careful not to cross me." Thus the religious life is bullied into silence. How many times have I heard priests and religious confide to me: "If we did (thus-and-such) or said (this-and-that), we'd suffer the same fate as the FFI."

---

† I drafted the following text on August 6, 2016, did not publish it at the time. When reviewing it and slightly updating it in December 2019, I was struck by how much worse the situation had become since the summer of 2016, and how all of my evaluations had been confirmed by subsequent events. Although the text could have been considerably expanded, it was better to leave it as a brisk pencil portrait of a Roman Pontiff who would beat the worst Renaissance popes at their own game.

2. The creation of stricter rules about bishops erecting institutes in their dioceses. It is true that this limitation cuts against *any* new orders, whatever "orientation" they may have. But since the most vigorous new blood in the Church is traditionalist, it is primarily directed at them (without seeming to be so).

3. The step taken against the spread of traditional contemplative sisters through *Vultum Dei Quaerere* and *Cor Orans*. This is perhaps the most diabolical of all the things Bergoglio has done to date.

If one wishes to prop up the liturgical revolution so that it may last, if it were humanly possible, until the end of time, one has to take steps to ensure that its false principles and tendencies are promoted—or at least that their dismantling, which had seemed a real possibility under Benedict, is made exceedingly difficult. Francis has made several moves on this front.

1. He first treated the rule about the washing of the feet (that only men, *viri*, should be chosen) with contempt, to show that violating liturgical rubrics is no big deal and that the people of God had outgrown such legalism. In this way he deliberately set a bad example (except that he seems to have thought it was a good example).

2. He then *changed* the rule about the washing of the feet (women may be included, but only "the faithful"), so that it would advance the feminist agenda and the dissolution of liturgical symbolism and tradition. Of course, he proceeded to violate this new rule, as well, which inculcates contempt for rules in general.

3. He pushed through a commission on deaconesses for no other reason, as far as anyone can tell, than to destabilize the faithful's convictions about the maleness of the hierarchy. This, of course, plays into the same feminist agenda. It is like saying: "You conservatives don't like female altar girls? You trads don't like women in the sanctuary at all? Well, guess what: not only are you forever going to have women acting like clergy, but I'm going to make a big deal about whether women can *become* clergy." In this way he is signifying his contempt of the "hermeneutic of continuity" project. The Amazon Synod then came along to put the icing on the cake.

4. The infamous Lombardi "clarification" (emanating from Francis) rebuking Cardinal Sarah for three things—recommending *ad orientem*, promoting the "reform of the reform" (ROTR), and endorsing the so-called Extraordinary Form—was the final twisting of the knife. Since *ad orientem* is the fundamental symbol of traditional Christian

worship, as embodied in the old Roman Rite and sought for in the (admittedly floundering) ROTR movement, this amounts to a declaration of war against traditional worship as such.

Authentic renewal comes by way of bishops. This is why Bergoglio has also destabilized the episcopacy.

1. He has made it easier, canonically, to yank traditional bishops from their sees on the slightest pretexts. In order to show that this is in fact his intention, he has yanked some of the best bishops from their sees, even though they had been guilty of far less bad behavior than certain liberal bishops whose positions have never been threatened. In this way, the pope has signified to traditionally-minded bishops: "Beware of what you do, for the Vatican is watching."[1]

2. He is encouraging "decentralization," which means empowering episcopal conferences to push their progressive agendas down the throats of unwilling conservatives. An indication of the likely results can be seen in the motu proprio *Magnum Principium*, turning over the approval of translations to episcopal conferences, without a Vatican doctrinal control.[2] (We may be tempted to say that the Vatican control is not reliable any more, and sadly that is true at the moment; but the CDW and the CDF when well staffed have prevented a great deal of liturgical nonsense that bubbled up from the lower levels.)

3. Francis relies on Wuerl and Cupich as bishop-makers, in order to recast the most influential local church, the American, in his own image and likeness, since it is rather too evident that he dislikes it as it stands. Because the traditional renewal is happening most of all in America, it was necessary to do all in his power to prevent its future growth. The easiest and most effective way to do this without drawing too much attention to himself is to ensure that American bishops are either progressives who hate the traditional liturgy or mild-mannered neo-conservatives who will do nothing to promote it.[3]

Finally, renewal takes hold in the family and spreads through

---

1 See chapter 60.   2 See chapter 58.

3 Sixteen months after this article was published, Pope Francis released his motu proprio *Traditionis Custodes*, which demonstrated that he and his advisers realized they could not solve the "problem" of the growing appeal of tradition without taking draconian measures; the hitherto less direct approach was not yielding the desired results. For full commentary, see *From Benedict's Peace to Francis's War*.

godly children. Thus Bergoglio had to aim his poison-tipped arrows at the mystery of marriage.

1. With the "reform" of the annulment process, he has welcomed the evil of no-fault divorce into the bosom of the Church. We have had this problem *de facto* for many decades, but popes always protested against it. The current pope endorses it, as he seems to entertain doubts about the validity of a great many marriages.

2. With the two Synods on the Family, the Synod on Youth, and the Amazon Synod, he has destabilized public perception of Catholic teaching and the adherence of the People of God to moral doctrine.

3. With *Amoris Laetitia* he created a masterpiece of postconciliar ambiguity that encourages clergy to continue in their laxism, while bringing a haze of uncertainty, sentimentalism, and pragmatism to the entire area of morality. In this way, his moral vision perfectly complements his liturgical vision, and both are supported by his ecclesiology.

With the cleverness of a serpent in the garden, Pope Francis has, through all of these steps, played upon the gullibility and credulity of faithful Catholics, the majority of whom will, he knows, follow him like witless sheep. The result has been an utter polarization among Catholics: an earnest minority who support and defend him (or at least find plausible ways to exonerate him), an equally earnest minority who see his plan and oppose it with all their might, and a majority who care very little about these issues and tend to view the pope as a benign grandfather who blesses their hedonism and relativism.

I have not even touched here on Bergoglio's errors about God, Christ, the Scriptures, and Catholic social teaching. (See "Denzinger Bergoglio" for a more thorough treatment.)

No one could write a dystopic novel as dystopic as our current situation is: a pope who holds what Robert Hugh Benson's Antichrist holds; a Church confused about its very identity and cut off from its tradition; a society wedded to every vice and calling it virtue.

Never have we had a pope who is so wrong about so many things. He has earned infamy and perdition. May God have mercy on his soul before he departs this life.

It will take a pope of the stature of Gregory the Great, Gregory IX, Innocent III, Pius V, or Pius X to set the Barque of the Church back on course again. Indeed, it will take several such popes. May Our Lord in His infinite mercy grant them to us, in spite of our unworthiness. *Dixi.*

53

What Was Pope Francis Doing, Asking for Buddhist Leader's Blessing?

LifeSiteNews

MARCH 24, 2020

O N NOVEMBER 21, 2019, POPE FRANCIS met with the Buddhist "Supreme Patriarch" at the Wat Ratchabophit Sathit Maha Simaram Temple in Bangkok and spoke vaguely of how "religions" are "beacons of hope" and "promoters and guarantors of fraternity."[1] He neglected to mention the basic truth that there is common brotherhood only in a common Father—the Father revealed in His Son Jesus Christ: "No one knoweth the Son, but the Father: neither doth any one know the Father, but the Son, and he to whom it shall please the Son to reveal him" (Mt. 11:27).

Admittedly, it's not necessary, and not even humanly possible, to speak every truth in every situation. Yet the salvation brought by Christ is not just one truth among many, but the central truth of our existence—the difference between a life lived well and a life lived in vain. One wonders what a pope is doing paying a personal visit to a Buddhist leader and requesting *his* blessing, as if he has something to give that Christ and His Church do not already have in a more perfect way, or as if there were no danger at all in such intercourse between fundamentally incompatible religions.

When Pope Francis next travels such a great distance, he might consider imitating his namesake, St. Francis of Assisi, who walked straight into the Muslim camp and preached the Gospel to convert the sultan.[2] But ardent believers are few and far between in this age of polite chitchat. The Lord who saith "I will shake the heavens and

---

1   See "Pope in Thailand: Catholics and Buddhists can live as 'good neighbours,'" *Vatican News*, November 21, 2019.
2   See the homily on this episode by Fr. Matthew McCarthy, FSSP, at www.stfrancislincoln.org/pdf/Sermon_2019_St_Francis_of_Assisi_Works_of_Mercy_2.pdf.

the earth" has been replaced by the handshake and the photo-op.

Thomas Merton toward the end of his career, until it was short-circuited in Bangkok, was interested in the question of what Buddhists and Christians—and more particularly, Buddhist and Christian monasticism—have in common. There is, after all, as St. Thomas Aquinas points out, *some* common ground between any two serious positions; it is just this common ground that often furnishes a foothold for the evangelist to begin making his case. It is well that we ask ourselves what the commonality consists in, and whether it hides a more profound opposition that deserves to be drawn out, so that we may avoid the error of seeing Christianity and Buddhism as two analogous paths toward the Ultimate and the Infinite, toward Personal Realization (or however someone in the Vatican Press Office might phrase it).

In order to accomplish this, we must look at the problem of desire, its effect of restlessness, the remedy of asceticism, and the result of peace.

St. Thomas teaches that common goods bring us together, while private goods drive us apart. Animals fight chiefly about goods that cannot be shared—namely food and sex.[3] This is true of human beings, too, insofar as they live like animals: their concern is to get as much enjoyment, or as many bodily goods, as they can get, and since these goods are unable to be had by many at once and in the same respect, and since there is nearly always a scarcity of at least some goods at any given time and place, this leads to conflict, division, resentment, injustice, and violence. It is, in short, the logic of raw capitalism and of Marxism alike, for in both systems men must find ways to vent their mounting frustration with the inability to gather and enjoy bodily goods in proportion to the "infinity of desire."

The remedy for this diseased condition is twofold: negatively, *a mortification of desire*, by which desire is restored to a healthy realism and moderation; positively, *a yearning for and an increasing possession of spiritual goods*, which are inherently limitless, ever available, and ever abundant and cause charity, peace, joy, and the other fruits of the Spirit mentioned by St. Paul in Galatians. The medieval mystic Meister Eckhart notes: "As far as you are in God, thus far you are at peace, and as far as you are outside God, thus far you

---

3   *Summa contra gentiles*, Bk. 3, ch. 124; *Summa theologiae* I, qu. 81, art. 2.

are outside peace" (*Talks of Instruction*, 23).

It is here that we first see what looks like a correspondence between Christianity and Buddhism. Classic Christian spirituality emphasizes mortification of the flesh in order to achieve self-mastery and illumination; in like manner, Buddhism seeks to bring the restless wheels of desire to a standstill in order to achieve enlightenment.

In spite of his Assisi escapades, Pope John Paul II reminded us in his 1994 blockbuster *Crossing the Threshold of Hope* (1994) that the contrast between the two religions is far greater than the likeness:

> The "enlightenment" experienced by Buddha comes down to the conviction that the world is bad, that it is the source of evil and of suffering for man. To liberate oneself from this evil, one must free oneself from this world, necessitating a break with the ties that join us to external reality—ties existing in our human nature, in our psyche, in our bodies. The more we are liberated from these ties, the more we become indifferent to what is in the world, and the more we are freed from suffering, from the evil that has its source in the world.
>
> Do we draw near to God in this way? This is not mentioned in the "enlightenment" conveyed by Buddha. Buddhism is in large measure an *"atheistic" system*. We do not free ourselves from evil through the good which comes from God; we liberate ourselves only through detachment from the world, which is bad. The fullness of such a detachment is not union with God, but what is called nirvana, a state of perfect indifference with regard to the world. *To save oneself* means, above all, to free oneself from evil by becoming *indifferent to the world, which is the source of evil.* This is the culmination of the spiritual process.

For Christians, the "culmination of the spiritual process" is not total detachment, but loving attachment to God—a personal God whom we can know and love, without being absorbed into Him and losing our identity like a drop dissolved into the ocean. We do not lose all desire; we refine and intensify desire for what is really worth desiring.

Next week, I will resume with John Paul II's intriguing assertion that the Carmelites *begin* where the Buddha *ends*.

54
Carmelite Mystics
Show How Christianity
Transcends Buddhism's Limits

LifeSiteNews
MARCH 31, 2020

I N HIS BOOK *CROSSING THE THRESHOLD OF Hope*, John Paul II reached the conclusion (as we saw last week[1]) that Buddhist liberation from evil through asceticism and detachment involves, in a way, breaking one's ties with external reality—including human nature—so as to acquire indifference and freedom from suffering. The pope claims that such liberation rests on an atheistic foundation; instead of salvation there is, ultimately, negation.

John Paul II contrasts the abysmal emptiness of the Buddhist path with the fullness of light and life promised by Christ to those who deny themselves *for His sake*—for the sake of finding themselves anew in Him. Not surprisingly, he takes up one of his favorite spiritual writers, St. John of the Cross, on whose conception of "faith" he wrote his doctoral dissertation under the great Thomist Fr. Réginald Garrigou-Lagrange, and shows how utterly different Christianity is from the impersonal a-theistic religion of Asia:

> When Saint John of the Cross, in the *Ascent of Mount Carmel* and in the *Dark Night of the Soul,* speaks of the need for purification, for detachment from the world of the senses, he does not conceive of that detachment as an end in itself. "To arrive at what now you do not enjoy, you must go where you do not enjoy. To reach what you do not know, you must go where you do not know. To come into possession of what you do not have, you must go where now you have nothing" (*Ascent of Mount Carmel*, I.13.11). In Eastern Asia these classic texts of Saint John of the Cross have been, at times, interpreted as a

---

1   See the preceding chapter.

confirmation of Eastern ascetic methods. But this Doctor of the Church does not merely propose detachment from the world. He proposes detachment from the world in order to unite oneself to that which is outside of the world—by this I do not mean nirvana, but a personal God. Union with Him comes about not only through purification, but through love.

Carmelite mysticism begins at the point where the reflections of Buddha end, together with his instructions for the spiritual life. In the active and passive purification of the human soul, in those specific nights of the senses and the spirit, Saint John of the Cross sees, above all, the preparation necessary for the human soul to be permeated with the living flame of love. And this is also the title of his major work—*The Living Flame of Love.*

Therefore, despite similar aspects, there is a fundamental difference. *Christian mysticism* from every period—beginning with the era of the Fathers of the Eastern and Western Church, to the great theologians of Scholasticism (such as Saint Thomas Aquinas), to the northern European mystics, to the Carmelite mystics—is not born of a purely negative "enlightenment." It is not born of an awareness of the evil which exists in man's attachment to the world through the senses, the intellect, and the spirit. Instead, Christian mysticism is born of the *Revelation of the living God.* This God opens Himself to union with man, arousing in him the capacity to be united with Him, especially by means of the theological virtues—faith, hope, and, above all, love.

Is it not remarkable to read again, in these dark days of the one whom history may refer to as "the Abu Dhabi pope," such a careful analysis of the more profound and indeed singular truth of the Christian Faith over its rivals? The Carmelites *begin* where the Buddha *ends*: that's the kind of language that might get you put into a Vatican prison cell these days. Yes, we are right to condemn the Assisi interreligious gatherings and other confusing signals given by John Paul II, but there can be no doubt that *as a thinker* he understands clearly the unbridgeable abyss that separates Far Eastern religions from Catholicism.

"This God opens Himself to union with man, especially by love." John Paul II shows that Christian asceticism is about detachment from selfishness for the sake of being all the more *attached in love to the beloved*. We need to be detached because, as beings who thrive on attachments, we need to make sure we are rightly attached to the right things, not because we are better off isolated and indifferent. Purification makes sense only in relation to purity, which means having a single heart that can be given wholly to another. Penance is a clearing away of whatever interferes with a union of love.

The contrast between Buddhist "salvation" and Christian salvation—entering fully into the plenitude of love, gaining one's identity in communion with the other—could not be more striking. In *Truth and Tolerance*, Joseph Ratzinger dwells in a similar way on the contrast between the path of mystical "identification," where the ego is lost in an ocean of impersonal "divinity," and the path of personal communion where the self, through a process of abandonment and purification, becomes for the first time *really and truly itself*, precisely by surrendering to and being caught up in the Beloved.[2]

Here is where the Christian faith is unique and superior: we find rest in a *person*, in a friendship founded on a love that knows no limits and will last forever.

> Come to me, all you who labor and are heavy laden,
> and I will give you rest.
> Take my yoke upon you, and learn from me;
> for I am gentle and lowly of heart,
> and you will find rest for your souls. (Mt. 11:28–29)

Certain themes run throughout much of Far Eastern thought and religion, in spite of its many varieties. One sees an emphasis on health, longevity, oneness with nature, and the sufficiency of the created or natural order; transcendence beyond this order is understood as a return to or merging with an impersonal oneness beyond being.

Christianity, in contrast, could be evoked with a few striking words: Cross, Heart, Flesh, Face, Spirit, Love, Heaven. Man was made by God for God, not by the cosmos for the cosmos. The Christian vocation is to find and hold onto God, who is personal,

---

2　To read more along these lines, see "Catholicism and Buddhism: Incompatibilities in Love" by John Michael Keba, *CatholicCulture.org*, September 21, 2006, item 7152.

ultimate reality—totally other, yet more interior to me than I am to myself. God takes on real human flesh to make it holy. The Christian is reformed by His grace, created anew, and called to bodily resurrection after death.

The idea of a 24-year-old victim of tuberculosis (St. Thérèse of Lisieux) presenting her sickness as a self-offering in reparation for damage done by sin; the idea of this life as a vale of tears through which we pass to the heavenly Jerusalem, where persons are more alive and more definite than ever—none of this can make sense to the Far East. The Cross is absurd, the resurrection no less so. "For the word of the Cross, to them indeed that perish, is foolishness; but to them that are saved, that is, to us, it is the power of God" (1 Cor. 1:18).

55

Pope Distorts Basic Christian Teaching in Homily

LifeSiteNews
MAY 4, 2020

IN HIS HOMILY AT MASS ON MAY 4, 2020, starting from the consoling truth that Christ died for all men, Pope Francis appears to have stated a doubly false conclusion: that we are not to convert unbelievers and that His death "justifies" everyone:

> Big, small, rich, poor, good and bad. All. This "all" is the vision of the Lord who died for all. "But did he die for that wretch who made my life impossible?" He died for him too. "And for that brigand?": He died for him. "For everyone?" The Lord died for all. And also for people who do not believe in Him or are of other religions: he died for everyone. That does not mean that proselytism must be done: no. But He died for everyone, He justified everyone.

There are some rather basic problems with these off-the-cuff statements, which do not appear in the Vatican's official transcript but may be heard in the video.

First, it seems that the pope has confused redemption with justification. Redemption is Christ's paying of humanity's debt of justice to the Father. This He accomplishes in His bloody sacrifice on the Cross, which is the one and only acceptable sacrifice of atonement. This objective redemption must be applied to the soul of each human being: this is what we call the *subjective* redemption, that is, the sharing of individuals in Christ's redemption through faith and the sacraments. In other words, the fact that Christ has given to the Father all that humanity owes Him does not automatically cancel out the debt each individual incurs from Adam and from his own personal sins. The individual must freely enter into the death and resurrection of Christ to be fully redeemed.

Justification, also known as regeneration, describes the application of the fruits of Christ's Passion to individual men by the power of the Holy Spirit. That is why we can truly say that Christ died for all, but not all will be saved, not all will be justified—only those who are united to Christ in faith, hope, and charity. This, moreover, is precisely why missionary and evangelistic efforts are necessary. As St. Paul teaches:

> "Every one who calls upon the name of the Lord will be saved." But how are men to call upon him in whom they have not believed? And how are they to believe in him of whom they have never heard? And how are they to hear without a preacher? And how can men preach unless they are sent? As it is written, "How beautiful are the feet of those who preach good news!" But they have not all heeded the gospel; for Isaiah says, "Lord, who has believed what he has heard from us?" So faith comes from what is heard, and what is heard comes by the preaching of Christ. (Rom. 10:13–17)

In other words, we must *call* on the Lord's name to be saved, we must *believe* the Gospel. For St. Paul, who was the greatest missionary in the history of the Church and who tirelessly sought the conversion of every Jew and Gentile with whom he came into contact, the only path to salvation is hearing the Gospel and assenting to it—which means not just *saying* that one assents to it, but endeavoring to live in accordance with the teaching of Christ.

The most authoritative exposition of the Catholic teaching on justification is the one given in the Sixth Session of the Council of Trent, by far the most ample and detailed teaching of the Magisterium on the question, prompted by heretical distortions prevalent in the sixteenth century. Chapter 1 reaffirms that in Adam all have sinned; all are unclean and under God's wrath; all are in the power of sin, the devil, and death. Chapter 2 states that Christ came precisely to rescue us from this abject slavery. Chapters 3 and 4 then speak directly contrary to the preaching of Pope Francis:

> But though "He died for all" (2 Cor. 5:15), yet all do not receive the benefit of His death, but those only to whom the merit of His Passion is communicated, because ... if they were not born again in Christ, they would never be justified, since in that new birth there is bestowed upon them, through the merit of His Passion, the grace

by which they are made just .... This translation [from
wrath to adoptive sonship] cannot, since the promulgation
of the Gospel, be effected except through the laver of
regeneration [baptism] or the desire for it, as it is written:
"Unless a man be born again of water and the Holy Ghost,
he cannot enter into the kingdom of God" (Jn. 3:5).

The Council of Trent goes on to say in Chapter 6 that adults
are prepared for justification by hearing the preaching of the
gospel and responding with repentance and a desire for baptism.
Chapter 7 furnishes a clear definition:

> Justification ... is not only a remission of sins but also
> the sanctification and renewal of the inward man through
> the voluntary reception of the grace and gifts whereby
> an unjust man becomes just and from being an enemy
> becomes a friend, that he may be "an heir according to
> hope of life everlasting" (Tit. 3:7).

This same chapter teaches what the *causes* of justification are:

- the final cause (purpose) is "the glory of God and of Christ
and life everlasting";
- the efficient cause (origin of action) is "the merciful God who
washes and sanctifies";
- the meritorious cause is "His most beloved Only-Begotten,
Our Lord Jesus Christ, who, 'when we were enemies, for the
exceeding charity wherewith he loved us' (Eph. 2:4), merited for us
justification by His most holy Passion on the wood of the Cross
and made satisfaction for us to God the Father";
- the instrumental cause is "the sacrament of baptism, which
is the sacrament of faith, *without which no man was ever justified*"
(emphasis added);
- the formal cause (that which makes the soul to be just) is
"the justice of God."

In light of the foregoing, the pope's words "He justified everyone"
could, with some squinting, be given an orthodox interpretation
if we took them to mean: "He was the meritorious cause of
the justification of everyone who is justified." Nevertheless, the
words as they stand—particularly adjacent to the statement about
not going out to convert unbelievers, which implicitly calls into

question the instrumental cause of baptism—seem to suggest a view more akin to universalism, i.e., that all men will be saved regardless of their faith or lack thereof, because Christ simply justifies everyone, *tout court.*

Trent reminds us also in Chapter 14 that those who fall into mortal sin lose sanctifying grace—"forfeit the received grace of justification"—and are restored to justification by the sacrament of penance, which Christ instituted precisely to give us a "second plank after the shipwreck of grace lost." In other words, unlike the Protestant view "once saved, always saved," the Catholic Church teaches that we must freely *remain* in the grace of God and persevere in it until death; that we can indeed fall away; and that we can be restored to spiritual life. As Augustine says: "He who created you without you, will not save you without you." It is not some sort of mechanized automated process.

The eminent Oratorian theologian Louis Bouyer adds valuable precisions:

> As for the faith whereby we receive justification, it is the faith of Christ (Rom. 3:22; cf. Gal. 2:16), i.e., the faith which leads us to be justified in him (Gal. 2:17), justified in his blood (Rom. 5:9). The fifth chapter of the Epistle to the Romans sheds light on this latter verse by showing us the Cross of Jesus as the *root* of our justification, just as the sin of Adam had been the root of our sin. We must further see it in connection with the following chapter, where St. Paul shows us how it is *through baptism* that the faith takes possession of God's gift, which brings us justification insofar as we are baptized (i.e., immersed) in his death, "so that as Christ was raised from the dead by the glory of the Father, we too might walk in newness of life" (v. 4). The whole context shows how justification by faith in the grace of God in Christ, quite far from excusing us from living in the holiness of Christ, requires and enables us to do so.[1]

Bouyer notes that the Sixth Session of Trent "set forth a particularly detailed and delicately worded doctrine of the different aspects inherent in justification":

---

[1]   Louis Bouyer, *Dictionary of Theology*, trans. Charles Underhill Quinn (N.p.: Desclée Co., 1965), 255.

In conformity with the much more unified conception of St. Paul, the Council affirmed that there is only one justification, which comes entirely from the merits of the crucified Christ alone, but which is realized in the positive justification that grace engenders in us, the principle of good works that will be its fruit, and, immediately, the principle of charity that is inseparable from the state of grace.[2]

The dogmatic teaching of Trent summarized above has been expressed innumerable times in other documents of the Church's Magisterium and expounded by reputable theologians of all periods. Readers may consult, for example, the systematic index of magisterial teachings in Denzinger's *Enchiridion symbolorum, definitionum et declarationum de rebus fidei et morum* (43rd ed., Ignatius Press), 1255–59 and the thorough presentation in Ludwig Ott's *Fundamentals of Catholic Dogma* (Baronius Press ed.), 269–89.

When listening to or reading transcripts of the homilies of Pope Francis, one often gets the sense of a man who, as soon as he speaks off the cuff, reveals the inadequacy of his own theological training and the sloppiness of his thinking. He seldom sounds like someone deliberately trying to dismantle traditional theology with the cleverness of a Karl Rahner; rather, he comes across as an embarrassing witness to the collapse of sound dogmatic and moral theology in the mid- to late twentieth century.

Popes in general would do well to speak only when their thoughts have been correctly formulated—it was not for any trivial reason that papal speeches and documents of any kind were always carefully reviewed by house theologians—and only on occasions when public speaking is pastorally necessary, rather than doing it day after day like a radio talk show or a tear-off calendar with affirming sentiments. If popes limited themselves in this time-honored way, their statements would have a greater resonating force and a greater possibility of fruitful ecclesial reception.

---

2   Bouyer, 257.

56

These Condemned Criminals Accepted "Inadmissible" Death Penalty and Became Saints

LifeSiteNews

AUGUST 11, 2020

I N THE BESTSELLING INTERVIEW OF BISHOP
Athanasius Schneider conducted by Diane Montagna, His
Excellency says the following about ruling out the death
penalty absolutely:

> Those who deny the death penalty in principle implicitly
> or explicitly absolutize the corporal and temporal life of
> man. They also deny to some extent the consequences
> of original sin. Those who deny the legitimacy of the
> death penalty also implicitly or explicitly deny the need
> and value of expiation and penance for sins, and espe-
> cially for monstrous crimes, still in this earthly life. The
> "good thief" who was crucified next to Our Lord is one
> of the most eloquent witnesses to the expiatory value of
> the death penalty, since through the acceptance of his
> own death sentence he gained eternal life and became
> in some sense the first canonized saint of the Church.
> Indeed, Our Lord said to him, "Today you will be with
> Me in paradise" (Lk. 23:43).[1]

Bishop Schneider draws our attention to a most important
aspect of the discussion—an aspect, note well, that progressive or
liberal opponents of capital punishment consistently ignore: *its
expiatory value in making reparation for sin.* The neglect of this truth
is perfectly consistent with the neglect of many other divinely
revealed and constantly taught truths of Catholicism, such as the
fact that all of our earthly sufferings are the result of sin, original
and personal, and that God, as providential Lord, wills physical

---

1 *Christus Vincit: Christ's Triumph over the Darkness of the Age* (Brooklyn, NY:
Angelico Press, 2019), 188.

evils for our just punishment and especially for our conversion and purification.[2]

His Excellency reminds us of this crucial dimension when he continues:

> There are plenty of moving examples of executed evil-doers and criminals who, through the acceptance of the death penalty, saved the life of their soul for all eternity. St. Joseph Cafasso is the patron of men condemned to death; his biography provides us with astonishing examples of conversions of such men. All of these examples bore witness to the truth that the short temporal life of the body is disproportionate to eternal life in heaven.[3]

Ms. Montagna asks if the bishop thinks more criminals would convert if they were allowed to live out long prison sentences rather than being put to death. His response is striking:

> We have the example of a "good thief" of the twentieth century in the case of Claude Newman, a murderer who in 1943 was put on death row in Vicksburg, Mississippi. Initially an unbeliever and non-Catholic, he experienced a conversion to the Catholic faith through the power of the Miraculous Medal. He died a holy death as a devout Catholic. He bore witness to the legitimacy and to the expiatory value of the death penalty.
>
> One can mention also the case of the Servant of God Jacques Fesch (1930–1957), a murderer who spent more than three years in solitary confinement. He experienced a profound conversion before his execution by guillotine in Paris. He left spiritually edifying notes and letters. Two months before his execution, he wrote: "Here is where the Cross and its mystery of suffering make their appearance. The whole of life has this piece of wood as its center.... Don't you think that, whatever you set out to do in the short time that is yours on earth, everything worthwhile is marked with this seal of suffering? There are no more illusions: you know with certainty that all

---

2   See "The Catholic View: We're All Guilty, and We All Must Suffer," *OnePeterFive*, April 29, 2020, and "Coronavirus pandemic: God's punishment or meaningless bad luck?," *LifeSiteNews*, March 17, 2020.

3   *Christus Vincit*, 188.

this world has to offer is as false and deceptive as the most fantastic dreams of a six-year-old girl. Then despair invades you, and you try to avoid the suffering that dogs your heels and licks at you with its flames, but every means of doing so is only a rejection of the Cross. We can have no genuine hope of peace and salvation apart from Christ crucified! Happy the man who understands this." On October 1, 1957, at 5:30 am, he climbs to the scaffold. "May my blood that is going to flow be accepted by God as a whole sacrifice, that every drop," he writes, "serves to erase a mortal sin." In his last journal entry, he wrote, "In five hours, I shall look upon Jesus!"[4]

It is true that not every criminal will admit his sins and seek repentance and forgiveness from God; but it is no less true that, as Dr. Samuel Johnson famously quipped, "Depend upon it, sir, when a man knows he is to be hanged in a fortnight, it concentrates his mind wonderfully." There is something more humane about confronting a murderer with the gravity of his crimes: "You have unjustly taken these lives, and now your life is justly required of you. You have two weeks in which to repent and prepare yourself to meet the divine Judge, of whom the earthly judge is only a faint echo." With a ten-, twenty-, or thirty-year prison sentence, many temptations and evils are spread out in a seemingly endless stretch in front of prisoners, who can end up morally worse, or at any rate not morally better, than when they entered. Is this more humane? Only if the worst evil is physical death—which it certainly is not.

In *Christus Vincit*, Bishop Schneider proceeds to remind us of an episode in the life of the Little Flower:

> We also know from the life of St. Thérèse of the Child Jesus that, as a young girl, she adopted her "first sinner," the murderer Pranzini, who in 1887 was sentenced to death. The saint writes in her autobiography, *The Story of a Soul*: "The day after his execution I hastily opened the paper and what did I see? Tears betrayed my emotion; I was obliged to run out of the room. Pranzini had mounted the scaffold without confessing or receiving absolution, and . . .

---

4   *Christus Vincit*, 189.

turned around, seized the crucifix which the priest was offering to him, and kissed Our Lord's Sacred Wounds three times. I had obtained the sign I asked for, and to me it was especially sweet. Was it not when I saw the Precious Blood flowing from the Wounds of Jesus that the thirst for souls first took possession of me?"[5]

Pranzini was a hardened criminal who had no interest in the "consolations of religion," but thanks to the prayers of a girl and the ministrations of a faithful priest who did not leave his side, he welcomed God's grace at the last moment and died having repented of his evil. Even as it can be a false mercy to want to keep someone alive who sinned against the very foundations of social life, it can be a true mercy to give a criminal a radical choice between repentance and hardness, so that the seriousness of what he has done and the need to put his soul in a right relationship with God before death will be apparent.

The examples narrated by Bishop Athanasius Schneider also show us in the most vivid way how important prison ministry is, which offers to convicts again and again the opportunity to be reconciled to God, against whom every sin is directed (cf. Ps. 50:6); it shows us that the prayer of the righteous man availeth much (cf. Jas. 5:16).

---

5   *Christus Vincit*, 189–90.

57

Seven Points to Consider about the "Canonization" of Paul VI

The Remnant

OCTOBER 13, 2020

TWO YEARS AGO, ON OCTOBER 14, 2018, Pope Francis undertook to canonize several people, including his predecessor, Pope Paul VI. Of course, it is a pope's prerogative to beatify or canonize anyone he thinks fit to be beatified or canonized. But this does not mean that, in every single case, there is no room for doubts or difficulties in the matter. In this column I will offer seven points that Catholics deserve to know.

First, it is an open theological question whether canonizations must be considered infallible acts of the papal magisterium. While theological consensus has favored infallibility, the Church herself has never made a binding determination on the matter, such that the opposite position would be ruled out *in principle*.[1] There may be grave reasons for which it would not be unreasonable for Catholics to question a particular canonization.[2]

Second, canonizations have always been understood to be an official response to a popular *cultus* or devotion. In recent times, however, certain beatifications and canonizations seem to have been driven by political motivations, in order to legitimize a certain "program." A little comparison may help: the Church canonized only two popes from a span of *700 years* (Pius V and Pius X), but now three popes from a span of *50 years* (John XXIII, Paul VI, and John Paul II) have been canonized. Commentators have spoken of the real intention, which was to "canonize Vatican II."[3]

---

1   For a complete treatment of this question in all of its aspects, see Peter Kwasniewski, ed., *Are Canonizations Infallible? Revisiting a Disputed Question* (Waterloo, ON: Arouca Press, 2021), esp. 219–41 on Paul VI.

2   See John Lamont, "The Authority of Canonizations" and "The Infallibility of Canonizations and the Morals of the Faithful," in Kwasniewski, *Are Canonizations Infallible?*, 151–74.

3   See Jake Neu, "Paul VI and the Canonization of Vatican II," *First Things*, October 12, 2018.

Third, the *process* by which beatifications and canonizations occur is not without significance. The traditional rigorous process, instituted by Pope Urban VIII (1623-1644) and brought to perfection by Prospero Lambertini (1734-1738, later Pope Benedict XIV, 1740-1758), was followed until 1969. Between 1969 and 1983 the process was in flux, until John Paul II established a new set of much-simplified procedures to speed up the making of saints. In particular, the role of the "devil's advocate" was minimized, the total number of miracles required for canonization was halved from four to two (i.e., one each for beatification and canonization), and the "magnitude" of miracle expected was downsized. These changes, taken together, increase the probability—even if it generally remains small—that a beatification or a canonization will be mistaken.

The cause for Giovanni Battista Montini in particular shows worrisome features. A source in the Vatican confirmed to me that the process was pushed ahead at such speed that the copious documentation from and about Paul VI in the Vatican archives was not exhaustively reviewed. An archive of such magnitude could still turn up problematic material—especially since, as historians know, Montini was involved in clandestine dealings with the Communists as part of the Vatican's failed *Ostpolitik*.[4]

Fourth, contrary to well-meaning attempts to sidestep difficulties, canonization does *not* mean simply that "a person's soul is in heaven." If such were the case, it would be possible to proceed forthwith to the canonization of thousands of individual Catholics who died devoutly receiving the Church's last rites. (Indeed, this is the kind of "canonization" that routinely happens at modern funeral Masses,[5] with or without evidence of the devout reception of last rites.) In truth, canonization has *always* meant that the saint is exemplary in the heroic exercise of the Christian virtues, and is therefore held up to the universal Church as a model to venerate and imitate, particularly by those who are in the same or similar positions or states of life. This, of course, is the fundamental reason why, historically, so few Christians have been named saints! Many people exercise some virtues sometimes,

---

4   See George Weigel, "The Ostpolitik Failed. Get Over It," *First Things*, July 20, 2016.
5   See "The scandal of the modern Catholic funeral," *LifeSiteNews*, November 2, 2018.

but very few exercise the panoply of virtues to an heroic degree. While saints need not be "flawless," they are still genuine "giants" of the supernatural life. When it comes to Paul VI, unfortunately, there is abundant evidence not only that he failed to exercise certain virtues heroically, but also that he displayed the *absence* of certain virtues in his discharge of the papal office—above all in regard to the unprecedented magnitude and violence of the liturgical reform in the period 1964–1974, wherein he acted not as a servant of tradition but as its master and possessor.

Fifth, if some Catholics have doubts about Paul VI's canonization, are they committed to thinking him a criminal and a villain? By no means. Paul VI did much that can be admired, or at least respected as compatible with his papal duties: his encyclical *Mysterium Fidei* of 1965, which reiterates traditional Eucharistic doctrine; his encyclical *Sacerdotalis Caelibatus* of 1967, which defends clerical celibacy; his *Credo of the People of God* of 1968, a resounding reaffirmation of the Catholic Faith; and most famously, his encyclical *Humanae Vitae* of 1968, which repeats the Church's teaching that any deliberate attempt to thwart the procreative end of the marital act is sinful. Nevertheless, the fact that a person (be he a layman, religious, or cleric) has done many great things for Christ and His Church does not constitute, in and of itself, a reason to beatify or canonize him. There are dozens of popes from history who have done as much good as Montini did, or rather, far more good—and without the blemishes that mark his papal record and disqualify him from public veneration.

Sixth, even in the case of *legitimate* beatifications and canonizations, Catholics are not required to have a personal devotion to any particular saint or to invoke him or her as part of their own prayer life, nor would the elevation of someone to the standing of public veneration endow his every action with normative value or his every opinion with indubitable truth. As others have pointed out, the policies of *canonized* popes—including their liturgical decisions—have been questioned or overturned by later popes.[6]

Seventh, we cannot go wrong venerating and imitating the great saints of the past whose heroic virtue is beyond any reasonable doubt, by objective standards and by the witness of generations

6   See Gregory DiPippo, "What Does the Canonization of Paul VI Mean for the Liturgy and Liturgical Reform?," *New Liturgical Movement*, October 14, 2018.

of devotees. We also cannot go wrong approving and lauding any Catholic whose words and deeds obviously harmonize with the well-known doctrine, discipline, and tradition of the Church. On the other hand, we would be wise to refrain from venerating or imitating anyone whose heroic virtue there *are* objective reasons to doubt, or whose opinions on matters of grave importance, such as the sacred liturgy, are saturated with erroneous philosophical theories such as rationalism or utilitarianism.

Two years later, then, we can frankly say: the case for Montini has gained no strength, nor has a robust *cultus* on the part of the faithful shown any hints of existence. Rather, this "canonization," like others, has merged into the general dystopian mess of this pontificate, the Augean stables that a future Roman pontiff will have the unenviable job of cleaning out.

58
Christ's Universal Dominion and the Modern Tower of Babel

OnePeterFive
DECEMBER 23, 2020

T RUTH IS THE FIRST CASUALTY OF WAR—SO goes an old saying. We see it verified again in the so-called "liturgy wars," where, at least on the progressive side, no lie is too big or too bald, if only it can be repeated often enough to convince most people. If one can add a certain sacrilegious touch to it, all the more thrilling!

A case in point, already forgotten in the ceaseless torrent, was Pope Francis's September 3, 2017 motu proprio *Magnum Principium*, concerning vernacular translations of the liturgy, and more specifically, the right of episcopal conferences to approve them for their own territories.[1] As is the custom with this pope, most of his documents appear to be named ironically or parodistically. The Apostolic Exhortation *Amoris Laetitia,* which should have been about the joy of that unbreakable charity that the grace of Christ makes us capable of living out, paved the way for dissoluble marriage and normalized Eucharistic sacrilege. The Apostolic Letter *Vultum Dei Quaerere* put into motion changes that, if not resisted and eventually overturned, will certainly lead to a dropping off of the number of women who are seeking the face of God in the contemplative life—particularly in orders undergoing renewal thanks to the rediscovery of their own deepest traditions. *Laudato Si'* starts off with a quotation from St. Francis of Assisi, who, as a mystic of the Holy Eucharist, would have repudiated much of the encyclical's Teilhardian eco-humanism. *Fratelli Tutti*, the telephone-book expansion of Abu Dhabi, opens with a blatantly false recasting of the story of St. Francis and the Sultan whom the saint, at the risk of his life, tried to convert to the true Faith. And on and on it goes.

So, too, with this motu proprio, the title of which alludes to the antiphon for the Fourth Sunday of Advent:

---

1   See my interview with Diane Montagna in *Tradition and Sanity*, 169–73.

Dominus veniet, occurrite illi, dicentes: Magnum principium, et regni ejus non erit finis: Deus, Fortis, Dominator, Princeps pacis, alleluia, alleluia.

The Lord will come, go ye out to meet Him, saying: Great in His dominion, and of His kingdom there shall be no end: He is the Mighty One, God, the Ruler, the Prince of Peace, alleluia, alleluia.

The great dominion of the Redeemer was powerfully witnessed in the Western world by the unity of Roman Catholic worship in a period of over 1,500 years—a unity of which the Latin language was the obvious icon and vehicle. How ironic, then, to take this particular phrase and apply it to the veritable explosion of more or less inadequate (but always tradition-rupturing) translations that followed the building of the Tower of Babel in the 1960s liturgical reform! The very title of the motu proprio carries an ominous ring: the Great Leader has deigned to tell us about *the* "Great Principle" of the Great Council, for the benefit of the Great People.

Magnum Principium opens with about as breathtaking a series of half-truths as one can find in a papal document of the past 2,000 years:

> The great principle, established by the Second Vatican Ecumenical Council, according to which liturgical prayer [should] be accommodated to the comprehension of the people so that it might be understood, required the weighty task of introducing the vernacular language into the liturgy and of preparing and approving the versions of the liturgical books, a charge that was entrusted to the Bishops. The Latin Church was aware of the attendant sacrifice involved in the partial loss of liturgical Latin, which had been in use throughout the world over the course of centuries. However, it willingly opened the door so that these versions, as part of the rites themselves, might become the voice of the Church celebrating the divine mysteries along with the Latin language. At the same time, especially given the various clearly expressed views of the Council Fathers with regard to the use of the vernacular language in the liturgy, the Church was aware of the difficulties that might present themselves in this regard.

How many half-truths, or, more accurately, lies, are we working with here?

1. The Constitution on the Sacred Liturgy of the Second Vatican Council never placed the verbal comprehension of the people above the principle of fidelity to tradition and the preservation of Latin. In spite of the problems in its reformatory inversion of principles,[2] the document nevertheless went out of its way to state that Latin was to remain the language of the liturgy and that the limits of the vernacular could be extended, especially in *missionary* regions. The truth is that what happened after the Council well exceeded, or perhaps we might say fell far short of, any natural reading of the texts.

2. At the Council, the Fathers (bishops and religious superiors) debated the Latin question at enormous length in the first session, and the "clearly expressed views" in the majority of their speeches were, in point of fact, in favor of preserving liturgical Latin. There were a few speakers who advocated a significant increase in the vernacular, and, if I recall rightly, *only a single one*, the Melkite patriarch Maximos IV Sayegh, who advocated complete vernacularization—which, surprise!, is what transpired under Paul VI and Bugnini. In no way could one read the debates in the aula and come away with the impression that "the Latin Church was aware of the attendant sacrifice involved in the partial loss of liturgical Latin, which had been in use throughout the world over the course of centuries"—simply because practically no Catholic at the Council dreamed of a world in which liturgical Latin would have disappeared.

3. The phrases "partial loss of Latin" and "along with the Latin" are sheer absurdity. I don't know what planet Pope Francis lives on, but in 99.9% of the Catholic world, not a single word of Latin is heard at any time; there are even bishops who severely persecute those who attempt to use Latin. Perhaps the pope is thinking too narrowly of the Vatican, which is one of the few places left where Latin *is* still sometimes encountered in the Novus Ordo.

Magnum Principium was the opening salvo of a liturgical campaign to match the moral campaign of *Amoris Laetitia.* As the latter document decentralized moral decisions to episcopal conferences, so the former began to do the same for liturgy. Just as one can

---

2 See "How *Not* to Understand Active Participation," in Kwasniewski, *Ministers of Christ,* 131–40.

be in adultery and forbidden from Communion in Poland but go across the border to Germany and be welcomed to Communion as a Christian adult who had self-annulled a marriage by one's own judgment of conscience, so it will happen that one may attend Mass in a certain country and hear a strictly accurate rendering of *pro multis*, while in the next country, where the bishops had decided that Jesus should have said *pro omnibus*, one will hear something different, even in the very sacramental form.

In the 1970s, before his fall from grace, Bugnini was openly saying that the revision of the liturgy was only the first step in a long process of evolution, the final stage of which was a totally "inculturated" liturgy that reflected the needs and demands of each unrepeatable local group (think: Amazonification). In other words, liturgical unity, uniformity, and universality are enemies of authentic individual faith and a worship relevant to modern times. Ratzinger criticized this idea fiercely, but it has always remained the hippie dream of the liturgical progressives, who now have one of their own on the papal throne. He is acting slowly, but with decisive steps—and I'm sure his stacking of the deck of cardinals is designed to ensure a successor as liberal as himself so that the project can be completed.

And I haven't even gotten into the nitty gritty! Francis says, for example:

> The goal of the translation of liturgical texts and of biblical texts for the Liturgy of the Word is to announce the word of salvation to the faithful in obedience to the faith and to express the prayer of the Church to the Lord. For this purpose it is necessary to communicate to a given people using its own language all that the Church intended to communicate to other people through the Latin language.

1. It is far from obvious that it is *"necessary"* to have *everything* in the people's language. It is good when the faithful can access the meaning of the liturgical texts, but this can and should happen in many ways, educational, catechetical, homiletic, and with hand missals—and most importantly, it should happen by a long and steady process of assimilation that goes beyond the surface-level of registering familiar words. The worst way to reach the goal of a deep understanding of the mysteries of Christ is to vernacularize the liturgy at a time of unprecedented secularization,

theological illiteracy, poetic impotence, and contempt for tradition.

2. One cannot communicate all that is contained in the traditional Latin prayers through any modern vernacular. Every translation is a betrayal; all the more so when we are looking at over 1,600 years of liturgical Latin. A hand missal can give the conceptual content fairly well, but the Latin prayer says more, says it better, more subtly and fully and strikingly. Does this make a difference? By all means. The one we are addressing principally is God, and how we speak to Him matters. When we offer Him solemn, beautiful, highly-valued and saint-spoken prayer, it is pleasing in the way that an unblemished lamb is pleasing—in the way that *the* unblemished Logos offered on the Cross was pleasing. The very fact that countless holy men and women had the very same words on their lips over the centuries endows them with a special efficacy. St. Mectilde of Hackeborn says that the court of heaven rejoices whenever it hears the same words it prayed while on earth.

3. As already intimated, there are many other and more important aspects of communication than mere verbal comprehension. The assumption at work in the motu proprio is that of modern rationalism, which is hardly surprising, since it is the operative philosophy of the entire liturgical reform.

4. Over time, the Church saw in her traditional Latin far more than a mere instrument of communication. It was a sign and principle of unity, a representation of her timeless empire of truth, which leads us always back to the roots and makes of us one flock everywhere. Many popes and bishops across the ages have taught the same, indicating that we are dealing with the ordinary universal Magisterium. Pope John XXIII's Apostolic Constitution *Veterum Sapientia*, another milestone of 1962, was no more abrogated than the classical *Missale Romanum* was.

The whole motu proprio *Magnum Principium* could be critiqued like this. It is either a piece of mendacity and double-dealing that reeks of sulfur, or an historic monument to the depths of ignorance and error to which the "spirit of Vatican II" has led its captives. With my forefathers in the Faith, I will gladly stick to the old missal and the old breviary, allowing the phrase to be reabsorbed into its higher and superior origin: *Dominus veniet, occurrite illi, dicentes: Magnum principium, et regni ejus non erit finis: Deus, Fortis, Dominator, Princeps pacis, alleluia, alleluia.*

59

Crocodile Tears and Hand-Wringing: No GPS Coordinates for the Unicorn

The Remnant

AUGUST 16, 2021

"**A**T THE SAME TIME, I ASK YOU TO BE VIGilant in ensuring that every liturgy be celebrated with decorum and fidelity to the liturgical books promulgated after Vatican Council II, without the eccentricities that can easily degenerate into abuses..." Thus spake Francis in the letter that accompanies his motu proprio *Traditionis Custodes* of July 16, 2021.

Two days later, on July 18, we were given a textbook example of eccentricity in a Sunday Mass held by pastor Rainer Maria Schießler at the Hofbräuhaus München, a famous brewery restaurant, where Mass is held once a month in the midst of mascots and Biersteins. Everyone sits at their picnic tables looking vaguely bored or amused, depending on what they've eaten and drunk beforehand. The vessels for the Eucharist sit on top of an improvised card table with two pillar candles. On July 23, we were given an example of abuse (to say the least) in a Gay Mass in the Archdiocese of Berlin, featuring rainbow-colored cloths leading up to the altar, hanging from the ambo, and decorating the base of the crucifix.

The fabled unicorn—code language for the reverent, traditional (-looking), Ratzingerian Novus Ordo, which is supposed to satisfy the yearnings of devout Catholics—is still wandering at large and rarely sighted. Even where eccentricity and abuse are not abundant, banality and verbosity prevail.

For fifty years, popes have been wringing their hands about various kinds of abuses and the prevailing lack of reverence and beauty in the Novus Ordo.[1] Yet nothing much has happened. Neither popes nor bishops have enforced the existing rules. They did not punish the recalcitrant or promote outstanding models. *Redemptionis*

---

1   See "Fidelity to Liturgical Law and the Rights of the Faithful," *OnePeterFive*, July 3, 2017.

Sacramentum of 2004 was supposed to be the great moment, in the wake of John Paul II's encyclical *Ecclesia de Eucharistia*, when the new Mass would *finally* be restored to rubrical rightness and resplendent reverence. What happened? Fields of crickets from one end of the earth to the other. A friend of mine called a chancery one day and asked if she could report a violation against *Redemptionis Sacramentum*. The person on the phone went around the office asking if anyone had heard of the document, and then told her: "No, we haven't heard of it. We're sorry." End of conversation.

Pope Francis added his crocodile tears to the hand-wringing of his predecessors:

> I am saddened by abuses in the celebration of the liturgy on all sides. In common with Benedict XVI, I deplore the fact that "in many places the prescriptions of the new Missal are not observed in celebration, but indeed come to be interpreted as an authorization for or even a requirement of creativity, which leads to almost unbearable distortions."

Saddening abuses. Deplorable facts. Unbearable distortions. Surely, then, they must be dealt with swiftly and mercilessly, in the same manner in which the pope has chosen to deal with the pressing problem of the traditionalists!

Such rhetorical tropes are as shallow as the feelings of comfort they evoke. How do we *know* that Pope Francis (or a like-minded Francis II) won't take the well-rooted problem of bad liturgy seriously?

Watch the daily papal Mass: the dull and horizontal ritual of a dying *Weltanschauung*. This is the pope who violated the rule about whose feet could be washed on Holy Thursday,[2] and then, having modified the rule,[3] proceeded to violate the new one.[4] This is the pope who does not kneel or genuflect before the Most Holy Sacrament of the Altar,[5] but who becomes surprisingly lithe when

---

2   See anon., "Pope breaks rules as he washes feet of disabled people in pre-Easter ritual," *CBS News*, April 17, 2014.

3   See Edward Pentin, "Pope Changes Rules for Washing of the Feet on Holy Thursday," *National Catholic Register*, January 21, 2016.

4   See Elahe Izadi, "Pope Francis washes the feet of Muslim migrants, says we are 'children of the same God,'" *The Washington Post*, March 25, 2016.

5   See anon., "Why Doesn't Pope Francis Kneel Before the Blessed Sacrament?," www.torchofthefaith.com/news.php?extend.1332.

it's time to kneel at the feet of politicians.[6] This is the pope on whose watch the Basilica of St. Peter, premiere pilgrimage church of Christendom, has outlawed Masses at side altars, undergrounded the Mass of the Ages, and nearly banished the use of Latin—at *St. Peter's*, the one place in the world where the Church's mother tongue has always been at home and would always be fitting. This is the pope under whom the Vatican's publishing house has decided not to reprint the Liturgy of the Hours in Latin—its *editio typica* or standard edition—since it might foster dangerous linguistic liaisons.[7]

No, this pope is no "guardian of tradition" (*traditionis custos*), nor will he lead the long-awaited crusade to bring forth "the spiritual richness and the theological depth of this [new] Missal" (to borrow a somewhat ironic phrase from Benedict XVI's letter to the bishops of July 7, 2007). Nor can we expect any better from the influential churchmen of his making, who are as eager to cancel Tridentine Masses as they are to allow or even celebrate Masses for any and every subculture, especially if it calls itself by a string of capital letters.[8]

The "high Novus Ordo" is not and never could be appealing to Latin Mass-goers. Where progressives hold that the liturgy is simply a means to an end, traditionalists view the Mass as a sublime end to which everything else should be ordered, because God Himself, Alpha and Omega, to whom all things bow, graces it and us with His very Presence. Because it is His gift to us of what is divine and most holy, the Mass must be rubrically inflexible, thoroughly scripted, as objective as the everlasting hills and the surging seas, carving out a space free of arbitrary personality in order to let the unchanging God of love act in our midst.

With the TLM, it makes almost no difference who the priest is, as long as he knows what he's doing. I can go (and I have been) to Latin Masses all over the world, and I know just what I'm getting. The priest does a ritual that corresponds to what is printed in

---

6   See Philip Pullella, "Pope kisses feet of South Sudan leaders, urging them to keep the peace," *Reuters*, April 11, 2019.

7   See Fr. John Zuhlsdorf, "ASK FATHER: Can't get 'Liturgy of the Hours' in Latin," *Fr. Z's Blog*, September 6, 2017; Fr. John Hunwicke, "Irreversibly Bye Bye to Vatican II," *Fr Hunwicke's Mutual Enrichment*, September 19, 2017.

8   See Jules Gomes, "Bishop backs LGBT Eucharist, bans Latin Mass," *Church Militant*, July 19, 2021.

my hand missal. I might barely see his face, and at a Low Mass might never hear him speak a vernacular language. He is, as St. Thomas says, an "animated instrument" of the High Priest: it is quite clear Who is in charge, Who is the primary actor. It is theocentric and Christocentric.

In contrast, the Novus Ordo is clericocentric, depending on the priest for its "reverent" realization. A lover of sights and sounds might praise Holy Loftitude Parish because *that* priest at *that* place does it *that* way: with smells and bells, *ad orientem*, a pinch of Latin for Roman Catholic effect, kneeling for Communion, and so forth. All of it is optional: at the option of the priest and his "team," at the option of a willing congregation without speed-dial Susans, at the option of a willing bishop. It quickly becomes a matter of "this good and holy priest does the Mass right," instead of "the good and holy God gave us in His Providence a good and holy liturgy, on which we can always rely."

The traditionalists' issue with the Novus Ordo has never fundamentally been at the level of good looks, even if we'd readily admit that a new Mass dressed like the old Mass can be a feast for sore eyes. No. It is about the traditional liturgy in its total integrity on every level, starting with its ancient and venerable *lex orandi* found in the corpus of prayers, the chants, ceremonies, rubrics, and customs. These are either utterly missing,[9] wildly mingled,[10] or woefully mangled[11] in the new liturgical books. The new and old rites (thankfully, Pope Francis has rid us of the clumsy "ordinary" and "extraordinary" jargon) are, in fact, nearly always different—and often radically so.[12]

In the month that has passed since July 16, there have been well-meaning priests and laity who say: "I'm very sorry that we have to stop the TLM but I'm sure you'll learn to adjust to the NO if you bring the right spirit."

9   See Hazell, "Mythbusting, Part II," *New Liturgical Movement*, October 1, 2021.

10   See Matthew Hazell, "The Prayers for the Feast of St Lawrence in the Post-Vatican II Liturgical Reforms," *Rorate Caeli*, August 10, 2021.

11   See Matthew Hazell, "The Scattering of the Propers: A Case Study in the Mass Formularies of the Ordinary Form," *New Liturgical Movement*, July 15, 2020.

12   See Lauren Pristas, *The Collects of the Roman Missals: A Comparative Study of the Sundays in Proper Seasons before and after the Second Vatican Council* (London/New York: Bloomsbury T&T Clark, 2013).

Whoever can speak thus doesn't have even the faintest clue about what it is that attracts Catholics to the old rite, about how deeply the rites are different, and how inadequate the modern rite will always seem in comparison. Or why educated, serious, and devout Catholics have been sparring over this issue for more than half a century. It's not the sort of thing about which one can shrug one's shoulders and "move on." You cannot unsee what you have seen,[13] unknow what you have come to know.[14] And that is why, in the absence of a competent pope, the troubles will continue and indeed multiply. Problems of this magnitude don't evaporate simply because a powerful person orders them to vanish. *They go away when truth and justice are recognized and accepted.* Physical healing may be more or less automatic, but moral and spiritual healing doesn't work that way.

Yes, God may be asking you to suffer, for a time, the loss of your local TLM. *But this loss is still an evil.* It is objectively evil to be cut off from the gift of tradition.[15] It is objectively evil to repudiate a liturgical rite organically developed over more than 1,600 years. It is objectively evil to be deprived of a strong daily link with our ancestors in the faith and of a rich source of spiritual nourishment on which we had come to rely. God does not and cannot will these evils as such (*pace* the Abu Dhabi declaration), for He does not deny Himself or repent of His gifts. Yes, He sometimes asks priests to suffer imprisonment in a concentration camp and to say no Mass, or to say a rushed and whispered Mass with a scrap of smuggled bread and a thimbleful of wine. Needless to say (or is it?), this is not the normal, natural, social, and cultural situation that is fitting for tradition-constituted rational animals. That is why God has not willed that most Christians most of the time should be incarcerated and deprived of their basic rights *or* rites.

We've all heard of "fiat currency." This pope believes in "fiat culture." As Tracey Rowland shows, the Fathers of Vatican II neither possessed nor were able to formulate a coherent conception of

---

13   See "Discovering Tradition: A Priest's Crisis of Conscience," *OnePeterFive*, March 27, 2019.

14   See "Comparison of Old and New Prayers for Blessing of Ashes," *OnePeterFive*, February 26, 2020.

15   See Kwasniewski, "The Gift of Liturgical Tradition," in *Reclaiming Our Roman Catholic Birthright*, 161–79.

culture and therefore of how Catholicism was supposed to permeate and animate culture.[16] This is why they ended up with an awkward view in which two forces—a religious subculture and a modern anti-culture—were supposed to blend and produce a new synthesis, which, however, must remain as crippled as either of its elements. Pope Francis's *Traditionis Custodes* shows that he thinks it's possible, by papal *ukase*, to tell Catholics who have embraced and internalized traditional ways of worshiping—which it is perfectly *dignum et justum* for them to do—that they must simply "transition" over to the modern liturgy of Paul VI, sooner or later. As if we just put on or put off our deepest thoughts and feelings, our surrounding world, like a piece of clothing. That, however, is modernity's view: we are what we will ourselves to be; we are disembodied minds that choose our identity.[17] So false is this view that it cannot be refuted by argument; it is refuted by the whole of reality at every moment.

The authors and promoters of *Traditionis Custodes* are not concerned only about whether or not Catholics "accept" Vatican II or the new liturgy. Of course they want us to say we do. But the goal is not verifying assent to some propositions and then moving on with life. The goal is to exterminate the possibility of living a traditional Catholic life in adherence to the perennial Magisterium. It is, in that sense, precisely an anti-Catholic campaign, as Sebastian Morello and Massimo Viglione bring out so well.[18] The partisans of Bergoglianity would rather see a sparsely-attended Novus Ordo church than a full one with the traditional Mass; a tiny family that worships contemporarily than a large family that worships timelessly; fewer priestly and religious vocations, as long as they are liberal and lavender, than an abundance of vocations cut from old-fashioned cloth, be it black, brown, or gray. The specious hermeneutic of continuity has been summarily swapped out for the hermeneutic of hatred—a hatred of the past, of memory and identity, of history, of reality.

A priest friend wrote to me:

---

16   See *Culture and the Thomist Tradition: After Vatican II* (London/New York: Routledge, 2003).

17   See Jason Morgan, "Triumph of the Will: The Novus Ordo, RIP," *The Remnant*, August 3, 2021.

18   See *From Benedict's Peace to Francis's War*, 94–99 and 103–11.

I think that people need to wake up to the fact that this is about so much more than the TLM—Francis is attempting to eliminate a whole way of being Catholic, even for people who never go to the TLM. The English liturgist Clifford Howell was wont to say that the use of vernacular in the Liturgy was pointing towards a new world order that couldn't otherwise be expressed coterminously with Latin. I realize now that what he meant is that essentially the new liturgy is a social movement based on the wholesale rejection of the Catholic worldview. The Old Mass is too off-message now to be allowed to continue.

To our conservative Catholic friends we say: thanks for the reminders about how the pope's motu proprio is a cross, willed by God, that we must carry. That's true. At the same time, let's not turn our religion, centered on the sacrifice of Calvary, into a version of Buddhism bedecked with a Christian symbol. We do not wave aside evils as illusions on the path to enlightenment and nirvana; we recognize them for what they are—ontological parasites—and we strive to overcome them by the grace of a personal God who reveals Himself to us. As Leo XIII says in his encyclical *Libertas Praestantissimum*, evils in a society may need to be tolerated for a time, but they may never be approved as regular fixtures, much less hailed as advantages. And if the injustice is deep enough, it must call forth our total effort at eradicating it.

Meanwhile, program your GPS to find the nearest Latin Mass. It will probably be easier to find, and will certainly be more Catholic, than the fabled unicorn.

60

Is the Pope the Vicar of Christ or CEO of Vatican, Inc.?[†]

Catholic Family News
MARCH 14, 2022

B Y NOW, MANY WILL HAVE HEARD OF THE arbitrary removal, by Pope Francis, of a young (57-year-old) bishop of Puerto Rico—Daniel Fernández Torres of the Diocese of Arecibo—because, apparently, he wasn't "sufficiently in union" with the pope and his fellow bishops on the island. By all accounts and by the bishop's own testimony, no objective canonically-classifiable wrongdoing or even hint or claim of wrongdoing has been pressed against him, as *The Pillar* summarizes in its article "Can the pope just fire a bishop?"[1] Rather, the bishop exercised a certain freedom of judgment by which he took a more conservative line than his fellow bishops: he would not send his seminarians to a new interdiocesan seminary; he would not enforce vaccinations; he would not collaborate in the suppression of the traditional Latin Mass; he would not buckle to the agenda of the lavender mafia.[2] This was enough to make him hated and feared. He had to be terminated, just like that. One might say his crime was to be a Catholic in the mold of the pope, Benedict XVI, who had appointed him.

Bishop Torres passionately and articulately defended himself in a crystal-clear statement on March 9, part of which reads (my translation):

> I regret very much that in a Church where mercy is so much preached, in practice some lack a minimal sense of justice. No process has been made against me, nor have I been formally accused of anything and simply one day the Apostolic Delegate verbally communicated to me that Rome was asking me to resign. A successor of the apostles

---

† New paragraphs on Pius XII have been added for this publication.

1 Published March 9, 2022.
2 See Inés San Martín, "Pope removes Puerto Rican bishop from office after he refused to resign," *Crux*, March 9, 2022.

is now being replaced without even undertaking what would be a due canonical process to remove a parish priest. I was informed that I had committed no crime but that I supposedly "had not been obedient to the pope nor had I been in sufficient communion with my brother bishops of Puerto Rico." It was suggested to me that if I resigned from the diocese I would remain at the service of the Church in case at some point I was needed in some other position—an offer that in fact proves my innocence. However, I did not resign because I did not want to become an accomplice in a totally unjust action, one that even now I am reluctant to think could happen in our Church.[3]

The Pillar article, which is quite revealing in itself, competently explains that removing a bishop is an extremely grave matter: he is, after all, a successor of the apostles who receives his authority *from Christ*, even if through the pope's appointment; he is not a middle manager appointed by the CEO of Vatican, Inc.[4] *The Pillar* treats us to fascinating historical details of the considerable pains taken by earlier popes *not* to fire bishops, because it would have been considered unthinkable to act that way toward one of the "high priests" in the Church of Christ: "*Ecce Sacerdos magnus,*" as the old antiphon for the entrance of a bishop exclaimed.

A telling example of this reverential attitude towards the episcopate comes to us from the reign of Pope Pius XII. As Yves Chiron narrates in his biography of Giovanni Battista Montini (a masterpiece of a book), the government of France at the end of World War II wanted to punish all the bishops who openly supported Marshal Pétain and the Vichy regime. Understandable enough. But when individuals in the new French government like Hubert Guérin, Pierre Bloch, René Massigli, and Georges Bidault made it known to the Vatican that they wished not only to swap out the papal nuncio but to see a slew of hierarchs removed from their offices—three cardinals and thirty bishops, to be exact—Pius XII responded indignantly:

---

3 "Declaración del Obispo Daniel Fernández Torres," www.diocesisdeare-cibo.org/2022/03/09/declaracion-del-obispo-daniel-fernandez-torres/, accessed March 21, 2022.
4 See Phil Lawler's take: "The Pope's arbitrary actions belie his call for 'synodal' governance," *CatholicCulture.org*, March 9, 2022.

> On the 27th [of November 1944], Pius XII received Msgr Théas. Concerning the change of the nuncio, the Pope "stated his displeasure with the attitude of the French government, which he regards as offensive, discourteous, injurious. He will change the nuncio because he has become *persona ingrata*, but he will not do it without pain or protest." As for purging the episcopacy, he declared: "There can be no question of changing the bishops. That has never been done. That will not be done. That would be an injustice. That would be without precedent. That is inadmissible."[5]

Pius XII, who knew and hated the Nazis like few others, had the instinct of a pope who also knew that even when a successor of the apostles has behaved dishonorably, one doesn't just fire him "at will"; he's not an employee of a corporation or a government official. Pius XII would not remove bishops who bore the real guilt of collaborating with Vichy, while Francis removes Bishop Torres who seems to have done nothing grievously wrong.

Let us return now to *The Pillar*. In glorious hyperpapalist fashion, we are told that *of course* the pope can remove a bishop *ad libitum* because the pope's the boss, with no limits to his power:

> Notwithstanding the absence of any evidence of a canonical crime, or the reticence of previous popes to remove diocesan bishops by papal fiat, Francis does have, according to canon law, "supreme, full, immediate, and universal ordinary power" in the Church, and specifically the "primacy of ordinary power over all particular churches [dioceses]."

The Pillar sidesteps the million-dollar question of what all these words—"supreme, full, immediate, universal, ordinary, power"—actually *mean*: if their interpretation were self-evident, they would not have been the object of canonical and theological scrutiny for centuries. Scholastics famous and obscure all took the position that there are limits to *any* human authority's exercise of power, even the pope's. It is astonishing that anyone could adhere to an interpretation that makes the pope a mortal god on earth, before whom every bishop must quake for fear that he will be arbitrarily removed from his office at the pope's next whim.

---

5   Yves Chiron, *Paul VI: The Divided Pope*, trans. James Walther (Brooklyn, NY: Angelico Press, 2022), 93.

The Pillar's simplistic ecclesiology (and would that it were limited only to journalists!) makes an utter hash of the episcopacy as part of the inherent constitution of the Church. If bishops have zero rights in the possession of their office—that is, if they can be "fired at will"—they are not actually governing the Church with divine authority in collegial communion with the vicar of Christ. They are, as the nineteenth-century caricature had it, "vicars of the pope" who govern their dioceses simply because the pope can't practically be everywhere at all times. According to that ecclesiology, if one may dignify it with such a name, the pope would be the real bishop of each and every diocese, who has delegated some of his authority, *pro tempore* and *ad hoc*, to these various individuals.

On this view of papal authority, no one in the Church has any objective rights except by papal sufferance. That is, as long as the pope is willing to let you have the appearance of rights, then you can live according to those appearances, and you might even be permitted to conduct a canon law case in reference to them; but the moment he says "Okay, enough of that make-believe; I deprive you of XYZ," then we must bow our heads and submit. Not only (on this view) does canon law have no say over the pope himself, it possesses force only by his continually willing it to have force, as if he were sustaining it in being. The pope is not the protector and promoter of the Church and her members, but the source and measure of all that belongs to them qua members of the Church. He *makes* and *unmakes* the members of the Church. In short, he is the sole actual possessor of authority and standing in the Church, while everyone else possesses it from his implicit grant, which may at any time be revoked.

Such is the *reductio ad absurdum* of a certain vein of ultramontanism. Thanks be to God it is not Catholicism, but only a rotten and sickly parody of it.

Let's explore this matter further. Who, in the Church, *has* absolute and unlimited power? Who is the source of all authority, all rights and duties? The answer is obvious: *Christ Himself*, the Head of the Church. The pope as *vicar* of Christ is one who stands in His place, exercising certain duties (and only those duties) that have been entrusted to him; but the pope is by no means the *equal* of Christ. Perhaps the chafing pain of this inherent limit explains

Pope Francis's curious removal of the title "Vicar of Christ" from the list of titles in the *Annuario Pontificio*, where he had it relegated to the category of "historical titles": he no longer wants to be or to be seen as just a representative of Christ. Rather, in some sense, he wishes to be His *equal*, to rule and control and remake the Church as if it were his own possession, his own bride. To be "friend of the bridegroom" (cf. Jn. 3:29) is not enough.

In spite of its democratic outward appearance, the synodal process fits snugly into this ultimate grab for power. Inasmuch as the Church could be described as monarchical in her papacy, aristocratic in her episcopacy, and democratic in the common access of all her members to the full treasury of Redemption poured forth in the liturgy and sacraments, the Church is by no means "synodal" in the newspeak sense of the term, where synodality is a process of "consultation" and "decision-making" emanating from the top down, and seeking to elicit and impose a progressivist vision of perpetual doctrinal and moral evolution validated by the will of the pope, who, taking the place of the "God of surprises," presides over the autodemolition of historic confessional Catholicism. That kind of synodality serves as both a smokescreen for and an engine of modernism.

The pope as *servus servorum Dei* who receives and hands on what he has received, the bishops as successors to the apostles who do the same, and the faithful as recipients of tradition and subjects of the *sensus fidei* have no place in this Rousseauian vision of a "general will" that emerges as if spontaneously from human meetings and human decisions. We might even say that the Bergoglian ecclesiology combines the worst features of the three social contract philosophers: it has Hobbes's autocratic Leviathan in the person of the pope who is not Christ's vicar but Christ's replacement; it has Locke's relativism about truth claims and the subordination of religion to political power; and it has Rousseau's autocratic regime masquerading as the people's will and voice.

There are those who celebrate the "reconciliation" of the Catholic Church with Enlightenment philosophy. We who recognize, in keeping with Vatican I, that the divine constitution of the Church is unchanging and unchangeable, should not be among them.

The Pillar concludes its article thus:

Bishop Torres may not like, or even understand the reasons for his removal. And it may be true that he has committed no canonical offense, and received no kind of due process. Torres might believe the decision to be entirely unjust, and it very well might be unjust. The Church does not hold that the charisms of the Holy Spirit protect popes from bad decisions in governance—and every pope in history has made some. But does the pope have the power to do it? He does.

Catholic journalism is not meant to be theology, granted, but it should at least try to avoid trumpeting absurdities. Here is a suggested alternative conclusion:

> When a pope wields his power arbitrarily, against the rights of his subjects (for they do retain their rights, which come to them from sources above and beyond the pope), he sins in doing so, harms the common good of the Church, and deserves to be resisted in any way possible, such as non-compliance. Such a pope would be in a state of mortal sin and would have to seek absolution for it.

After all, Karl Rahner—no traditionalist he—argued the same about a pope who should dare to obliterate an Eastern Rite.[6]

---

6   Fr. Zuhlsdorf cites the text in "What the mighty Jesuit Karl Rahner would say, said, about suppressing *Summorum Pontificum*," *Fr. Z's Blog*, July 1, 2021.

61

Innovations Will Continue Until Morale Improves: On Francis's New Constitution for the Roman Curia

Catholic Family News
APRIL 19, 2022

ON MARCH 19, 2022, POPE FRANCIS released the text of the long-awaited reform of the Roman Curia in an Apostolic Constitution entitled *Praedicate Evangelium* ("Preach the Gospel": hereafter, *PE*). I say "long-awaited" because this reform was one of the main reasons the cardinals elected Bergoglio back in 2013, when he talked tough about the need for change in the Vatican. So it's been in the works for nine years—elaborated by a council of cardinals (some of whom ended in disgrace) and reviewed by the world episcopacy. (No one knows precisely how wide or serious this episcopal consultation was; if the highly erratic and misrepresented survey on *Summorum Pontificum* and the traditional Mass is any indication, the Vatican seems to practice "synodality" in inverse proportion to how much it talks about it.[1])

The fact that, after nine years of thrashing around, the Constitution was released suddenly, in Italian only, and in the midst of the highly distracting situation of a war in Eastern Europe, does not exactly inspire confidence in its "above-boardness." We have seen similar tactics used in this pontificate for augmenting chaos and disarming opposition, as when *Traditionis Custodes* was released on July 16 effective immediately, or when the responses to the supposed *dubia* were released a week before Christmas by the Congregation for Divine Worship and the Discipline of the Sacraments (usually abbreviated CDW).

In spite of nearly a decade of work on it, the document betrayed telltale signs of haste and clumsiness. For example, it still referred

---

1 For details on the 2020 survey of bishops regarding the Traditional Latin Mass, see Diane Montagna, "*Traditionis Custodes*: Separating Fact from Fiction," *The Remnant*, October 7, 2021.

to "the extraordinary form" [*sic*] of the Roman rite when discussing the competencies of the CDW's successor, the Dicastery for Divine Worship (we will need to get used to writing DDW), even though Francis's *motu proprio* of July 16 had obliterated the terminology introduced by *Summorum Pontificum*. (It was about time that someone officially stated the truth that there is only one form of the Roman rite. This one form, of course, is the traditional Latin liturgy. Unfortunately, Francis picked the wrong member of the pair by selecting Paul VI's modern rite, which has only the loosest of connections to the Roman rite.)

A POSTMODERN HIERARCHY OF OFFICES

There are several key features to the curial reform that deserve our closest attention.

The reduction of all the branches of the Roman Curia to *equal* "dicasteries" with no ranking among themselves except that they are all inferior to the Secretariat of State and the Dicastery of Evangelization is strangely post-modern. Post-modern philosophy is skeptical of hierarchy, dependency or subordination, truth claims, and dogma. It tends to privilege pluralism, relativism, freedom, equality, and social action, in spite of the fact that each of these ideas eventually clashes with all of the others when followed with any seriousness.

In reality, there *is* a hierarchy among these various Vatican offices, as is plain for anyone who thinks theologically: the Gospel itself is revealed truth that must be first understood, and rightly understood, before it can be proclaimed and put into practice. The new arrangement suggests a vision in which action and politics hold primacy over contemplation and doctrine; in which nothing is apolitical, everything politicized. As one commentator pointed out, if most of the dicasteries are now to be considered equal yet all must serve the Secretariat of State, there will be even more jockeying for power and influence than before, as each tries to get the best seat at the Secretariat's table. As Phil Lawler mildly puts it:

> The Dicastery for the Doctrine of the Faith...will have a somewhat diminished role. While the existing Congregation for the Doctrine of the Faith has had the final say on all doctrinal statements, the dicastery will now be

charged with collaborating with other Vatican offices and with local churches on questions of doctrine.[2]

This jockeying will intensify in connection with major papal documents, for the reason that Loup Besmond de Senneville of *La Croix* explains:

> The Secretariat of State is defined as the "papal secretariat," underlining this office's role in helping the Roman Pontiff carry out his mission. Francis also wants the Secretariat to focus particularly on the preparation of the major texts of the magisterium.[3]

The Secretariat—think: the people in charge of the deal with Beijing that sold out the Chinese Church, either because of high-level blackmail or Vatican financial dependency—will prepare the "major texts of the magisterium." What could possibly go wrong, in a world where enormous wealth and power is concentrated in the hands of the globalists of the New World Order to whom the Secretariat of State has been playing the coquette for some time now?

SEVERING CURIAL LEADERSHIP FROM CLERICAL STATUS

PE takes the audacious step of severing curial leadership from clerical status.[4] The progressives are popping corks around the globe at the prospect of laywomen taking charge of entire Vatican dicasteries (as they have already done at many mainstream parishes). Just think of it: Sr. Hildegard Waffenmund from the highest ranks of the German Church might be put in charge of the DDW, making sanctuaries a safe place for women of all ages, races, orientations, and religions! A lay theologian like Massimo Faggioli might even be tapped to lead the Dicastery for the Doctrine of the Faith.

Lawler points to this provision as an example of the document's slapdash nature, which sadly has come to characterize so many messy "reforms" of this pontificate:

---

2   "Pope Francis releases document reforming Curial reform," *Catholic-Culture.org*, March 21, 2022.

3   "Roman Curia reformed: Pope Francis' revolution," *La Croix International*, March 21, 2022.

4   Michael Haynes, "Pope Francis reforms Roman Curia, says any layperson can hold 'governance' positions in Vatican," *LifeSiteNews*, March 19, 2022.

The document says that lay people may take roles in Church governance, but the Code of Canon Law reserves the authority of governance to the ordained clergy, saying that lay people "can *cooperate* in the exercise of that same power." Of course the Pope, as the supreme legislator of the Church, can amend canon law to resolve that apparent contradiction. But no such amendment has yet been suggested.[5]

The severance of curial leadership from clerical status suggests that the curia is being reconceived as a gigantic secretariat for the pope, instead of being seen as sharing in the hierarchical function of governing and teaching (*sub et cum Petro*). That is, although the curia has never been seen to have authority *over against* the pope, it has had in the past a certain "weight" to it that is appropriate to a body competent to issue instructions, clarifications, laws, rulings, and so forth. As Fr. Hunwicke has well explained, the curia of the Vatican is a natural outgrowth of the curia of the pope as the Bishop of Rome: every bishop is surrounded by his clergy who assist him in the tasks of ruling, teaching, and sanctifying. According to Cardinal Gerhard Müller, however, the changes put in motion by *PE* transform the Roman Curia "from an ecclesial entity of the Holy Roman Church into a worldly administrative apparatus."[6]

The idea that lay people can take charge of the dicasteries seems to make the latter more like think-tanks or study groups, while concentrating power solely in the pope's hands—a continuation of the now more than 150-year-old trajectory by which the diversified and complementary authorities spread throughout the Church by divine design, partly in order to give the Church due protection from the rare occurrence of wayward popes, have been weakened to such an extent that their power is treated as if it emanates from the pope and operates solely by his sufferance. I have written about this elsewhere in connection with the scandalous removal of Bishop Daniel Fernández Torres.[7]

---

5   See, in addition to Lawler, Andrea Gagliarducci's "Is Pope Francis' pragmatic approach creating a crisis for canon law?," *Catholic News Agency*, November 19, 2021.
6   Edward Pentin, "'Praedicate Evangelium' Poses Problems, Some Church Analysts Warn," *National Catholic Register*, April 6, 2022.
7   See the preceding chapter.

Notably, Fr. Pius Pietrzyk, O. P., professor of canon law at the Dominican House of Studies in Washington, D. C., holds that the view, stated by *PE*'s defender Fr. Gianfranco Ghirlanda, that the pope can endow a layman with the power to head a dicastery of the Roman Curia "destroys the link between episcopal consecration and the sacred offices of the bishop, to teach, sanctify, and govern, and makes the pope 'the source of all authority,'" as Edward Pentin reports.[8] Ironically, a pope who wishes to be remembered as the one who completed the unfinished business of Vatican II has, according to canonist Fr. Gerald Murray, approved provisions that contradict the teaching of that Council as given in *Christus Dominus*, the decree on the pastoral office of bishops.[9] Nor should we be surprised, since even *The Pillar* recognized that the CDW's *Responses to the "Dubia"* violate Vatican II's presentation of the rights and responsibilities of bishops.[10]

Moreover, having lay people on committees that are drafting and voting on policies that will apply to clergy and religious should strike us as problematic, not because we are clericalists who think that laymen can have nothing helpful to say about clergy and religious, but because it is a principle of good order (not to mention common sense) that the higher ranks should not be ruled by the lower ranks, even if the former ought to take fully into account the latter's professional expertise and insights. This almost cavalier separation of governance from ordained ministry is another step in the progressives' campaign to separate the offices of ruling, teaching, and sanctifying.[11]

The separation of the power of governance from the power of ordination—an idea strongly espoused by the German Synodal

---

8   Pentin, "'Praedicate Evangelium.'"

9   Ibid.

10   See Ed Condon, "Roche's Rules: Does the new Extraordinary Form instruction line up with Vatican II?," *The Pillar*, December 20, 2021. See also the extremely important interview of Diane Montagna with Fr. Gerald Murray, "Guarding the Flock: A Canon Lawyer's Advice to Bishops on Latest Vatican Crackdown on Tradition," February 15, 2022.

11   For a full treatment of this subject, see Kwasniewski, *Ministers of Christ*, including its Foreword by Leila Marie Lawler, "The Nuptial Mystery Will Always Be True." The innovators want laity to be able to preach at Mass and run parishes; they would like women to be ordained as deaconesses; etc. In many places these things are happening already informally or operationally.

Way—has received a potent theological critique from the former vicar general of the diocese of Chur in Switzerland, Fr. Martin Grichting, who maintains that this separation is not some brilliant new idea but a resurrection of an old error that the Church has had to fight energetically in European history.[12] Fr. Grichting likewise points to the irony that this German proposal, now embraced by *PE*, directly contradicts the teaching of Vatican II's *Lumen Gentium*. One might think that the men in charge are trying to signal that it's time to leave the Council behind—a proposition with which traditionalists would agree, but for quite different reasons.

As with *Spiritus Domini* in the domain of worship,[13] there is in *PE* a systematic conflation of the value and dignity of the laity with exercising positions of authority in the Church's government. This politicization and democratization of Church office could occur only in a time period when the truly supernatural mystery of Holy Orders—a direct participation in the priestly, kingly, and prophetic offices of Christ—has been obscured owing to the corruption of Catholic liturgy by the acids of naturalism and secularism.

IS EVANGELIZATION REALLY THE PRIMARY TASK?

On another point, it seems odd, too, that *PE* makes the pope *ex officio* head of the Dicastery for Evangelization, which, with the Secretariat of State, rules the roost. Is the pope's primary task to evangelize? It seems like his traditional function was (to repeat it once again) to rule, teach, and sanctify the members of the Church, creating a favorable environment, so to speak, for the evangelizing efforts of subsidiary members—both those we call *missionaries* and the laity in everyday life as they rub shoulders with unbelievers, separated brethren, and the fallen-away. Think of this parallel: a secular ruler's job is not to run the factories or sell the products; rather, he presides over a just society that can provide for its own needs out of its own resources.

The pope may well evangelize incidentally just by being a good model of an ecclesiastical leader, living a life of virtue and

---

12   See Maike Hickson, "Swiss priest warns against German bishops' plan to separate Church governance from ordination," *LifeSiteNews*, April 7, 2022.
13   See Kwasniewski, *Ministers of Christ*, ch. 6: "Lay Ministries Obscure Both the Laity's Calling and the Clergy's."

celebrating the divine mysteries with befitting splendor and majesty; but he is not a street preacher to the six populated continents. The orienting theme of *PE* looks like an attempt to reduce to institutional form the globetrotting John Paul II-style papacy. However much good his travels may have accomplished, John Paul II was known to have neglected urgent work in Rome, above all the appointment of truly good bishops—and this, in spite of the fact that the great authority on canonization, Prospero Lambertini (the future Benedict XIV), took great pains to say that the number one job of a pope, and the number one criterion for papal sanctity, is the appointment of good bishops.[14]

Loup Besmond de Senneville rhapsodizes:

> The 250 articles clearly show that the goal of the Curia is not to be an administrative apparatus, but to contribute to active evangelization.... Another sign that evangelization is considered a fundamental axis of the Roman Curia's work is that this new dicastery [for Evangelization] appears at the top of the organizational chart, taking the place that was previously occupied by the Congregation for the Doctrine of the Faith. The change is a way of signifying that all the Church's work, including development and defense of doctrine, is at the service of evangelization.

It is very difficult, as mentioned earlier, to understand how evangelization could ever take precedence—even administratively—over doctrine, and thus, how the dicastery overseeing the latter could be subordinate to that tasked with the former. Is this shift a realization of the much-vaunted fourth principle of Pope Francis: "Reality is more important than ideas"?[15] That is a page taken straight out of Marxism's playbook, in which praxis is superior to theory, or, in Catholic terms, action to contemplation. Can we not see here a sort of fusion of ecclesial identity and evangelization, as if the Church's only activity were mission? But this is false: she has tasks *ad intra* as well as supreme actions *versus Deum*. The Church's first and most important work is divine worship, the *opus Dei*; her second task is to educate and nourish the members of "the household of the faith"

---

14   See *Are Canonizations Infallible?*, 249–51.
15   Jeanne Smits, "'A political scam': French author exposes the four principles that guide Pope Francis' thinking," *LifeSiteNews*, March 30, 2022.

(Gal. 6:10); her third task is to bring others into the Mystical Body. If the priority is inverted, disaster will ensue.

A huge irony of our situation can be missed by no one: the more evangelization is talked about, the less evangelizing actually takes place. In reality, the more Catholics evangelize, the less time or inclination they will have to talk about it. Preaching the Gospel is real work that takes a person out of himself into opportunity, danger, and heroism, as the Word of God crashes against the internal and external fortifications constructed by "the prince of this world" (John 12:31, 14:30, 16:11) and his infernal craftsmen; talking about preaching the Gospel is largely busy work that takes a person out of his office and into a meeting room. After Vatican II there have been endless meetings, initiatives, pastoral plans, and synods, printed on the paper of countless forests, yet the decades-long decline of the mainstream Church continues unabated.

Let's be honest: all this grandstanding about evangelizing is a typhoon of hot air. If the pope and his men were seriously interested in evangelizing, they would welcome with open arms everything that helps modern people rediscover and live the Catholic Faith with zeal. At least in Europe and America, such renewal is unquestionably seen in Traditional Latin Mass communities, which, if they are simply allowed to exist, soon flourish with young adults, large families, converts, and reverts, not to mention vocations to priestly and religious life.

One would think, surely, that a form of Latin-rite worship and Catholic life that proved effective in nourishing the faithful for over 1,600 years would receive a place of honor in the New Evangelization, to which, paradoxically, it has proved so well suited.[16] Yet the pope and his curia mercilessly attack this thriving part of the faithful, while encouraging Amazonian inculturation, LGBTQ outreach, and every other fashionable and controversial progressive program, to the confusion and division of believers. This indicates that, in point of fact, it is not the unchanging

---

16   See Kwasniewski, *Noble Beauty, Transcendent Holiness: Why the Modern Age Needs the Mass of Ages* (Kettering, OH: Angelico Press, 2017), ch. 1: "Why the New Evangelization Needs the Old Mass"; Tracey Rowland, "The *Usus Antiquior* and the New Evangelization," in *Sacred Liturgy: Source and Summit of the Life and Mission of the Church*, ed. Alcuin Reid (San Francisco: Ignatius Press, 2014), 115–37.

Catholic Faith and the Christ who is "the same yesterday, today, and forever" (Heb. 13:8) that the Vatican wishes to preach, but a modernist substitute for both: a Faith that has "evolved" to leave behind the Church's heritage, and a Christ who is no longer the sole Savior of mankind, the one Way to the Father (cf. Jn. 14:6), apart from whom there is no salvation (cf. Acts 4:2).

It must never be forgotten that the primary justification given for the massive liturgical reform was that it would be "evangelical": Catholic worship would finally reach out to Modern Man and meet him just where he was, and thousands, even millions, would come rushing into the embrace of a Church that had formerly alienated them with cryptic and cobwebbed ceremonies, held in dark churches in a dead language. Not only did this utopia of active participation never materialize, the opposite transpired. The congregational song of renewal is burdened with a monotonous refrain of church closures, parish mergers, payoffs, and settlements.[17]

Pardon me, then, if I refuse to believe a single word about "evangelization" that comes forth from the mouths of wolves and serpents who attack the sheep they should love, misappropriate their titles and our funds, and leave a charred wasteland wherever they implement their "vision."

WHAT THE CHURCH REALLY NEEDS

When it comes to preaching the gospel, maybe, just maybe, a radically different approach is called for... How about imitating the priorities of the great missionaries of the past: celebrate glorious traditional liturgies; preach sound doctrine "in season, out of season" (2 Tim. 4:2); support Christian marriages and families; show forth the beauty of holiness? This is the short version of the *Praedicate Evangelium* that the Church needs in the Western world.

It is quite true that *PE* is, in some respects, not as radical a document as had been predicted or feared. Nuttier ideas tossed about

---

17   It is also misleading to cite Third World countries as examples of "success" after the Council. The Church that was planted by pre-Vatican II missionaries continues to grow in those countries as their populations grow, but there is every reason to believe the harvest would have been still greater—and the desertion to Protestant pentecostalism far less—had the practice of the Faith remained traditional. See my article "Did the Reformed Liturgical Rites Cause a Boom in Missionary Lands?," *New Liturgical Movement*, July 6, 2020.

several years ago met the fate of many a committee brainstorm as the document got passed round and round. Nevertheless, it is radical enough in certain respects, as my comments have shown. De Senneville notes:

> The new constitution profoundly changes the very concept of the Curia's role and purpose.... National and regional episcopal conferences appear in *Praedicate evangelium* as full partners of the Roman See, and not just as structures over which Rome has hierarchical authority. The text also specifies that "documents of major importance" must henceforth be "prepared with the advice of the episcopal conferences."

This sounds like an absolute bureaucratic nightmare, synodality on steroids. Anyone who knows anything about committee documents knows how bland, weak, blunted, and turgid they tend to become, the larger the committee is and the longer it labors to reach consensus. This is not how the best Roman documents were composed. Think of the social encyclicals of Leo XIII: he would find an orthodox Catholic ghostwriter he could trust who shared his vision; he let him produce a draft; and the pope, with impeccable Latinity, revised it. That's all.

It also seems telling that there have been four major curial reforms since Pope Sixtus V structured the Roman Curia in 1588. Note the dates: St. Pius X (1908), Paul VI (1967), John Paul II (1988), Francis (2022). Is there any significance to the fact that the Church was able to "get on" with Sixtus's scheme for 320 years, while three reforms were felt to be needed in the space of only 55 years? To me, that rather sums up the Vatican II problem: a liquefied/liquefying Church, uncertain of itself, uncertain of its direction, uncertain of the hierarchy of reality that should be reflected in its structures of governance. It will be necessary at some point for well-equipped political philosophers and dogmatic theologians—such as those of the *Josias* integralist school—to ponder the implications of the new "political structure" of the Roman Curia.

GOOD GOVERNMENT HINGES ON GOOD LEADERS

Let us recall an important principle from Leo XIII's encyclical *Au Milieu des Sollicitudes*:

> In so much does legislation differ from political power
> and its form, that under a system of government most
> excellent in form legislation could be detestable; while
> quite the opposite under a regime most imperfect in
> form, might be found excellent legislation... Legislation
> is the work of men invested with power, and who, in fact,
> govern the nation; therefore it follows that, practically,
> the quality of the laws depends more upon the quality of
> these men than upon the power [i.e., the constitutional
> arrangement]. The laws will be good or bad accordingly
> as the minds of the legislators are imbued with good or
> bad principles, and as they allow themselves to be guided
> by political prudence or by passion.[18]

Although the *ralliement* of Pope Leo XIII—that is, his effort to convince French Catholics to participate in the Masonic republican government of the time—was a predictable failure,[19] his words nevertheless help us to remember that it is not ultimately a structure or a constitution that rules, but actual human beings invested with power, exercising their offices. A poorly-structured government could still be ruled by men of prudence and sanctity who would use their positions to do good, even as an admirably structured government could be administered by corrupt criminals and insane ideologues. At the end of the day, what will matter far more than Francis's new arrangement of deck chairs is who exactly will be sitting in them and what decisions they will reach.

Regardless, therefore, of the arguably bad or good aspects of the new curial structure, the decisive question is who will succeed Francis, who will that pope put into positions of authority, and what policies will they form and follow. We must hope and pray more than ever that the next pope and the future heads of dicasteries, in whatever system they work in, will truly give glory to God and build up the Mystical Body of Christ on earth.

---

18   Encyclical Letter *Au Milieu des Sollicitudes* to the French Bishops, Clergy, and Faithful, February 16, 1892, nn. 21-22; text from the Vatican website.
19   See Roberto de Mattei, "The *Ralliement* of Leo XIII: A Pastoral Experiment That Moved Away from Doctrine," in *Love for the Papacy*, 87-91; José Antonio Ureta, "Leo XIII: The First Liberal Pope Who Went Beyond His Authority," *OnePeterFive*, October 19, 2021.

62

Pius X to Francis:
From Modernism Expelled
to Modernism Enthroned†

I F WE WISH TO UNDERSTAND POPE FRANCIS
and the direction in which he has tried to lead the Church,
it is not enough to look at Argentina, or the Jesuits, or the
Second Vatican Council. We must step further back and take into
view the problem, or better, the plague, of Modernism. In order
to impose limits, I will start with Pope Pius X at the start of the
twentieth century. I assure you that, by the end of the talk, we
will be in possession of a key to understanding the meltdown
through which we are passing.

With his inaugural encyclical *E Supremi* of October 4, 1903, the
Supreme Pontiff who succeeded Leo XIII eloquently outlined the
program of the new pontificate: *Instaurare omnia in Christo*, "to
restore all things in Christ." As subsequent years would prove,
Giuseppe Melchiorre Sarto (1835–1914), who reigned as Pius X
from 1903 until his death just after the start of World War I in
1914, committed himself bravely and energetically to this mission.
Pius X looked with tender love on his flock, ready to guide it into
pastures of sound doctrine and holiness, while he gazed out with
anguish upon the ever-growing multitudes of unbelievers, lost
sheep for whom he felt the Good Shepherd's compassion. The
first pope in many hundreds of years to have been canonized
(due to the lofty and stringent norms for canonizations in place
before Vatican II), Pius X was singlemindedly dedicated to the
reform of the Church, above all in her liturgical and devotional
life.[1] His writings indicate that he always considered the internal

---

† This lecture was given in Sacramento, California, on April 29, 2022.

---

1 Here may be noted his promotion of sacred music and of Gregorian
chant in particular, and his encouragement of the more frequent worthy
reception of Holy Communion. The problems with Pius X's reform of the
Roman Breviary need not detain us here; suffice it to say that he was making a good-faith effort to respond to a seemingly intractable problem, the

strengthening of the Church, the deepening of her life of prayer and sacrifice, to be her best and, in truth, her *only* safeguard against attacks from without and dissensions from within.

Pius X knew the fundamental importance of preserving and preaching the *Catholic Faith* in its purity and fullness, for this is the gift that the Church can give mankind. No matter how much the world changes in its structures, no matter what technology is developed and deployed, the human condition is ever the same: man the sinner is always in need of God's mercy, always in need of the salvation Christ offers to us through the ministry of the Church He founded, and through her constant confession of the true religion revealed by God. It is in light of this stubborn adherence to the immutable essence of the Catholic Faith that we must understand Pius X's battle against the "Modernists."

Modernism was a complex movement that never had an official platform or a centralized organization; it was a loosely-defined set of tendencies and views, a method and a mentality, that criss-crossed the Catholic intelligentsia of Europe at the end of the nineteenth and the start of the twentieth centuries, casting a long shadow for many decades to come, down to the present day. The Modernists believed that Christianity must be reinterpreted in accordance with the (perceived) discoveries and needs of the modern age. This, in turn, implies that Christianity is not a religion revealed by God but a product of human minds cogitating on divine subjects, and therefore mirroring the evolution and vicissitudes of human thought and experience. For the Modernist, religion as such is an organized social expression of personal, immanent, subjective experiences of the divine. This expression can be more or less refined according to time and place, so that one might attempt to rank religions by the clarity and loftiness of their assorted conceptions of the divine. Doctrinal formulations, moral standards, acts of worship: all of these emerge from, correspond to, and follow the lead of an inner exigency or urge of the human spirit called the "religious sense."

---

manner in which the weekly cycle of psalms had effectively been sunk by the constant use of the festal office. While his motivations were defensible, his solution of radically reordering the Divine Office is open to criticism because of its rupture with the immemorial tradition of the Roman Church. The goal could have been achieved in other less violent ways.

The Modernists saw themselves as having the mission of bringing Christianity "up to date" and into conformity with the Zeitgeist, the spirit of the age. To them, the march of modern progress, most plainly seen in the ever-expanding discoveries of the natural sciences, forced a reinterpretation or redefinition of every major tenet of Christian doctrine, from the creation account to the inspiration of Scripture, from the Virgin Birth to the Resurrection, from ecclesiology to eschatology. Nothing, including the liturgy, was to be left unmodernized—or, in a term that would become fashionable later on, "updated" (according to the Italian term *aggiornamento*). However, the attempt to fashion a modernized Christianity—more "spiritual" and "authentic," less "mythical," miraculous, and supernatural—meant sooner or later rejecting the very idea of an inerrant deposit of faith contained in Scripture and Tradition and of a Magisterium that understands and teaches this deposit without error and also without contradicting itself over the ages. As a consequence, it was not uncommon for Modernists to reject the great historic Creeds, drift away from the Faith, and turn into hardened skeptics. The most outspoken of them, Alfred Loisy, quipped that he believed nothing in the Creed except that Jesus suffered under Pontius Pilate. Historian Yves Chiron tells us more about this controversial figure:

> In November 1902, Fr. Loisy published two new books: a collection entitled *Études évangéliques* and, most notoriously, *L'Évangile et l'Église*, called "the little red book" because of its orange-red cover. This latter work claimed to be a reply to *Das Wesen des Christentums* ("What is Christianity?"), a collection of lectures published by a famous German Protestant, Professor Harnack.... These are the conclusions he [Loisy] draws at the end of each of his five chapters: the Gospel is not "a unique and immutable truth, but a living faith, concrete and complex" which undergoes an "evolution"; the divinity of Christ and his resurrection are acts of faith: "the resurrection is not a fact that could have been directly and formally established"; the Church is nothing other than the "collective and continuous life of the Gospel," and "the decisions taken by authority only sanction, so to speak, and consecrate the movement of the community's thought and piety"; "the Church does not

demand belief in its formulas as if they were an adequate expression of absolute truth," and there is an "unceasing evolution of Christian doctrine"; finally, the Church endeavors to "regulate" the external forms of devotion: they must not be seen as opposed to true piety and faith, but as forms of the "immense development which has gone on in the Church," a development which has not come to an end, "for it has always been necessary to adapt the Gospel to the changing conditions of humanity, and today it is even more necessary."[2]

Loisy also wrote:

> It appears evident to me that the notion of God has never been more than a sort of ideal projection, a replication of the human personality, and that theology has never been, nor could it ever be, more than a mythology that becomes with time more and more sanitized.

The Paris Archdiocese issued a ruling condemning Loisy's book, concluding with this statement: "We condemn this book and forbid it to be read by the clergy and faithful of our diocese." The judgment was quickly adopted by other dioceses in France. Seven months later, Cardinal Sarto was elected Pope Pius X; and on December 16, 1903, *L'Évangile et l'Église*, along with several others by the same author, was placed on the *Index of Prohibited Books* by a decree of the Holy Office. In the words of Chiron:

> Pius X well knew that Loisy's case was by no means an isolated one. He saw, behind the theses propounded by the French exegete, a tendency, a "system" raising its head. He expressed this at the beginning of 1905 in a letter addressed to the rector of the Institut Catholique of Paris. After having praised the Institut, its "select masters, who were capable of bringing honor to scholarship and religion," he deplored the fact that some in the Catholic Church "seem to want unreservedly to approve the current dictum that *what is false today will be held as true tomorrow*. This explains the system, which has spread everywhere, of removing everything that is ancient and promoting

---

2 Yves Chiron, *Saint Pius X, Restorer of the Church* (Kansas City, MO: Angelus Press, 2002), 191.

everything that is new, almost for no other reason but its novelty; as if scholarship ought to consist in a kind of disdain for antiquity."[3]

About a year and a half later, in a letter to the Italian bishops, *Pieni l'Animo* of July 28, 1906, Pope Pius X repeated and developed this point:

> As regards Catholic publications, it is necessary to reprove all language which, animated by a spirit of unhealthy novelty, mocks the piety of the faithful and speaks of new orientations of the Christian life, of new directions for the Church, of new aspirations of the modern soul, of a new social vocation for the clergy, of a new Christian civilization, and other similar things.[4]

In an allocution to cardinals on April 17, 1907, Pius X furnished an exact portrait of the modernist, in words that are chilling to read in 2022:

> These rebels profess and repeat, in subtle formulas, monstrous errors on the evolution of dogma, on the return to the pure Gospel—that is, as they say, a Gospel purified of theological explication, Council definitions, and the maxims of the moral life—and on the emancipation of the Church. This they do in their new fashion: they do not engage in revolt, lest they should be ejected, and yet they do not submit either, so that they do not have to abandon their convictions. In their calls for the Church to adapt to modern conditions, in everything they speak and write, preaching a charity without faith, they are very indulgent towards believers, but in reality they are opening up for everyone the path to eternal ruin.[5]

The modernist claims can be distilled into four points:

1. dogma must undergo evolution in its formulation;
2. there must be a return to the "pure Gospel";
3. people must be emancipated from the Church's authority;
4. the Church must adapt her teaching to the present time.[6]

---

3   Letter *Solemne Illud*, February 22, 1905, in Chiron, 197.
4   Chiron, 199.   5   Chiron, 200.   6   Chiron, 199.

Only a few months later, in July and September of 1907, Pius X was to give the Church the double gift of the Decree of the Holy Office *Lamentabili Sane* and the encyclical *Pascendi Dominici Gregis*, documents that, shining like moon and sun in a darkening world, guided countless souls away from the precipice of error and kept them under the sweet yoke of Jesus Christ, the Way, the Truth, and the Life.

Giuseppe Sarto's battle against modernism—begun while he was Bishop of Mantua, continued as Cardinal Patriarch of Venice, and brought to its highest pitch in his papacy—was a battle for the very soul of the Church, concerning as it did the immutability and constancy of divinely revealed truth, without which Christianity, and more particularly the Catholic Faith, cannot exist. It is grimly fascinating to read about the modernist crisis of the early twentieth century and to see how comparable its features are to the relaxed everyday modernism that surrounds us like polluted air in the Church today. One is also struck by the diligence and zeal with which St. Pius X and the Curia under him took action to discover, thwart, punish, and obliterate any and all traces of modernism—a campaign that might have eventually succeeded, had the successors of Pius X been willing to follow his path. (We see more than once in Church history that the great momentum for reform built up by one pope is then squandered or opposed by his successor. While not a new phenomenon, it is never an edifying one.)

The Modernists never formed a definite school with a definite system; there was much variation in opinion from individual to individual, country to country, discipline to discipline. Nevertheless, their ideas tended to emerge from the same widespread currents of modern thought—above all, the strong influence of German philosophers Kant and Hegel—and tended to yield similar proposals for "reinterpretation," revision, and reform. As a result, it was possible for Pius X to publish a survey of the overall system to which these ideas would of necessity give rise, and then to demonstrate how it is utterly irreconcileable with confessional Christianity, or even with sound philosophy. The originality and power of the encyclical *Pascendi* consists primarily in its exposition of a fully consistent Modernism that probably did not exist as such in any individual's mind, but which was the complete package if one took the time to assemble all the pieces.

The hundredth anniversary of this encyclical in 2007 came and went without public celebration or official commemoration; relatively few Catholics nowadays have heard of it. Theologians and historians who deign to mention the document often dismiss it as an embarrassing papal temper tantrum, an unfair caricature that fell wide of its mark, an unsympathetic and even uncomprehending refusal to assimilate the findings of honorably-motivated modern theologians—and, in any case, they think that it quickly lost whatever relevance it may have had. A Jesuit historian in 2007 opined that "the movement of the 'innovators' (at least the doctrinal and theological movement) remained confined to the restricted circles of Catholic scholars, mostly young priests or seminarians," and therefore had no real impact on wider Catholic life and thought. The same historian "highlighted the elements judged as most outdated: its excessively 'doctrinaire' structure, its excessively 'harsh and censorious' tone, and its 'excessively fundamentalist and hard-line' application."[7] (Whenever you hear someone apply the word "fundamentalist" to a Catholic, you know that you are dealing with a soft or hard Modernist.[8])

It can hardly escape the notice of one who reads it attentively that the encyclical *Pascendi* is not only *not* irrelevant, it is vastly *more* relevant now than it was at its promulgation over a century ago. The errors in doctrine and practice that Pius X condemned are far more prevalent in the Church of today, and in Catholic educational institutions, than they were in the heyday of Alfred Loisy, George Tyrrell, and Friedrich von Hügel. As for the Jesuit's remark, one is perhaps reminded of those who say that the Americanism condemned by Leo XIII was a "ghost heresy" that only existed on European paper and never really existed on American soil. On the contrary, I challenge anyone who reads the Apostolic Letter *Testem Benevolentiae* today to make a case that the principles targeted by Leo XIII do *not* permeate and dominate the Church in the USA.[9]

---

7   See Sandro Magister, "The Encyclical Against the 'Modernists' Turns 100—But Without Fanfare," *Settimo Cielo*, October 23, 2007. The Jesuit historian's name is Giovanni Sale.

8   See "Catholics who hold fast to truths of faith are now condemned as 'fundamentalists,'" *LifeSiteNews*, November 28, 2018; "Why Catholicism is necessarily dogmatic, with a definite content," *LifeSiteNews*, February 12, 2019.

9   For an explanation of how *Testem Benevolentiae* in fact perfectly applies to us today, see "Contemplation of Unchanging Truth" in Peter Kwasniewski,

Leo XIII and his successor Pius X were astute doctors of the body politic and the body ecclesiastic: they knew the cancerous effects of false principles left unchecked. That is why they did their utmost to lead the Church away from the many reductive and destructive "-isms" of modernity (rationalism, liberalism, utilitarianism, materialism, and so forth) toward the only whole that precontains and validates all partial truths: the Catholic Faith.

The encyclical *Pascendi* portrays the Modernist reinterpretation of Christianity as follows. Faith is an interior "sense" originating in a need for the divine; it is not a gift from without, but an immanent surge, an intuition of the heart, a subjective "experience." Religion, accordingly, is when this "sense" rises to the level of consciousness and becomes an expression of a worldview. What, then, is revelation? The awakening consciousness of the divine within me. Doctrine, in turn, is the intellect's ongoing elaboration of that awakening, while dogmatic formulas are mere symbols or instruments by which the intellect tries to capture the meaning of religious experience. Hence, of necessity, dogma evolves in response to the pressure of vital forces, with ever-changing beliefs corresponding to ever-changing understandings of reality and of subjective experience. What become of Scripture and Tradition? Tradition is the sharing with others of an original experience in such a way that it becomes the experience of others too, while Scripture is the written record of particularly powerful experiences, expressed with poetic inspiration. Sacraments, finally, are public gestures by which the assembled faith community represents to itself a certain worldview and excites in itself an awareness of the divine.

No wonder the 1907 document *Lamentabili Sane* from the Holy Office condemned the following Modernist proposition (with many others akin to it): "Truth is no more unchangeable than man himself, since it evolves with him, in him, and through him." As Cardinal Désiré-Joseph Mercier, Archbishop of Mechelen, Belgium, wrote in the same year:

> Modernism consists essentially in affirming that the religious soul must draw from itself, from nothing but itself, the object and motive of its faith. It rejects all revelation

---

Resurgent in the Midst of Crisis: Sacred Liturgy, the Traditional Latin Mass, and Renewal in the Church (Kettering, OH: Angelico Press, 2014), 57–70.

imposed upon the conscience, and thus, as a necessary consequence, becomes the negation of the doctrinal authority of the Church established by Jesus Christ, and it denies, moreover, to the divinely constituted hierarchy the right to govern Christian society.

Cardinal Mercier continued his perspicacious comments:

> Christ did not represent Himself to the world as the head of a philosophy and uncertain of His teaching! He did not leave a modifiable system of opinions to the discussion of His disciples. On the contrary, strong in His divine wisdom and sovereign power, He pronounced and imposed upon men the revealed word that assures eternal salvation, and indicated to them the unique way to attain it. He promulgated for them a code of morals, giving them certain helps without which it is impossible to put these precepts into practice. Grace, and the Sacraments which confer it upon us—or restore it to us, when, having sinned, we again find it through repentance—form together these helps, this economy of salvation. He instituted a Church, and as He had only a few years to dwell with us upon earth, He conferred His power upon His Apostles, and after them on their successors, the Pontiffs and Bishops....

Cardinal Mercier went on to say that every child when preparing for his first Communion was taught that the Catholic Faith is passed on to us by tradition, and that we must hold fast to tradition; and this is why the pope had to condemn Modernism.

Writing many decades later, the great Dominican traditionalist Fr. Roger-Thomas Calmel had this to say about our subject:

> Modernism is deadlier than Protestantism; in effect, it does not proceed by open negation but by interior sterilization. Dogmas and sacraments are not denied outright, but, by a diabolical process of dismantling, modernism leads gradually to their denaturing and the voiding of their proper mystery.[10]

---

10   Fr. Roger-Thomas Calmel, O. P., in *The Angelus,* vol. 38, n. 1 (January-February 2015), 43. See, moreover, Pink, "Vatican II and Crisis in the Theology of Baptism," on the reduction of sacraments to "salvation theatre."

For these errors and still others, Pius X in *Pascendi* condemned the entire system of Modernism as "the synthesis of all heresies," or, to translate more accurately the pope's Latin phrase, *omnium haereseon conlectum*, "the collector of all heresies." It was declared incompatible with the first truth of the Catholic Faith, namely that *God*, in the freedom of His love, willed to reveal Himself to man, to whom He also provided the gift of faith and reasonable motives of belief so that man may freely and reasonably respond to that revelation with intellectual assent and base his life upon it.

But why did Pius X brand Modernism with the striking and perhaps perplexing phrase "the collector of all heresies"? Br. André-Marie explains it well:

> The Holy Father says that the Modernists "lay the ax not to the branches and shoots, but to the very root, that is, to the faith and its deepest fibers." There is, then, something *fundamental* to the heresy. It is not a question of the Modernists literally professing every single historical heresy, something mentally impossible, since many of them are mutually exclusive; it is, rather, a question of Modernism being *radical*—in the literal sense of going to the *radix* (root)—in its denial of the faith. This is so because "[the Modernists'] whole system has been born of the alliance between faith and false philosophy," a philosophy that fundamentally denies knowledge, the supernatural order, the stability of truth, the principle of non-contradiction, and the metaphysics of common sense.... The manifold results of this evil union between faith and an unworthy handmaid are the fruits of a tree which is corrupt at its very roots.[11]

I will come back later on to the "false philosophy" involved.

When St. Thérèse of Lisieux spoke her memorable words "all is grace," she might well have been summing up Pius X's objections to Modernism. That God made us; that He reached out to us in our wretched condition; that He was made flesh and died for us; that he poured His Spirit of love into our hearts; that He offers us a share in His life through the sacraments of the Church—all

---

11   "What Did St. Pius X Mean When He Called Modernism 'the Synthesis of All Heresies'?," *Catholicism.org*, September 9, 2007.

this is pure grace, pure gift, coming down to us from the Father of Lights, the giver of every good gift, to whom we make a gift of ourselves through obedience, filial love, and adoration. For the Modernist, everything is upside down; one is in a hall of mirrors where all is self, welling up from self, trapped in time, ever evolving, a confusion of becomings, a cacophony of opinions. Behind the catechetical, liturgical, doctrinal, and moral chaos of the Catholic Church today, it is easy to detect the lingering influence of the Modernist ideas that even Pius X's strict disciplinary efforts—and similar efforts of Pius XII decades later—were unable to eradicate.

Given the enormous influence of Modernism in the Church, *Pascendi* is an encyclical that no educated Catholic can afford to ignore, even if it does not make for light reading. Page by page, the encyclical distinguishes, defines, and dismantles each part of the Modernist system, showing how one warped idea leads to the next, and how each contradicts the doctrine of the Faith—and often, the truth of sound philosophy as well. To be sure, there are other ingredients in our pot of crisis from the past century, but Modernism is more than just salt and pepper, it's the beef in the stew.

I was once teaching *Pascendi* to a group of college students. After we had finished laying out the Modernist redefinitions of traditional terms like faith and revelation, I asked them: "So, what do you think of all this?" Sure enough, one student said: "Well, it sounds a lot like what we learned in my high school religious ed class." Another said: "Yeah, I've heard stuff like that preached from the pulpit." Still another: "My friend had a book about the Mass that was exactly the same as what you said." Then I asked: "Why does St. Pius X reject all of it, lock, stock, and barrel?" A student piped up: "Because it's all subjective, it's all in your head, and where's God?" To which a neighboring student added: "It completely does away with the idea of faith as a gift bestowed upon us, as something *God* is doing for *us*, a message He entrusts to *us*. The Modernists created their own God and their own religion, so they don't have to submit their minds to the real one. It takes humility to abandon oneself in faith and not to think that modern man is so special and different." As our discussion went on, this much became painfully clear to me and to my students as well: all the errors that Pius X analyzes in *Pascendi* are still being taught today—indeed, in the most scandalous dereliction of duty yet seen in Church history, by the current Pope himself, not just once or twice, but frequently, across a wide range of subjects.

Part of Pius X's effort to extinguish Modernism and uphold Tradition was the institution of the famous (or, to its opponents, infamous) "Oath against Modernism," issued on September 1, 1910. The Oath had to be "sworn by all clergy, pastors, confessors, preachers, religious superiors, and professors in philosophical-theological seminaries." I would like to quote just a few choice portions of this remarkable text, which opens: "I... firmly embrace and accept each and every definition that has been set forth and declared by the unerring teaching authority of the Church, especially those principal truths which are directly opposed to the errors of this day." In particular, pay heed to the fourth article of the Oath:

> I sincerely hold that the doctrine of faith was handed down to us from the apostles through the orthodox Fathers in exactly the same meaning and always in the same purport. Therefore, I entirely reject the heretical misrepresentation that dogmas evolve and change from one meaning to another different from the one which the Church held previously. I also condemn every error according to which, in place of the divine deposit which has been given to the spouse of Christ to be carefully guarded by her, there is put a philosophical figment or product of a human consciousness that has gradually been developed by human effort and will continue to develop indefinitely.

In that language, we can hear echoes of the First Vatican Council's constitution *Dei Filius*, but even further back, echoes of St. Vincent of Lérins, who said in his fifth-century treatise the *Commonitory* that no legitimate development in theology can ever take the form of a *mutatio* or change in nature, but had to be in the form of a *profectus*, organic growth, so that even if a new explanation is more ample or more penetrating, the meaning that was taught in the past will never be contradicted by it, and the "upshot" (as we would say) will never be different. So too, the Creed of the Council of Trent from 1563 is more ample than the Creed of Constantinople from 381, and that is more ample than the Creed of Nicaea from 325, and that, in turn, is more ample than the Apostles' Creed—but all of them are completely consistent with one another, the later only making explicit what the former implied. Such has always been the understanding that the Church has had of the way in which progress is possible and desirable. It is the kind of growth that never requires us to throw out our old catechisms to make room for new ones that say something else; all the catechisms remain valid and useful for various purposes, because they are in harmony.

The Oath against Modernism continues:

> I hold with certainty and sincerely confess that faith is not a blind sentiment of religion welling up from the depths of the subconscious under the impulse of the heart and the motion of a will trained to morality; but faith is a genuine assent of the intellect to truth received by hearing from an external source. By this assent, because of the authority of the supremely truthful God, we believe to be true that which has been revealed and attested to by a personal God, our Creator and Lord.

In this article of the Oath we hear a resounding affirmation of the objective and intellectual character of Catholicism. By this, I mean that our faith is not a bunch of warm feelings about vague religious things but a definite, concrete, articulated content of truths that God communicates to us accompanied by signs of credibility and an inherent power of converting and convincing our minds, and that while we cannot *comprehend* the Faith in the sense of "getting to the bottom of it," neither are we lost in foggy clouds of uncertainty and constant change. Nor is God some kind of cosmic force or world spirit that evolves together with us, the blind leading the blind; He is *personal*, infinitely perfect, free, loving, truthful, and desirous of our salvation.

Taken all together, the eleven articles of the Oath against Modernism perfectly sum up the system of errors in which men like Loisy were entangled, and which later emerged again with a vengeance in someone like Teilhard de Chardin. The final lines of the Oath say:

> I promise that I shall keep all these articles faithfully, entirely, and sincerely, and guard them inviolate, in no way deviating from them in teaching or in any way in word or in writing. Thus I promise, this I swear, so help

me God, and these holy Gospels of God which I touch with my hand.

Now, it is a striking fact that all of the soft Modernists who were busy behind the scenes at the Second Vatican Council as *periti* or experts, working on drafts, hobnobbing with bishops and cardinals, disseminating their "spin" through the media—all of these men had taken this Oath; and so had Paul VI, who was not himself a dyed-in-the-wool Modernist, but who certainly had Modernist sympathies and alliances, particularly in the domain of the liturgy, where his entire vision rested on the premise that the Roman rite in its full Tridentine maturity no longer suited the needs and capacities of "modern man," and for that reason had to be replaced with something artificially created by "scientific experts" from the field of pastoral liturgy. All of these men had taken the Oath—and therefore, arguably, all of them were guilty of perjury inasmuch as they knowingly departed from the affirmations to which they had solemnly committed themselves, placing their hand on the holy Gospels. It is still more serious, not to say sinister, that Paul VI abolished the Oath against Modernism on July 17, 1967 (he had already abolished the Index of Forbidden Books the year before). The abolition of the Oath, which had been in place for 57 years, came at the same time as the Consilium (the body in charge of implementing the liturgical reform) was busy pushing forward new Eucharistic Prayers to supplant the Roman Canon, which had been the definitive core of the Roman rite for at least 1,600 years. Only a few days later, on July 23, 1967, the fateful "Land O' Lakes Statement" was signed in Wisconsin—a statement that essentially severed Catholic colleges and universities from the Magisterium and from the obligation to hold and teach the Catholic Faith. The Oath's abolition came not long before the revolution of 1968, of which, as Archbishop Viganò (among others) has convincingly argued, the Council was a necessary precondition.[12] In short, the Oath against Modernism was abolished

---

12   Viganò makes this point in an essay dated December 7, 2020 and published a month later; for the full text, see Maike Hickson, "Abp. Viganò: Abolition of anti-Modernist Oath is 'a desertion, a betrayal of unheard-of gravity,'" *LifeSiteNews*, January 6, 2021. Mentions and citations of the controversial archbishop are by no means to be construed as a blanket endorsement of all his positions, especially his unconscionable stance on the Russian

exactly at the culmination of the doctrinal, moral, and liturgical triumph of Modernism—as if to free the consciences of "clergy, pastors, confessors, preachers, religious superiors, and professors in seminaries" from the burden of forswearing themselves on the Gospels. Archbishop Viganò poignantly writes:

> The abolition of the *Iusiurandum Antimodernisticum* was part of a plan to dismantle the disciplinary structure of the Church, precisely at the moment in which the threat of the adulteration of faith and morals by the innovators was greatest. This operation confirms the intention of those who, in the face of the ultra-progressive attack initiated at the Council, not only allowed the enemy to have freedom of action but also deprived the Hierarchy of the disciplinary means with which to guard and defend itself. And it was a desertion, a betrayal of unheard-of gravity, especially in those terrible years: as if in the middle of full combat the commander-in-chief ordered his men to lay their arms down before the enemy just as they were getting ready to invade the citadel.[13]

His Excellency adds:

> The Revolution of 1968 found its ideological base in the Catholic universities and formed its most excited protagonists there, some of whom were political exponents of the extreme left. Not asking the professors of these universities and the chaplains of the lay associations to swear the Oath was the equivalent of authorizing them to transmit their heterodox ideas, suggesting that the condemnation of Modernism had fallen. This allowed the innovators to take power, according to the methods analyzed by Antonio Gramsci, who identified in the apparatus of the State—schools, parties, trade unions, the press, associations—the "casemates" of the enemy to be conquered in a parallel action to the war in the trenches.[14]

Orthodox Church and Vladimir Putin's war of aggression against the nation of Ukraine. Nevertheless, intellectual honesty demands that we recognize the value and incisiveness of many of his writings, such as those collected in McCall's *A Voice in the Wilderness.*

13   From the essay mentioned in the preceding note.

14   Ibid.

I find it fascinating that, as a matter of historical fact, both the encyclical *Pascendi* and the Oath against Modernism were implemented only partially and with many exceptions in the land of Germany, where today we see the world's most liberal local church. Joseph Ratzinger himself, in 1955, was accused of Modernism by the assistant supervisor of his habilitation dissertation, Professor Michael Schmaus. In a detailed article, Maike Hickson summarizes the many connections Ratzinger had to the neo-Modernist movement after World War II, and from which he partially turned away in later years.[15] Archbishop Viganò aptly writes concerning Ratzinger:

> It also seems to me undeniable that there are many of his writings in which both his Hegelian formation as well as the influence of Modernism emerge, as Professor Enrico Maria Radaelli has illustrated very well in his essays and as the new biography of Pope Benedict XVI by Peter Seewald confirms with an abundance of particulars and numerous sources. In this regard, I believe it is obvious that the declarations of the young Joseph Ratzinger reported by Seewald largely contradict the *hermeneutic of continuity* which Benedict XVI later theorized, perhaps as a prudent retraction of his former enthusiasm.

As mentioned earlier, one of the characteristic features of Modernism is its reliance on an evolutionary model of thought, in which truth is not static but dynamic: the Church does not possess the Truth at any given moment, but is ever searching for it, and ever stumbling upon new aspects of Truth that can even amount to a reversal of what the Church used to hold as true.[16]

We can see this approach vividly in Pope Francis, who maintains that the Church was actually wrong to support the use of the death penalty for its entire history, since we "now know" that the death penalty is contrary to human dignity, and therefore always and everywhere inadmissible (but this can be true only if it is *per se malum*, something evil in and of itself; for if it were not, it would

---

15   See Maike Hickson, "The Great Influence of Joseph Ratzinger in the Revolutionary Upheaval of the Second Vatican Council," *Rorate Caeli*, December 11, 2020.

16   For a superb treatment of the defined dogmatic truths to which Modernism is opposed, see Lamont and Pierantoni, *Defending the Faith*, 103–13, 268–69.

sometimes be admissible). Or rather, it is perhaps more accurate to say that for a Modernist, the Church at a more primitive period of the development of human consciousness was right to promote the death penalty—it was bound to look legitimate to culturally immature people—but now in our stage of higher consciousness, which involves the apprehension of universal human rights, the brotherhood of all men, the non-divine source of political authority, and the universal benevolence of the Creator-God, we can see that the death penalty is wrong.[17]

Another example is the false teaching of the eighth chapter of *Amoris Laetitia*, which overturns the hitherto unbroken exclusion from reception of the sacraments of Catholics who are living in an objective state of adultery. The Modernist, however, would say that notions of mortal sin, objective sinfulness, worthiness, pre-conditions for sacramental reception, have all "evolved" under the influence of an ever-more comprehensive grasp of God's merciful love, which "stops at nothing" (as they would say) and "is never earned or lost by our actions," etc.[18]

The universalism espoused at Abu Dhabi is yet another example: the Church once taught that it alone possesses and teaches the true religion given to us by God for our salvation, but "now we know" that God speaks to man through all religions and goes beyond them all, so each is a path to salvation for those who follow it sincerely. At best, Jesus is the "privileged path" of salvation, as Bishop Robert Barron said.[19] One can detect here the influence of the subjective, emotional, and pragmatic theory of religion Pius X diagnosed in *Pascendi*.

One could multiply such examples of modern teachings, present already before the Council but emerging into the open afterwards, that bear this evolutionary stamp. Br. André-Marie writes:

> Where Kant made all things static, Hegel introduced a dynamic element into his metaphysics (like Heraclitus). For Hegel, all things evolve in the dialectic of thesis, antithesis, and synthesis. History, truth, thought, indeed all reality is explained by this principle. In the history of

---

17   See chapter 40.

18   See, inter alia, chapters 10 and 11.

19   See "Is Jesus Christ the 'privileged way' to salvation—or the only way?," *LifeSiteNews*, December 17, 2018.

thought, the Hegelian dialectic gives rise to "Historical Consciousness," an acute awareness of change as a constant, describing all reality as in continual development. It further produces "Historicism," the theory in which general laws of historical development are the determinant of events. In this theory, all things are subject to progressive evolutionary processes.

Indeed, we can see how even Benedict XVI's theory of the "hermeneutic of continuity" imports or retains an element of Hegelianism. In the famous address he gave to the Roman Curia on December 22, 2005, he spoke not of a "hermeneutic of continuity" (although he used that expression at other times),[20] but of a "hermeneutic of reform, of renewal in the continuity of the one subject-Church which the Lord has given to us." As Brian McCall explains, this is not quite as promising as it might sound: "Benedict XVI is arguing that the object of belief can change over time as long as the Church remains the same subject proposing those developing beliefs. It seeks revisions of teaching over time through a process that keeps the structure of the Church in place."[21] So, although Benedict in the same speech rejects what he calls the "hermeneutic of rupture" that makes of the Church during and after the Council a totally different entity with totally different beliefs from the Church before the Council, he goes on to say that in regard to more contingent matters such as the Church's relationship with the modern world, there is in fact a blend of rupture and continuity—certain ruptures are necessary in order to secure a deeper continuity, as it were. Or in his words: "It is precisely in this combination of continuity and discontinuity at different levels that the very nature of true reform consists."

Let me give some examples of how this Hegelian dialectic works in Ratzinger.

1. In his book *Principles of Catholic Theology*, Ratzinger called the Pastoral Constitution on the Church in the Modern World,

---

20   For documentation, see "The Ongoing Saga of 'the Hermeneutic of Continuity,'" *New Liturgical Movement*, November 26, 2013—written at a time when I still believed that Francis might continue in the same line as Benedict and that Benedict's own line was unobjectionable. The passage of time together with further study has clarified much.

21   *A Voice in the Wilderness*, 109.

Gaudium et Spes, a "countersyllabus" to Pius IX's *Syllabus of Errors*.[22] The Thesis is Pius IX's Anti-Liberalism; the Antithesis is modern Liberalism; the dialectical process is the struggle to integrate modernity into Catholicism; the resulting Synthesis is a Higher Liberalism that is somehow also Catholic.

2. In the motu proprio *Summorum Pontificum* and the accompanying letter to bishops, *Con Grande Fiducia*, we have a Thesis: the Tridentine Roman rite; an Antithesis: the Novus Ordo; a dialectical process: "mutual enrichment"; and an eventual Synthesis: a future Roman rite that is both old and new, with the supposed "best qualities" of each.[23]

3. In the position Benedict XVI takes about heaven, hell, and purgatory in the encyclical letter *Spe Salvi*, we can reconstruct the latent structure this way. Thesis: the historically dominant view that the human race is a *"massa damnata,"* in other words, a race justly destined for perdition due to original and actual sin, from which a minority is saved. Antithesis: the universalism of Origen, David Bentley Hart, Hans Urs von Balthasar, and Bishop Barron: either everyone will be saved, or at least it's reasonable to hope that that will be the case. The dialectical process is the ever-widening inclusiveness of salvific grace. The final Synthesis: *most* people are saved, though the few who are terribly wicked, like Hitler and Stalin, are lost; they cannot sit at the same heavenly banquet.[24]

4. Regarding human evolution, the Thesis is that man and woman were created directly by God, and the whole human race takes its

---

22   "If it is desirable to offer a diagnosis of the text [*Gaudium et Spes*] as a whole, we might say that (in conjunction with the texts on religious liberty and world religions) it is a revision of the *Syllabus* of Pius IX, a kind of countersyllabus.... [T]he *Syllabus* established a line of demarcation against the determining forces of the nineteenth century: against the scientific and political world view of liberalism. In the struggle against modernism this twofold delimitation was ratified and strengthened.... Let us be content to say here that the text serves as a countersyllabus and, as such, represents, on the part of the Church, an attempt at an official reconciliation with the new era inaugurated in 1789" (*Principles of Catholic Theology: Building Stones for a Fundamental Theology*, trans. Sr. Mary Frances McCarthy, S. N. D. [San Francisco: Ignatius Press, 1987], 381–82).

23   See my lecture "Beyond *Summorum Pontificum*: The Work of Retrieving the Tridentine Heritage," *Rorate Caeli*, July 14, 2021.

24   See the Encyclical Letter *Spe Salvi* (November 30, 2007), nn. 44–46; cf. my article "On Hell: Clarity Is Mercy in an Age of 'Dare We Hope,'" *OnePeterFive*, August 7, 2019.

origin from them. The Antithesis is that human beings are nothing but a cosmic accident, the unplanned outcome of material particles interacting by chance. The Synthesis is theistic evolution, where God somehow upholds and directs the random material process until at some point He intervenes to establish "first humans."

We see this kind of dialectical pattern throughout Joseph Ratzinger's writings; it is very true that as different as he is from Cardinal Walter Kasper, they share a profound core of Germanic philosophy but apply it in different ways. Kasper, for example, describes the shift from the apostolic period to the post-apostolic period of the early Church councils as a "continuity in discontinuity," where the original *kerygma* or message of salvation was translated into Greek categories of thought in order to be "adapted to the mentality of the day"; and he says that this is what every age must do: translate the Gospel into a new language, discarding no longer relevant or meaningful concepts and adopting novel ones to fit the requirements of the times.

Now, I have spent a good deal of time talking about the history, personalities, and philosophical method of Modernism because if we do not see these things clearly, we will not be able to recognize the wide range of forms—at times, sophisticated and subtle—that Modernism assumes in our own day. There are out-and-out Modernists like Kasper, but there are also many who have been influenced or formed by Modernism without realizing it, or who believe they can somehow "salvage" or "rehabilitate" its "positive aspects" while still maintaining Catholic orthodoxy and tradition (Ratzinger, I think, would fall into this category, as would most so-called conservatives). As I have been at pains to show, Modernism is not a tidy, closed system that must be held or rejected in full; rather, it is a mish-mash of ideas about how faith and religion operate, how salvation occurs, how Scripture is formed, how dogmatic definitions emerge and are refined, how the law of development of thought—the expansion and refinement of the moral conscience—compels the modernization of human beings and their institutions, including the Church. It's unlikely that one will find all of these views equally in all who might be called Modernists or semi-Modernists; it's even more unlikely that everyone who holds such views will be aware of their origins and their implications.

Nevertheless, there are those individuals who are very well aware of what they are doing and how they intend to determine the future of the Church. I suggest we think of them in three categories: the Black Modernists of 120 years ago; the Scarlet Modernists of 60 years ago; and the Lavender Modernists of today.[25]

The Black Modernists of 120 years ago were men of the cloth, like Alfred Loisy and George Tyrrell, who embraced rationalism, scientism, historicism, revisionism, and relativism. These men and their writings and conferences made it possible for an attitude of distrust, suspicion, and contempt toward tradition to make head-way in the Church. Their views prompted a growing restlessness for Church reform and often for liturgical reform—a movement that Pius XI and Pius XII tried to moderate and placate in their pontificates, with mixed results.[26]

It was John XXIII who, though personally of a more traditional piety, made the fatal mistake of convening an ecumenical council at a time when the neo-Modernist agenda had picked up steam once again (we can see this by examining mid-twentieth-century theologians like Rahner, Congar, Chenu, Küng, Schillebeeckx, Häring, De Lubac, and Ratzinger, among many others), and then compounded his error by allowing these *periti* and their bishops to cancel out the preparatory documents of the Council, staging a "coup" that determined its fundamental direction and cast of mind. At this point, sixty years out from the start of Vatican II, we could

---

25   I first mentioned this division into three categories in volume 1, chapter 4.

26   Modernists were not uniformly in favor of liturgical reform or experi-mentation. Since their concern was to deny the literal meaning of dogmas and to emphasize subjective religious and ethical experience, it was easy enough for them to revel in the religious symbolism the traditional rites provided. At the same time, Modernism's general evolutionary framework, in which mankind's present condition and future state are seen as superior to the past, readily lends itself to liturgical *aggiornamento*. Ironically, we see in the official policy of the Society of St. Pius X an inversion of the Modernist problem: the focus is placed so strongly on "doctrine" that liturgical deformation, such as the Pius XII Holy Week (a trial run for the Novus Ordo), is accepted without protest. It's as if they maintain that a pope can be an absolute monarch with no responsibilities to the Church's tradition of worship, *as long as* dogma is untouched; he could create a new liturgy *de novo* and it would have to be accepted if no doctrinal objections could be made to it. Such is the essence of liturgical nominalism and voluntarism; and such a view is not Catholic.

speak of Scarlet Modernists, in the sense of bishops and cardinals of that period who, usually of impeccable personal morality and a strong sense of duty, were sympathetic to more progressive or liberal points of view at the Council—and even more can we speak of bishops and cardinals consecrated or created in the decades immediately after the Council, who would most fully implement its vision, normalizing milder forms of the ideas condemned in Pius X's *Pascendi*—a version that might be called "soft Modernism," which is the theological soundtrack to "beige Catholicism" (to use a phrase of Bishop Barron's). *This* Modernism is, in fact, nothing less than the Creed of the Anti-Church, the operative principles of the churchmen and ecclesiastical structures that are masquerading as the Church of Christ and living parasitically off of her historical capital and financial assets. We can recognize the Anti-Church by its self-contradictory traits: the dogmatic undogmatism, the rigid laxism, the exclusive inclusiveness, the systematic antischolasticism and eclecticism, the anti-traditional spirit that has by now practically become a substitute tradition, since it has been around long enough to win a certain veneer of respectability (note that the politicized canonizations of several Vatican II popes were a crucial step in transmitting the pretense of divine approval).

Intellectual errors followed by ecclesiastical restructuring—including the episcopate-destroying pursuit of "collegiality" and "synodality"—and the betrayal of the sacred liturgy have led to the moral vacuum, or worse, the demon-infested vacuum, that we now know as the clerical sexual abuse scandal, which it would be more proper to call the "abuse pandemic." The sexual abuse epitomized in former Cardinal McCarrick and now sustained by his well-placed collaborators in the USCCB and at the Vatican is of course bound up with the vice of sodomy, which has always flared up in the worst periods of Church history: times when knowledge, virtue, and commitment to Christ had dissipated, when the Faith was like a tiny spark nurtured by a faithful remnant, out of which reform and renewal eventually came by God's great mercy. This is why I speak of today's "Lavender Modernists": they have much in common with the two preceding types, the Black and the Scarlet, but they are altogether worse, for they combine intellectual infidelity, institutional ambition, liturgical corruption, and moral deviancy. And in this way, they are the promulgators and precipitants of the Great Apostasy.

How, then, do we combat this multi-generational parasite of Modernism? In a time of such confusion and wickedness, one thing is absolutely clear: we must hold fast to the settled and articulate tradition of the Church: in her doctrine, which we find in all of the ecumenical Councils that taught dogmatically and in the Catechism of Trent and all the good catechisms of the past; in our moral life, according to the constant teaching and example of the saints; above all, in the Church's authentic age-old rites of worship, be they Eastern or Western. This is what we are asked to do: remain faithful to the inheritance we have received, prior to the period of anarchy. The one and only safe path is to stick to what we *know* to be certainly true; to implore God's help and intervention daily; to entrust ourselves to the Virgin Mary; and never to abandon the Church of Christ for imaginary green pastures elsewhere. What good could any move away from the Catholic Church accomplish? It would only remove good people from what they need the most and where they are most needed—the visible Body of Christ—and would only contribute to the growing anarchy. What is needed is steadfast attachment to the Bride of Christ in spite of her marred countenance on earth, unswerving loyalty to her eternal Head, total acceptance of the doctrine He entrusted to her in its integrity. In short, we need to do what St. Pius X taught us to do over a hundred years ago. Truth is perpetually youthful, with a radiant countenance of beauty and delight; it is error that grows prematurely old, gnarled, and hideous.

There is more need than ever for the counterwitness of Catholics who speak the truth with love, and live it with joy. These will be the torchbearers who bring the light of the Faith into the remaining decades of the twenty-first century and beyond, while the Modernist sect implodes upon itself. After all, as our Lord said in no uncertain terms: *Veritas liberabit vos,* the truth will set you free (Jn 8:32). He Himself is that truth—*Ego sum via, et veritas, et vita* (Jn 14:6)—and His Church is the "pillar and bulwark of the truth" (1 Tim 3:15). Because of the flight from God that began with Adam's rebellion and worms its way into the children of Eve, we will not be surprised if the world prefers the slavery of subjectivism to the truth that sets us free: "The time is coming when people will not endure sound doctrine, but having itching ears they will accumulate for themselves teachers to suit their own likings, and will turn away from listening to the truth and wander into myths" (2 Tim. 3:3–4). Surely it is not too much to ask of loyal Catholics that they not follow suit; that, instead, they seek out, study, and promote sound doctrine in all faith and humility; that they turn away from fashionable modern myths to embrace a heritage of perennial truths; that they accumulate teachers who, unashamed to be lowly pupils in the school of Christ, feed upon every word that comes from the mouth of God, and nourish their disciples with the same life-giving food.

A sober examination of the Church on earth at this time discloses the existence of a major "schism." Yet, contrary to the propaganda of the progressives, it is not faithful and traditional Catholics who are in schism, but those members of the hierarchy and of the laity who, under the intoxicating influence of Modernism, have abandoned the rock of truth and the ark of salvation. We cannot expect *them* to be humbly admitting their errors and repenting of their sins. This, surely, is an apocalyptic storm from which only an omnipotent God can deliver us, in answer to the prayers He calls forth from our weary but unvanquished souls. As Archbishop Viganò says:

> The Church is shrouded in the darkness of modernism, but the victory belongs to Our Lord and His Bride. We desire to continue to profess the perennial faith of the Church in the face of the roaring evil that besieges her. We desire to keep vigil with her and with Jesus, in this new Gethsemane of the end times; to pray and do penance in reparation for the many offenses caused to them.... We know...that even the "synthesis of all heresies" represented by Modernism and its updated conciliar version can never definitively obscure the splendor of the Bride of Christ, but only for the brief period of the eclipse that Providence, in its infinite wisdom, has allowed, to draw from it a greater good.[27]

Our growth in holiness through trials, our recommitment to prayer, our study and proclamation of the truth, our grateful adherence to all that God has lavished upon us in our Catholic Tradition—may all this be the evidence in our own lives that He has indeed drawn from the crisis a greater good.

---

27   *A Voice in the Wilderness,* 157; 256.

SELECT BIBLIOGRAPHY

The following bibliography does not list all the works cited throughout this volume. Its purpose, rather, is to list works that the author has found especially helpful in furnishing background to or developing further the topics taken up in these pages. It is the same as the bibliography included in volume 1.

ON THE PAPACY

Chamberlin, E. R. *The Bad Popes*. Dorchester: Dorset Press, 1994.

Chiron, Yves. *Pope Pius IX: The Man and the Myth*. Translated by Graham Harrison. Kansas City, MO: Angelus Press, 2005.

———. *Saint Pius X: Restorer of the Church*. Translated by Graham Harrison. Kansas City, MO: Angelus Press, 2002.

Cleenewerck, Laurent A. *His Broken Body: Understanding and Healing the Schism between the Roman Catholic and Eastern Orthodox Churches*. Washington, DC: Euclid University Consortium Press, 2007.

Coulombe, Charles A. *Vicars of Christ: A History of the Popes*. Arcadia, CA: Tumblar House, 2014.

da Silveira, Arnaldo Vidigal Xavier. *Can Documents of the Magisterium of the Church Contain Errors? Can the Catholic Faithful Resist Them?* Translated by John R. Spann and José A. Schelini. Spring Grove, PA: The American Society for the Defense of Tradition, Family and Property, 2015.

———. *Can a Pope Be . . . a Heretic? The Theological Hypothesis of a Heretical Pope*. Translated by John Spann. Porto: Caminhos Romanos, 2018.

de Mattei, Roberto. *Love for the Papacy and Filial Resistance to the Pope in the History of the Church*. Brooklyn, NY: Angelico Press, 2019.

———. *Saint Pius V*. Translated by Giuseppe Pellegrino. Manchester, NH: Sophia Institute Press, 2021.

Hull, Geoffrey. *The Banished Heart: Origins of Heteropraxis in the Catholic Church*. London/New York: T&T Clark, 2010.

Journet, Charles. *The Church of the Word Incarnate: An Essay in Speculative Theology*. Translated by A.H.C. Downes. Volume 1: The Apostolic Hierarchy. London/New York: Sheed and Ward, 1955.

———. *The Theology of the Church*. Translated by Victor Szczurek, O.Praem. San Francisco: Ignatius Press, 2004.

Joy, John. *On the Ordinary and Extraordinary Magisterium from Joseph Kleutgen to the Second Vatican Council*. Studia Oecumenica Friburgensia 84. Münster: Aschendorff Verlag, 2017.

Kwasniewski, Peter A., ed. *Are Canonizations Infallible? Revisiting a Disputed Question*. Waterloo, ON: Arouca Press, 2021.

McCaffrey, Neil. *And Rightly So: Selected Letters and Articles of Neil McCaffrey.* Edited by Peter A. Kwasniewski. Fort Collins, CO: Roman Catholic Books, 2019. [The second section, "Reformation and Deformation in the Catholic Church," 135–220, contains penetrating observations on the postconciliar popes and especially on the liturgical reform.]

Mosebach, Martin. *Subversive Catholicism: Papacy, Liturgy, Church.* Translated by Sebastian Condon and Graham Harrison. Brooklyn: Angelico Press, 2019.

Ratzinger, Joseph. *Called to Communion: Understanding the Church Today.* Translated by Adrian Walker. San Francisco: Ignatius Press, 1996.

Siecienski, A. Edward. *The Papacy and the Orthodox. Sources and History of a Debate.* New York: Oxford University Press, 2017.

ON POPE FRANCIS

Borghesi, Massimo. *The Mind of Pope Francis: Jorge Mario Bergoglio's Intellectual Journey.* Translated by Barry Hudock. Collegeville, MN: Liturgical Press Academic, 2018.

de Valladares, Martha Alegría Reichmann. *Sacred Betrayals: A Widow Raises Her Voice against the Corruption of the Francis Papacy.* Translated by Matthew Cullinan Hoffman. Front Royal, VA: Faithful Insight Books, 2021.

Douthat, Ross. *To Change the Church: Pope Francis and the Future of Catholicism.* New York: Simon & Schuster, 2018.

Faggioli, Massimo. *The Liminal Papacy of Pope Francis: Moving Toward Global Catholicity.* Maryknoll, NY: Orbis Books, 2020.

Lamont, John R.T. and Claudio Pierantoni, eds. *Defending the Faith against Present Heresies.* Waterloo, ON: Arouca Press, 2021.

Lanzetta, Serafino M. *The Symphony of Truth: Theological Essays.* Waterloo, ON: Arouca Press, 2021.

Lawler, Philip F. *Lost Shepherd: How Pope Francis Is Misleading His Flock.* Washington, DC: Regnery Gateway, 2018.

Lee, Brian Y., and Thomas L. Knoebel, eds. *Discovering Pope Francis: The Roots of Jorge Mario Bergoglio's Thinking.* Collegeville, MN: Liturgical Press Academic, 2019.

Meloni, Julia. *The St. Gallen Mafia: Exposing the Secret Reform Group within the Church.* Gastonia, NC: TAN Books, 2021.

Neumayr, George. *The Political Pope: How Pope Francis Is Delighting the Liberal Left and Abandoning Conservatives.* New York: Hachette Book Group, 2017.

Sire, Henry. *The Dictator Pope: The Inside Story of the Francis Papacy.* Washington, DC: Regnery Publishing, 2018.

Ureta, José Antonio. *Pope Francis's "Paradigm Shift": Continuity or Rupture in the Mission of the Church?* Translated by José A. Schelini. Spring Grove, PA: The American Society for the Defense of Tradition, Family and Property, 2018.

Yiannopoulos, Milo. *Diabolical: How Pope Francis Has Betrayed Clerical Abuse Victims Like Me—and Why He Has To Go.* New York: Bombardier Books, 2018.

MODERN CHURCH HISTORY AND CONTROVERSY

Amerio, Romano. *Iota Unum: A Study of Changes in the Catholic Church in the XXth Century*. Trans. John P. Parsons. Kansas City: Sarto House, 1996.

Buck, Roger. *Cor Jesu Sacratissimum: From Secularism and the New Age to Christendom Renewed*. Kettering, OH: Angelico Press, 2016.

de Mattei, Roberto. *Apologia for Tradition. A Defense of Tradition Grounded in the Historical Context of the Faith*. Translated by Michael J. Miller. Kansas City, MO: Angelus Press, 2019.

———. *The Second Vatican Council: An Unwritten Story*. Translated by Patrick T. Brannan, SJ., Michael J. Miller, and Kenneth D. Whitehead. Edited by Michael J. Miller. Fitzwilliam, NH: Loreto Publications, 2012.

Ferrara, Christopher, and Thomas Woods. *The Great Façade: The Regime of Novelty in the Catholic Church from Vatican II to the Francis Revolution*. Second ed. Kettering, OH: Angelico Press, 2015.

Feser, Edward, and Joseph Bessette. *By Man Shall His Blood Be Shed: A Catholic Defense of Capital Punishment*. San Francisco: Ignatius Press, 2017.

Guimarães, Atila Sinke, Michael J. Matt, John Vennari, Marian Therese Horvat. *We Resist You to the Face*. Los Angeles: Tradition In Action, 2000.

Haynes, Michael. *A Catechism of Errors: A Critique of the Principal Errors of the Catechism of the Catholic Church*. Fitzwilliam, NH: Loreto Publications, 2021.

Lawler, Philip F. *The Smoke of Satan: How Corrupt and Cowardly Bishops Betrayed Christ, His Church, and the Faithful . . . and What Can Be Done About It*. Charlotte, NC: TAN Books, 2018.

Malloy, Christopher J. *False Mercy: Recent Heresies Distorting Catholic Truth*. Manchester, NH: Sophia Institute Press, 2021.

McGinley, Brandon. *The Prodigal Church: Restoring Catholic Tradition in an Age of Deception*. Manchester, NH: Sophia Institute Press, 2020.

Muggeridge, Anne Roche. *The Desolate City: Revolution in the Catholic Church*. Revised and expanded. New York: HarperCollins, 1990.

Murr, Charles Theodore. *The Godmother: Madre Pascalina, A Feminine Tour de Force*. N.p.: Independently published, 2017.

———. *Murder in the 33rd Degree: The Gagnon Investigation into Vatican Freemasonry*. N.p.: Independently published, 2022.

Sammons, Eric. *Deadly Indifference: How the Church Lost Her Mission and How We Can Reclaim It*. Manchester, NH: Crisis Publications, 2021.

Schneider, Most Rev. Athanasius, and Diane Montagna. *Christus Vincit. Christ's Triumph Over the Darkness of the Age*. Brooklyn, NY: Angelico Press, 2019.

Sire, H.J.A. [Henry]. *Phoenix from the Ashes: The Making, Unmaking, and Restoration of Catholic Tradition*. Kettering, OH: Angelico Press, 2015.

Trower, Philip. *The Catholic Church and the Counter-faith: A Study of the Roots of Modern Secularism, Relativism and de-Christianisation*. Oxford: Family Publications, 2006.

———. *Turmoil and Truth: The Historical Roots of the Modern Crisis in the Catholic Church.* Oxford: Family Publications and San Francisco: Ignatius Press, 2003.

Valli, Aldo Maria and Aurelio Porfiri. *Uprooted: Dialogues on the Liquid Church.* Translated by Giuseppe Pellegrino. Hong Kong: Chorabooks, 2019.

ON LITURGICAL QUESTIONS

Casini, Tito. *The Torn Tunic. Letter of a Catholic on the "Liturgical Reform."* Originally published by Fidelity Books in 1967; repr. Brooklyn, NY: Angelico Press, 2020.

Cekada, Anthony. *Work of Human Hands: A Theological Critique of the Mass of Paul VI.* West Chester, OH: Philothea Press, 2010.

Chiron, Yves. *Annibale Bugnini, Reformer of the Liturgy.* Translated by John Pepino. Brooklyn, NY: Angelico Press, 2018.

Davies, Michael. *Cranmer's Godly Order: The Destruction of Catholicism through Liturgical Change.* Fort Collins, CO: Roman Catholic Books, 1995.

———. *Pope Paul's New Mass.* Kansas City, MO: Angelus Press, 2009.

Dulac, Raymond. *In Defence of the Roman Mass.* Translated by Peadar Walsh. N.p.: Te Deum Press, 2020.

Fiedrowicz, Michael. *The Traditional Mass: History, Form, and Theology of the Classical Roman Rite.* Translated by Rose Pfeifer. Brooklyn, NY: Angelico Press, 2020.

Kwasniewski, Peter A., ed. *From Benedict's Peace to Francis's War: Catholics Respond to the Motu Proprio* Traditionis Custodes *on the Latin Mass.* Brooklyn, NY: Angelico Press, 2021.

———. *Holy Bread of Eternal Life: Restoring Eucharistic Reverence in an Age of Impiety.* Manchester, NH: Sophia Institute Press, 2020.

———. *Ministers of Christ: Recovering the Roles of Clergy and Laity in an Age of Confusion.* Manchester, NH: Crisis Publications, 2021.

———. *Noble Beauty, Transcendent Holiness: Why the Modern Age Needs the Mass of Ages.* Kettering, OH: Angelico Press, 2017.

———. *Reclaiming Our Roman Catholic Birthright: The Genius and Timeliness of the Traditional Latin Mass.* Brooklyn, NY: Angelico Press, 2020.

———. *Resurgent in the Midst of Crisis: Sacred Liturgy, the Traditional Latin Mass, and Renewal in the Church.* Kettering, OH: Angelico Press, 2014.

———. *Tradition and Sanity: Conversations and Dialogues of a Postconciliar Exile.* Brooklyn, NY: Angelico Press, 2018.

———. *True Obedience in the Church: A Guide to Discernment in Challenging Times.* Manchester, NH: Sophia Institute Press, 2021.

Mosebach, Martin. *The Heresy of Formlessness: The Roman Liturgy and Its Enemy.* Revised and expanded edition. Translated by Graham Harrison. Brooklyn, NY: Angelico Press, 2018.

INDEX OF PROPER NAMES
(for Volume 2)

ABOUT THE AUTHOR

Peter A. Kwasniewski holds a B. A. in Liberal Arts from Thomas Aquinas College and an M. A. and Ph.D. in Philosophy from the Catholic University of America, with a specialization in the thought of St. Thomas Aquinas. After teaching at the International Theological Institute in Austria from 1999–2006, he joined the founding team of Wyoming Catholic College, where he taught theology, philosophy, music, and art history and directed the choir and schola until 2018. Today, he is a full-time writer and speaker whose work is seen at websites and in periodicals such as *New Liturgical Movement, OnePeterFive, Rorate Caeli, The Remnant, Catholic Family News*, and *Latin Mass Magazine*. Dr. Kwasniewski has published extensively in academic and popular venues on sacramental and liturgical theology, the history and aesthetics of music, Catholic Social Teaching, and issues in the modern Church. He has written or edited many books and his work has been translated into at least eighteen languages. For more information, visit his website: www.peterkwasniewski.com.

Lightning Source UK Ltd.
Milton Keynes UK
UKHW012216081122
411883UK00017B/104/J